JOKES AND THE LINGUISTIC MIND

Through the lens of cognitive science, *Jokes and the Linguistic Mind* investigates jokes that play on some aspect of the structure and function of language. In so doing, Debra Aarons shows that these "linguistic jokes" can evoke our tacit knowledge of the language we use. Analyzing hilarious examples from movies, plays and books, *Jokes and the Linguistic Mind* demonstrates that tacit linguistic knowledge must become conscious for linguistic jokes to be understood. The book examines jokes that exploit pragmatic, semantic, morphological, phonological and semantic features of language, as well as jokes that use more than one language and jokes that are about language itself. Additionally, the text explores the relationship between cryptic crossword clues and linguistic jokes in order to demonstrate the difference between tacit knowledge of language and rules of language use that are articulated for a particular purpose. With its use of jokes as data and its highly accessible explanations of complex linguistic concepts, this book is an engaging supplementary text for introductory courses in linguistics, psycholinguistics and cognitive science. It will also be of interest to scholars in translation studies, applied linguistics and philosophy of language.

Debra Aarons is Lecturer in Linguistics at the University of New South Wales in Australia.

JOKES AND THE LINGUISTIC MIND

Debra Aarons

Routledge
Taylor & Francis Group

NEW YORK AND LONDON

First published 2012
by Routledge
711 Third Avenue, New York, NY 10017

Simultaneously published in the UK
by Routledge
2 Park Square, Milton Park, Abingdon, Oxon OX14 4RN

Routledge is an imprint of the Taylor & Francis Group, an informa business

Library of Congress Cataloging-in-Publication Data
 Aarons, Debra, 1956–
 Jokes and the linguistic mind / Debra Aarons.
   p. cm.
 1. Discourse analysis, Literary. 2. Wit and humor—History and criticism—Theory, etc. 3. Linguistics. I. Title.
 P302.5.A16 2011
 809.7—dc22   2010052712

ISBN: 978-0-415-89048-9 (hbk)
ISBN: 978-0-415-89049-6 (pbk)
ISBN: 978-0-203-81474-1 (ebk)

Typeset in Bembo
by RefineCatch Limited, Bungay, Suffolk

In memory of my mother, Minnie Aarons (1933–2009)
and for Joshua, Saul, Ilan and Adam.

CONTENTS

ACKNOWLEDGMENTS

Like raising a child, it takes a global village to raise a book, or at least, this book. I have had so much support in writing it that, truly, its healthy existence is owed to many creative and nurturing individuals. Its flaws, and length, however, are my responsibility.

First, I thank Mengistu Amberber, Ludmila Stern and Hilary Janks, my colleagues and very dear friends, who got me going, which was no mean task. They recognized that what I considered to be a lifetime pastime had potential as a linguistic project. It took a long time to persuade me that I could write an academic book about jokes. Had it not been for their ongoing interest and support, and commitment to my work and my wellbeing, this book would never have been written.

My great friend, one-time teacher and intercontinental colleague, Hilary Janks, has spurred me on for years, from afar, and intensively so, when nearby.

Mengistu Amberber, my colleague and very caring friend, has mentored me, read every word I sent him, and been a constant source of wisdom, support and encouragement. Ludmila Stern has kept me going, providing me with extraordinary friendship, warmth and optimism. They have held my hands, kept my head on my shoulders and my feet on the ground.

I specially thank Nick Riemer, who kindly read parts of this book and gave me the benefit of his astute insights and lucid erudition. He too has the humor of a six-year-old. Paul Taylor read a chapter whilst denying he knew anything about the topic and gave me excellent advice. Roger Lass, in addition to sending me exceedingly terrible jokes, has been a wonderful friend and mentor.

Adam Aarons provided me with much needed technical support, jokes and opinions. Marc Mierowsky read drafts and paid me back in kind for the years I have criticized his use of commas and hypotactic constructions.

I thank the Cognitive Science Reading Group at the University of New South Wales for years of stimulating and challenging discussion, and for their great sociability, especially Peter Slezak, Mengistu Amberber, Iain Giblin, Nick Riemer and Eran Asoulin.

I'd like to thank my editors at Taylor and Francis, Ivy Ip and Mike Andrews, for their efficiency, helpfulness and concern. I am also grateful to the anonymous readers who provided very useful feedback. My colleagues in the School of Languages and Linguistics at UNSW, Peter Collins, Barbara Mullock, Nicoletta Romeo and James Lee have been interested in my work, and have shown me friendship and staunch support.

My family kept me supplied with fresh jokes, and had some faith that this book would eventually see the light of day. My sister Michelle provided me with the eye of a professional eagle, and daily gave me the benefit of her fine mind and her kind nature, lovingly tolerating my neuroses. My sister Zahava and brother-in-law Anthony kept me fuelled with jokes, their own special brand of wit, and generously shared their home, their family and their opinions with me. My brother Alan and sister-in-law Debbie gave me a home when I first migrated to Australia and provided me with familial care and warmth. They kept straight faces when they heard I was writing a book about jokes, but engaged with enthusiasm in the project, and ensured that the jokes they gave me maintained the standards of the average eight-year-old.

Samuel Aarons apprenticed me very young into solving cryptic crosswords. Of this, he is still the master. For encouraging my love of language and language play, I will always be grateful to him.

I thank my nephews, Adam, Ilan, Saul and Joshua, data suppliers *extraordinaires*, connoisseurs of the silly joke, language makers and breakers, all of whom, at some stage have outgrown my sense of humor.

I also thank the children, most of them well into their adult lives now, who gave me many of these jokes and who were a source of inspiration and joy: Gregory Janks, Daniel Janks, Andrew Schalkwyk, James Schalkwyk, Marc Mierowsky, and Ruth Mierowsky.

I commend the eternal six-year-olds, Brian Siritzky, Colin Mierowsky, Alan Aarons, Zahava Aarons, Daniel Janks, Mary-Ann Kemp, Stephen Bloch, and David Schalkwyk, who still think that "What is brown and sticky?" is the funniest joke ever.

For their long term generosity and hospitality, including holidays in wonderful places (while I was, and also wasn't, and should have been, writing this book) my gratitude to Mary-Ann Kemp, Brian and Roanne Siritzky, John and Hilary Janks, Cecile and Michiel le Roux, and Eliott and Marina McIntire.

I cannot begin to contemplate how much I have laughed and marveled at the wit of Mary-Ann Kemp, Stephen Bloch, Felicity Kaganas, David Schalkwyk, Christina Murray, Brian Siritzky and Roanne Plotnitzky. They are not only the wittiest people I know, they are also my beloved friends. I consider myself very lucky.

In Sydney, my life has been enriched by my wonderful friends, Ilan Katz and Julia Meyerowitz-Katz, Steven and Margot Segal, Denise Meyerson and Paul Taylor, Colin and Rosemary Mierowsky and Jerome and Ludmila Stern. They and their families have made it possible for me to function in unpropitious times and their ongoing care has sustained me.

Siamak Movahedi and Ian de Saxe have ideas about why I work on jokes. My own feeling is that this work is play.

My friends Ruth Morgan, Hilary Janks, and Mary-Ann Kemp are always with me, even though we are at such a geographical distance. Sharon Cort is my comrade in struggle and in laughter, and generally, the difference escapes us.

Permissions

Extracts from Spike Milligan and the Goon Show by permission of Spike Milligan Productions.

Extracts from *Monty Python's Flying Circus – Jest the Words* by Graham Chapman, John Cleese, Terry Gilliam, Eric Idle, Terry Jones and Michael Palin and *A Pocketful of Python* by John Cleese by permission of their publisher, Methuen.

Extracts from Victor Borge by permission of Borge Productions, Inc. courtesy of Janet Crowle.

Cover image credit: © Andrew Lipson (www.andrewlipson.com)

Every effort has been made to obtain permission for use of previously published material. Any permission holder who feels it has not been properly acknowledged is invited to contact Routledge, who will endeavor to correct any omission in future editions of this work.

INTRODUCTION

It was the philosopher Wittgenstein who remarked that, "a serious and good philosophical work could be written that consisted entirely of jokes" (Malcolm, 2001). This remark has become a conventional way of introducing a scholarly work that concerns itself with jokes. No doubt Wittgenstein's remark could be validated, although I'm not sure that such a book has actually been written. I'd like to make another, somewhat less ambitious claim. I want to show that a book about linguistics can be written that consists of jokes, although in order to show that it can be done, alas, the jokes must be analyzed. This puts Wittgenstein's "entirely" in question. Instead, in this work, I want to take seriously the idea that many of the crucial concepts of linguistics can be illustrated by jokes.

In this book, I analyze jokes that play on some aspect of language. My purpose is to exemplify some of the central ideas of linguistics, and most particularly, to show that jokes can be utilized to provide evidence of tacit linguistic knowledge in users of a language. I identify and investigate the particular linguistic points that a joke turns on and, consequently, illustrates. In so doing, I show how linguistic jokes provide additional evidence for the idea that there is knowledge we have about language that is not directly accessible to consciousness.

The book is intended to be a contribution to a broadly Chomskyan approach to the notion of "competence" (Chomsky, 1965, and various formulations thereafter) and my claim, essentially, is that linguistic jokes which disrupt the normal automatized elimination of ambiguity can give us sudden access to aspects of our competence, making tacit knowledge conscious.

In general, I have restricted the data to jokes, witticisms, one-liners, and short excerpts from movie scripts, plays or books. In one case, I have analyzed an entire comedy sketch in order to show the sustained play at various levels of the grammar. There is no reason other than practicality that I have drawn the line at shorter examples, since length is neither a sufficient or necessary condition for the kind of humorous play in question.

The book is structured as follows. In Chapter 1, I introduce the topic of jokes and what they tell us about the linguistic mind. In Chapter 2, I discuss how playing with linguistic pragmatics creates humor. In Chapter 3, I explore semantic play and humor creation. Chapter 4 contains an analysis of phonological and morphological play in the creation of humor. Chapter 5 is concerned with the creation of humor by syntactic play. In Chapter 6, I provide a case study in order to show how a sustained piece of verbal humor exploits multiple linguistic features. In Chapter 7, I analyze jokes involving more than one language, and in Chapter 8, I look specifically at jokes that are about language. In Chapter 9, I explain the basic mechanisms of cryptic crosswords and the play of letters.

Readers will no doubt be able to think of even better, funnier jokes to illustrate the points I have raised. If that is the case, I shall consider that my aim is well on its way to being met.

1

JOKES AND THE LINGUISTIC MIND

1.0 Introduction

In this chapter I discuss my interest in the topic of jokes and what they tell us about the linguistic mind, and present the outline of my central claims. I detail the theoretical concerns and approach of this investigation and show how it makes a contribution to the study of Linguistics and Cognitive Science. I explain why the book is crucially about linguistics and not about humor, *per se*. In so doing, as a contrast, and for interested readers, I provide a very brief outline of some of the work in Humor Studies.

2.0 What Can the Study of Jokes Teach Us About Linguistics?

2.1 Linguistic Analysis and Evidence as Revealed Through Jokes

2.1.1 Analyzing the Language of Jokes

For years now, as a teacher of linguistics, I have noticed that every major idea in linguistics can be illustrated elegantly and memorably through an appropriate joke.[1] The joke usually makes the linguistic point in a pithier way than an explanation can. This has always made sense to me on an intuitive level. In studying linguistics,[2] after all, as well as viewing language as a window into the mind, we also observe, describe and analyze it as an object, made up of other smaller objects. Analyzing language performance is an indirect way for us to speculate on the mental representations underlying actual or possible utterances. It has been persuasively argued by Fromkin (1980, 1997, 2000) that the analysis of speech errors (*e.g.*, slips of the tongue) provides access to the mental representation and organization of some important linguistic features. Salvatore Attardo, in his comprehensive work, *Linguistic Theories of Humor* (1994), remarks on the use of puns as a source of linguistic evidence for mental representations.[3]

> A possible drawback in the use of puns as linguistic evidence may be the fact that, as has been stressed, puns are a conscious phenomenon, and so the data they present may be contaminated; the conscious nature of the use of puns should not be confused with an awareness of the mechanisms at play in the production and understanding of puns… they [speakers] are not at all aware of the rules that govern the appropriate strings for punning, of what qualifies as "similar" strings, or of how the two senses of the utterance are brought together. This allows the safe conclusion that puns do not present a worse quality of data than speech errors. As a matter of fact, they may provide a broader range of data (for instance, on pragmatic facts) and may not be subject in the same measure to the drawbacks that speech errors present when used as linguistic evidence.
>
> *(Attardo 1994, pp. 141–2)*

I extend this claim to a range of jokes, encompassing different kinds of linguistic phenomena, in an attempt to demonstrate that linguistic humor[4]—humor that is *de dicto* (verbal) as opposed to *de re* (referential)—is a valuable source of evidence for our tacit knowledge of the mental representations of phonology, morphology, semantics, syntax and pragmalinguistics, and the rules which govern these.

2.1.2 Playing with the Parts of Language

Treating language as an object, or a collection of objects, allows us to play with these objects, much like a child plays with toys. We can arrange the objects in different ways, build, construct, disassemble, bend, stretch and even break them. We can work with toys of all sizes, shapes, colors, textures, flexibility and rigidity. We can use them as weapons, vehicles or dolls. Watching a child play with the most basic of toys, including items such as matchboxes and bottle tops, we see that imagination is the limit of what can be done. Interestingly, it seems to me, a child playing with language does the same: the sounds are arranged, rearranged, repeated, turned inside out and upside down, sung, shouted, whispered, stretched and lengthened, simply as play for its own sake. Minimally, all the child has is a set of elements; some finite limitations provided by the elements themselves; and his/her own mind.[5]

It occurs to me that some kinds of jokes are just this: they are the product of playing around with language to see what is possible and what happens. Playing is fun: it results in delight. Play of the kind I discuss here is not particularly purposive. Every person has a set of toys (the parts of language and the rules for their combination) at their immediate disposal; not all of us recognize that the objects that we use for serious and telic activities are also available as toys. The semiotician,

Pierre Guiraud (1976, 1981), has called this activity the "defunctionalization" of language—that is the use of language for play, not for other purposes. The ways in which people play with objects can tell us something about the nature of the objects, as well as the nature of the mind of the player. Jokes are self-contained units that give us information about the nature of language and the nature of the mind that processes it. What I refer to as "linguistic jokes" provide excellent data for the exploration of the nature of linguistic knowledge and the human mind from which it is inseparable.[6] Although people may chuckle at private jokes on their own, jokes are an essentially social phenomenon, as is language use in most of its functions. We can and do use language ideationally in a solitary way, but this constitutes only one of language's many functions. Typically, jokes are shared in interaction. Language play, however, is not restricted to either communicative or private functions. Aquinas describes the playful use of language thus.

> Those words and deeds in which nothing is sought beyond the soul's pleasure called playful or humorous and it is necessary to make use of them at times for solace of soul.
>
> *(Aquinas,* Summa Theologia, *Question 168)*

Of course, using language in a defunctionalized way is also one of language's functions, and although language use might be for its own sake, it may not always be for the speaker's sake only. Although we entertain ourselves by playing, it is much more fun to play with others. In that sense, play with language may be both interactional and reflective.

Play with language, or the ludic use of language, has been discussed by a number of scholars. The Dutch cultural historian, Huizinga (1938), produced a magnum opus, *Homo Ludens*, in which he identified the essence of the human as playfulness. Huizinga claimed that playfulness was the fundamental human drive and that human cultural history emerged and developed out of play. Although his work was not specifically concerned with language, but rather with human cultural development as a whole, this encompassed language use. Playing, with language and in language, is, then, part of the basic human drive.

Gregory Bateson (1976), the anthropologist and polymath, discusses play, and also, more specifically, the notion of language play. Bateson shows that play (of the type that is found in jokes, etc.) is characterized by the addition of a meta-communicative act, a comment (or a new frame) that is outside the denotative level of communication. "These actions, in which we now engage, do not denote what would be denoted by these actions which these actions denote. The playful nip denotes the bite, but it does not denote what would be denoted by the bite" (Bateson, 1976 p. 121). For Bateson, language play is about the tension between the communication and the meta-communication. In language play, there is constant tugging between *la langue* and all the different tokens of *parole* (Saussure, 1993). What makes it play is that, "(a) the messages or signals exchanged in play are in a certain sense untrue or not meant; and (b) that which is denoted by these signals is non-existent" (Bateson, 1976, p. 123).

Karl Groos, a psychologist working within a tradition of evolutionary biology, regarded play as preparation for the ongoing activities of life (Groos, 1901). Nevertheless, despite his overall instrumentalist vision of play, he saw the virtue of the purely ludic use of language. In talking about the humorous use of language, he remarked that it is close to the way children play with words. Groos seems to have had a direct influence on Freud and his views of play. We see this in Freud's view of language play, specifically with respect to the non-tendentious or innocent uses of jokes, although it seems that play with language is not incompatible with jokes that are tendentious (Freud 1905/2002). Apter and Smith (1977) and Apter (1982) in comparing playfulness and serious-mindedness, consider humor to be paratelic, *i.e.*, concerned with play.

Indeed, Raskin's (1985) characterization of linguistic humor as *Non bona fide* (NBF) communication, is a modern version of the notion of ludic language, a form of play with language in which we engage, that seems to be governed by its own rules. Raskin does not make any claims, one way or the other, about the purpose of the humorous exchange, as his concern is essentialist, and deliberately uncommitted to theories of teleology. Talking about the purpose of humor, as he points out, does not tell us much about the essential nature of the phenomenon, linguistic humor—for that we need to analyze the phenomenon itself.

Crystal (1998) in his book, *Language Play*, is concerned to demonstrate that everybody plays with language, and he dwells on the questions of why this is so. Finally, he makes a case for why the ludic (or playful) function of language is of interest to our thinking about linguistic issues. He proposes, crucially, that it is language play that is the fundamental instinct that drives language acquisition.

2.2 The Linguistic Data

In this book, I use the term "linguistic humor" to refer to any kind of humor that reveals play with language objects at any and all of the different levels of language structure and additionally, that exploits playing around with rules governing pragmatic force. Here I am concerned only with humor that is *de dicto*.

2.2.1 Jokes de dicto and de re

Since jokes occur in the medium of language, they all use language. However, some jokes are dependent for their humor on the form of the language in which they are told, and others are independent of linguistic form as the source of humor. Those jokes that are independent of linguistic form for their humor are known as jokes *de re* (about things).

Joke 1, below, plausibly retains its humorous effect if expressed in any language. It is also not necessarily reliant on cultural stereotypes, but these are handy shortcuts into the joke atmosphere.

Joke 1 – *de re* humor

Texas tourist: *Back home it takes me the best part of a day to drive from one side of my ranch to the other.*
Local farmer: *Ah sure, I had a car like that once…!*[7]

In contrast, the humor in Joke 2 below is entirely dependent on the linguistic form of the relevant parts of the joke. Jokes of this sort are known as jokes *de dicto* (jokes that are about words). I refer to this kind of humor as "linguistic humor".

Joke 2 – *de dicto* humor

Q: *What do ducks do before they grow up?*
A: *They grow down.*

3.0 Linguistic Humor: Evidence for Tacit Knowledge of Language

3.1 The Study of Jokes from a Linguistic Perspective

The study of jokes from the perspective of linguistic theory opens up some interesting areas of exploration. I look at those uses of language that I find to be clever, surprising, witty and fresh, and which are distinguished from straightforward, predictable *bona fide* communication by being non-casual uses of language, that are aesthetic or artistic.[8] By *aesthetic* I mean linguistically patterned above and beyond what is strictly necessary for the direct and conventional communication of the message. In this sense, jokes are language artifacts. They are not simply unintended "found language"; their originators intend them to be special utterances. The kinds of jokes I analyze in this work are all crafted (except in the cases of accidental humor, which I treat as lucky accidents that bear analysis) in that they highlight a particular aspect of language structure or function of which we are normally unaware.[9]

3.2 The Phenomenon: Linguistic Jokes

3.2.1 What will Analyzing the Phenomenon Linguistically Tell Us?

In focussing on the phenomenon of linguistic humor I attend most specifically to jokes that turn on some element expressible in terms of linguistic rules. My central concern is to show that although much of our knowledge of language is tacit, it can be activated by these kinds of jokes.

Of course, jokes are always part of performance, as are any utterance tokens. However, it seems to me that jokes activate something that normal interactions don't: they cause us to reflect on language.

Apart from those in the reflections-on-language business, not everyone is aware that, when we engage with these kinds of jokes, reflecting on language is an important part of what we do. I think it is entirely reasonable to suggest that although not everyone is a joke maker, any person who knows his or her native language can, in principle, get a joke. Raskin (1985) has, in fact, proposed that we all have an innate humor competence that simply needs to be activated.[10] I don't take issue with this claim, however my assumption is a little more minimal. I am simply assuming that humans appear to have the capacity to play with language and be amused by language play. I assume as well, that jokes work by means of certain mechanisms, although the particular mechanisms I am interested in are specifically linguistic and not necessarily driven by psychological considerations such as processing.

There is no reason to assume, outside of the study of formal linguistics, that people have any idea what the formal concepts—phone, phoneme, syllable, morpheme, lexeme, and phrase—refer to. Yet, it can be demonstrated that when a joke plays around with linguistic rules, joke hearers do notice, even though they may not be able to explain what the rules are, or even describe what it is that they feel is not quite right. Grammaticality judgment experiments to elicit tacit knowledge of rules can, of course, be conducted without resorting to jokes, and are standardly used by those seeking the linguistic intuitions of native speakers. These experiments are of a laboratory nature with all the concomitant benefits and disadvantages. Various studies testing aspects of joke processing among normal subjects have been conducted, and these have produced information about response latency and the parts of the brain that are involved, depending on the type of humorous stimulus (Tanenhaus *et al.*, 1979; Giora, 2003; Vaid, 2003; Hatzidaki, 2007, *inter alia*). These sorts of inquiries, however, do not tell us about the nature of our knowledge of language, but about how we respond to humorous stimuli.

Analyzing examples of linguistic humor allows us to find evidence for the claim that we all have unconscious knowledge of the rules of our language. Linguistic description and analysis of the relevant part of a joke may be sufficient for the purpose of uncovering this evidence. Describing and analyzing the linguistic phenomenon at issue allows us to see that in order for the joke to be comprehended the listener must have resort to linguistic knowledge, which is, in the minimal case, tacit.

Graeme Ritchie (2004) has undertaken a detailed description of linguistic jokes with the purpose of formulating their grammar.[11] By this he means to propose that the joke has a certain grammar, and the way he comes to a formulation of this grammar is by analogy with the conduct of linguistic inquiry in the Generativist tradition. Although Ritchie's book is entitled *The Linguistics of Jokes*, his project and mine are very different. He shows that jokes have their own grammar, which is part of an overall theory of jokes. In contrast, I show that jokes illuminate aspects of linguistic theory and provide a source of insight into cognitive science, specifically with regard to knowledge of language.

3.2.2 Basic Theoretical Constructs

The basis of modern linguistics rests on the fact that language is a discrete combinatorial system, that is, "a finite number of discrete elements (for example, phones, morphemes, or words) are combined to form larger and complex structures with properties that are quite distinct from those of their elements" (Pinker, 1994, p. 84).

Thus, individual phonemes do not have sense, except in allowable language specific combinations with other phonemes, resulting in one or more morphemes. A morpheme is a representation of a sense-bearing unit in a particular language; its sense is consistent in all occurrences within that language. However, from a certain angle, language may be described as a stream of sounds that do not come labeled with instructions such as, *I am a morpheme, I am a word, I am a noun phrase*, etc. It is the mind, with its knowledge of a particular language that assigns structure, and therefore, sense, to a stream of sounds.

As phonemes are meaningless units, they contribute to meaning only in particular language-specific combinations. Morphemes are units of meaning but, naturally, they are language-specific in both their form and their rules of combination. Semanticity, *i.e.*, consistent interpretation of signals with sense is a crucial feature of language, but is inordinately difficult to characterize because every language is a combination of discrete elements according to specific rules of combination.

There is no necessary connection between the form of a signal and its sense. That is to say, a word does not resemble its referent. This is what Saussure referred to as the arbitrariness of the sign (Saussure, 1910/1993). Thus, there is no necessary connection between the sound and form of the word *tree* in English and its referent. Indeed, speakers of other languages will use a different word to refer to the same referent; French *arbre*; German *baum*, etc.[12] Nevertheless language has semanticity, *i.e.*, within a given language there is consistency in the interpretation of the signifier however a signifier can only be interpreted within a context of use. The form of an item (*e.g.*, a word) is not necessarily connected to only one sense. Thus, mapping from form to sense is consistent only within a context. Sound-sense mapping is not fixed at a phonological level, since phonemes are meaningless units, and is fixed only within a context at morphological levels. It is not the case that there is an obvious one-to-one mapping between word and sense, and in some cases there is no direct mapping between phrase, clause or sentence and meaning.[13] The lack of transparent one-to-one correspondence between sound form and sense leads us to one of the great mysteries of language use: how do we use language to make sense? Since language is generated by a small set of elements and finite means, sense-making is clearly not a matter of simply combining phonemes into morphemes and morphemes into words that are then arranged in sentences.

The products of the language faculty may be described or analyzed physically, at many levels of detail, including those of the acoustic signal, pause structure, and contrastive tone structure, *inter alia*. It is the mind of the perceiver that provides a structure within which a series of sounds may be heard as yielding one meaning or another (Isac & Reiss, 2008). This claim has been made elegantly, by linguists and cognitive scientists working in a Rationalist tradition, and especially by those working within a Generativist framework (*e.g.*, Jackendoff, 1992). It is part of a broader claim about cognition that has been made in the field of vision (Hoffmann, 1988; Marr, 1982) and audition (Bregman, 1990; Iverson *et al.*, 2004; Sacks, 2008). In this regard, the case is comprehensively made by Zenon Pylyshyn's work, in particular his 1984 *Computation and Cognition: Toward a Foundation for Cognitive Science.*

It is the mind of the speaker or listener that is able to combine strings of meaningless elements in order to create meaning. If the minds of speakers or listeners were not specifically geared to this task, sounds or movements would be simply that, sounds or movements. It is, however, innate in humans that having acquired a particular language, they are able to assign a structure to sound streams, resulting in their being able to hear and produce utterances in that language. The still more mysterious part is that hearers can assign the same structures as speakers intend.

Competent speakers of a language may not be able to analyze the structure of their language consciously and fully. Indeed, it is not necessary that they do so, and at some level, it is not possible. Thus, according to Pylyshyn,

> We should view it as a major discovery of twentieth-century cognitive science that most of what goes on when we act intelligently is not available to conscious inspection. And since what goes on is reasoning, we have every reason to believe that it takes place in a system of symbols – that's the only way we know of doing it without hiding a homunculus inside the machine.
>
> *(Pylyshyn, 1984, p. 19)*

Once language has been acquired, for many of us it becomes so much a part of ourselves that we don't think about it; we simply use it. It is not necessary to understand the structure of one's own language: producing it is like using a volitional biological function, such as walking; perceiving others' use is somewhat less volitional, like breathing or feeling. It is possible to study the components of walking, but it is not necessary to do so in order to walk.

This is a basic tenet of Chomskyan theory, expressly mentioned, or else implied, in all his work, from the very first (Chomsky, 1957 and following). It entails, essentially, that we all have knowledge of the rules of our grammar and that we did not learn these rules consciously. Additionally, in the Chomskyan framework, part of the language faculty is said to be a separate module in the mind, interfacing with other cognitive systems, but not identical to them.[14] Thus, it has been proposed, not uncontroversially, that language does not operate according to the rules proposed for general cognition, but is a self-contained computational system, interfacing primarily with the sensorimotor system and the conceptual/intentional system (Chomsky, 1995).

Chomsky, in 1965, made the distinction between 'competence' and 'performance': competence is our tacit knowledge of the rules of our language, and performance is the use to which this knowledge is put. Jokes are, of course, examples of language in performance, or as Chomsky (1986) would put it, they are E-language rather than I-language. A number of variables affect E-language (language utterances in use) including one-off performance features, processing limitations, individual preferences, world knowledge, and many other kinds of contextual factors. These variables all play a major part in the construction, delivery, reception and appreciation of a joke. However, the crucial element of a linguistic joke is that it relies for its humorous impact on listeners' competence, *i.e.*, listeners' tacit knowledge of the rules of their language. I claim that such jokes evoke a listener's competence, making an aspect of tacit linguistic knowledge conscious. I argue that it is this sudden consciousness of normally unconscious or tacit knowledge that causes a disruption and makes us laugh, or, at least, alerts us to the surprise and novelty. It is when we suddenly view language in a new and different way, rather than relating to it as an automatic and transparent means of communication and thought, that the "aha" moment takes place.[15]

When we think about the elements involved in walking, or any automatic activity, our relationship to the activity changes, as we become conscious. In the case of language, we may become aware that a stream of sounds could just as soon be heard in a different way, *i.e.*, the joke cues us into noticing another way in which the stream of sound might be analyzed by the computational system. This is not unlike the sort of cognitive activity involved in processing a Necker cube, or other ambiguous perceptual data. We are then able to entertain more than one possibility, and might think something like, "Hey, that's odd (or funny). I never thought about it like that".[16]

An interesting variation on the notion of tacit knowledge of language is to be found in interlingual or bilingual jokes. Since monolinguals actually constitute only one class of human beings to be analyzed, it is revealing to look at linguistic humor created and appreciated by people who know more than one language. In these cases we see the interplay created between the knowledge of two different languages and the ways in which the tacit knowledge of each language can be evoked by one joke.[17]

In a particular subclass of linguistic jokes we find jokes that are about language itself. These jokes take language as their subject matter. Some are rather clever in that they make the joke twice, *i.e.*, in terms of both medium and message. Of all the linguistic jokes, these most require conscious metalinguistic knowledge in order to be produced and appreciated. This is not to say that they do not tap tacit linguistic knowledge, but that, in addition they require on the part of the participants, conscious knowledge of some of the rules of language, as well.[18]

In contrast to language play that involves tacit knowledge of language, there is a particular kind of ludic language that is probably the most extreme example of playing with language form. This peculiar blend of pure play and the blind application of literalism is to be found in the cryptic crossword which blurs all the distinctions between linguistic levels, uses rebuses and cratylic language, swings between spoken and written modalities and is deliberately vague about the difference between use and mention. Cryptic crossword clues force solvers to work against all their grammatical intuitions, in viewing language elements as pieces to be joined with total disregard for rules of linguistic structure and use. When working with language as bits of code, puzzlers are thrown into their intuitions constantly, and consciously have to fight against them: cryptic crosswords really do not carve up language at the joints. In this way, they serve as an interesting and puzzling contrast to linguistic jokes.[19]

3.2.3 Overlap with Other Linguistic Areas

The proposals made here about jokes may have some overlap with other broad areas of applied linguistics and might shed additional light on some old problems.[20] Exploring associated branches of study in the terms of this line of enquiry could prove fruitful.

3.2.3.1 Translation

Most, if not all, linguistic jokes are untranslatable.[21] This is because languages do not all employ the same surface structures or phonological and morphological combinations. As de Saussure pointed out, there is, in general, an arbitrary relationship between signifier and signified, or between form and meaning. It is also well known that speech acts are not readily directly translated by use of the same structures as those used in the source language. Since linguistic jokes exploit the linguistic structure of a particular language, it would stand to reason that they would not be directly translatable whilst still maintaining the linguistic point of the joke. This issue has been noted and explored by many scholars, since Cicero, including Jakobson (1959), Steiner (1975), and in the specific field of humor translation, Laurian and Nilsen (1989) and Chiaro (1992, 2005, 2008). Translating a linguistic joke faithfully, thus, would, of necessity, entail losing the exact joke. The translation cannot tap tacit linguistic knowledge that is identical to that evoked by the original joke. Good translation can sometimes create parallel linguistic effects, and evoke tacit knowledge of a particular linguistic rule in the target language, but I hypothesize that the fundamental arbitrariness of language ensures that a faithful translation cannot itself replicate the joke, and, therefore, it cannot evoke tacit access to the identical rule. These are hypotheses, of course, and are open to empirical inquiry.

3.2.3.2 Appreciation of Linguistic Jokes by Non-native Speakers

Another area that overlaps with the investigation of jokes and tacit knowledge explored in this book is the extent to which non-native users of a language have tacit access to the non-native language. A non-native user of a language needs to be fairly proficient to grasp a linguistic joke in the non-native language. Linguistic jokes often play on extremely basic patterns in language, and are not universally regarded by adult native speakers as being particularly mature or sophisticated. Nevertheless, they require a particular kind of linguistic sophistication on the part of the listener to be perceived as jokes. These are the kinds of jokes that children of about 8 years old (and adults like me) find extremely amusing. To wit, *Q: What's brown and sticky? A: A stick.*

Although as we know, many jokes are culturally bound, and cannot be understood without recourse to cultural knowledge, a joke like this, it seems to me, is strictly linguistic. Nevertheless, many users of English as a second language do not find it particularly funny, although when dissected it can be useful in contexts where explanation is appropriate.[22] I can only speculate on why non-native speakers don't find this kind of joke terribly amusing, but I suspect it is because their knowledge of English does not draw on the same source as children's does.

3.2.3.3 Children's Linguistic Creations

A number of linguistic creations made by children employ the same features as are found in linguistic jokes. These reveal unconscious knowledge of the rules of language at work. Often these linguistic creations are used in the analysis of child language to show the developmental nature of first language acquisition, *i.e.*, the developing stages of the child's competence.[23] For instance, my two-year-old nephew said, *I wooded my finger*, when he meant that he had found a splinter in his finger. The same child, clearly generalizing a particular rule, in the same week, said, *I roofed the ball*, when he meant that he had thrown the ball onto the roof. Although neither of these utterances is commonly used, it is obvious what he intended, and we can see the rule he is following, *i.e.*, the alternation between, *e.g.*, *I put the paper in a file* and *I filed the paper*; *I bottled the fruit* and *I put the fruit in a bottle*; *I boxed the presents* and *I put the presents in a box*. Conceivably, he was following a rule that sentences have Verb Phrases that consist of Verb+Noun Phrase (V+NP), rather than the more complex Verb+Noun Phrase+Preposition Phrase (V+NP+PP). Bowerman (1982) provides examples such as *Giggle me*, meaning "cause me to giggle", produced by a child, presumably following the rule of *tickle me* or *carry me*, but not yet understanding the rule for the formation of causatives in English. These sorts of examples make transparent the language acquisition process of the child who is still sorting out the argument structure of English verbs. Invariably, adults find these creations amusing. I believe it is because these creations too, in their freshness and particular local logic, tap the tacit linguistic knowledge of the adult speaker.

3.2.3.4 Second Language Speakers' Creations

Some of the features of linguistic jokes are also to be found in the errors made by people in the developing or fossilized stages of second language acquisition. Paying attention to interlanguage errors is a way of finding some evidence of the unconscious knowledge of the rules of the new language. This evidence is, of course, muddied by interference from the first language, nonetheless, analysis of some errors reveal the not yet perfect use of tacit rules. Aberrant utterances (often unintentionally funny) are used by proficient speakers to mock the less than perfect productions of the second language user. Proliferating collections of these (in written form, and therefore compounded in their egregiousness) do the rounds on the Internet, and contribute to well-developed prejudices held by native speakers about non-native speakers. I attach a few randomly pulled off the Internet.

Funny signs from Hotels around the World

In a Tokyo Hotel:
Is forbidden to steal hotel towels please. If you are not a person to do such thing is please not to read notis.

In a Bucharest hotel lobby:
The lift is being fixed for the next day. During that time we regret that you will be unbearable.

In a Leipzig elevator:
Do not enter the lift backwards, and only when lit up.

In a Belgrade hotel elevator:
To move the cabin, push button for wishing floor. If the cabin should enter more persons, each one should press a number of wishing floor. Driving is then going alphabetically by national order.

In a Paris hotel elevator:
Please leave your values at the front desk.

In a hotel in Athens:
Visitors are expected to complain at the office between the hours of 9 and 11 A.M. daily.

In a Yugoslavian hotel:
The flattening of underwear with pleasure is the job of the chambermaid.

In a Japanese hotel:
You are invited to take advantage of the chambermaid.[24]

These errors too, tap the tacit knowledge of the native or highly proficient speaker, but have the effect of making us feel superior, rather than surprised.[25]

3.2.3.5 Linguistic Humor and Neurological Impairment

The proposals made here might also be relevant to the study of the cognitive neuroscience of language breakdown—*i.e.*, they might be helpful in studying the extent to which people are unable to produce/comprehend jokes and in providing leads to a study of the relevant corresponding deficit in the neuro-anatomy of the brain. Analysis of language impairment as a result of neurological damage, strokes and brain damage also yield examples of linguistic humor, although these are unintended. Interestingly, these utterances also show the linguistic features found in linguistic jokes, child language creations and second language speaker errors. These examples are simply a subclass of the general data that are available from people with neurological impairments since their humorous import is generally unintended, but they do give us an insight into the linguistic system within which they are operating.

Of significance to cognitive science and linguistics, a great deal of experimental research has been conducted on the **processing** of humor in people with neurological impairments. These studies provide some insight into the parts of the brain that are responsible for the processing of humor, and are an excellent source of evidence for the psychological reality of linguistic representations, and the fact that the location of damage can selectively affect the processing of humor at different levels. Whereas, in general, in right-handers, the comprehension of pragmatics has been regarded as a right hemisphere function, and jokes, being speech acts, require global understanding, certain jokes appear to be processed in the left hemisphere. It has long been thought that any metaphorical use of language is a right hemisphere function, and as would be expected, it has been shown that irony, non-literal and poetic language are processed in the right hemisphere (Brownell *et al.*, 1983; Burgess & Simpson, 1988; Coulson & Lovett, 2004; Goel & Dolan, 2001; Shammi & Stuss, 1999; Coulson & Williams, 2005). Most of these experiments have been conducted using Event Related Potentials, which measure electrical activity in the brain.

However, recent work has shown, additionally, that both hemispheres are involved in semantic activation during the course of jokes (Kandhadai & Federmeier, 2008), and that the processing of metaphoric language does not activate the hemispheres in the same way as jokes do. Right hemisphere privilege is shown to be less striking for the processing of metaphoric language, and the processing is finally similarly taxing for both hemispheres (Coulson & van Petten, 2007). Linguistic processing of linguistic jokes must, of course, implicate the left hemisphere as well. This has been shown for puns, specifically, by Coulson and Severens (2007), who have demonstrated that although the left hemisphere is at first involved in disambiguating the two different meanings of a word, the right hemisphere is concerned initially only with the most highly related meaning. However, ultimately, both meanings are active in both hemispheres.

Of course, since brain science is rapidly developing powerful technologies, it is likely that we will know much more about the areas of the brain that are implicated in the processing of language in general. Much research remains to be done on linguistic humor and the brain.

Overall, it seems that humor processing requires a person to have both a left and a right hemisphere, fully intact.

> Whereas the left hemisphere might appreciate some of Groucho's puns, and the right hemisphere might be entertained by the antics of Harpo, only the two hemispheres unified can appreciate an entire Marx Brothers routine.
>
> *(Gardner et al., 1983)*

4.0 Limitations, or What the Reader Can Find Elsewhere

I'm not a humor researcher: I'm a linguist, and in this book I offer only linguistic insights, and these only inasmuch as they illuminate my central questions.

Since my focus is on the fundamental problem of access to tacit linguistic knowledge, and what jokes can tell us about this knowledge, I have limited my scope to allow me to concentrate in depth on a few central questions. I point the reader to research in areas that have already become part of well-planned research programs. I have borrowed liberally and eclectically from established traditions.

The field of Humor Studies is a broad and amorphous one. Along with the philosopher Ted Cohen (1999), I do not believe it is possible to construct an overarching theory of humor, in fact, I don't even know what such a theory would look like. In a piecemeal, step-by-step way, however, researchers into aspects of humor have carefully proposed theoretical paradigms and testable hypotheses that have each begun to account for large numbers of specific joke types. The most developed of these, within a linguistic tradition, is the *General Theory of Verbal Humor* (previously the *Semantic Script Theory of Humor*) (Attardo & Raskin, 1991). Although no one theory has been shown to account for the structure of all jokes, the GTVH and, separately, with different proposals, the project begun by Ritchie and his associates (1999, 2004) are ongoing attempts to formulate such a theory.

The work in this book capitalizes on, but does not contribute to Humor Studies. Raskin states that an application of a disciplinary theory, (*e.g.*, a psychological, sociological or linguistic one) to Humor Studies is not of much value if all it demonstrates is that the original theory can be applied to the study of humor. For it to be considered as part of Humor Studies it must advance the study of humor. The application of disciplinary theories, thus, should contribute to theory building in Humor Studies (Raskin 1985, pp. 51–53, p.16 in Attardo, 1994).

The sort of linguistic analysis presented in this book does not contribute directly to advancing overall theories of humor, nor to extending existing linguistic theories of humor. It's fundamentally a matter of perspective: we can ask what language tells us about jokes or what jokes tell us about language. Linguistic theories of humor are concerned (*inter alia*) with the first, the linguistic study of jokes is concerned with the second.

Also within the framework of Linguistic Theories of Humor, scholars (Lew, 1997; Attardo, 1994; Chiaro, 1992) have provided various taxonomies of joke types, with Attardo, particularly (see Attardo, 1994, chapter 3), remarking on the limitations of taxonomies. For a processing account of how jokes are understood, see Giora, 2003; Lippman & Dunn, 2000; Long & Graesser, 1989; Mahoney, 1999.

Although I provide no original experimental psycholinguistic evidence for what I claim here, the analysis of my data (*i.e.*, the jokes) however, yields linguistic evidence that unconscious knowledge of the rules of language is required in order for these sorts of jokes to be acknowledged or noticed.

As a linguist, I focus on the linguistic insights provided by the philosophers of language or the linguistic philosophers. Although, in itself, this is not a philosophical work, it has important philosophical implications. The reader is directed to the work of John Moreall (1983, 1987, 2008a) on the philosophy of humor, for useful, comprehensive and interesting presentations on the history of the philosophies of humor. Also of interest in this regard is an extended essay by Jim Holt (2008).

Readers are urged to read the work of Davies (1990, 1998, 2002, 2008), Kuipers (2006, 2008) and Oring (1984, 1992, 2003, 2008), for comprehensive and sensitive accounts of humor from sociological, anthropological, folklorical and psychoanalytic perspectives. As will be seen, and as might be expected, much work on humor focuses on analyses of the social and psychological purposes and effects of jokes.

A large proportion of the work, much of it empirical, conducted in humor studies, has been directed towards investigating aspects of the psychology of humor. Ruch (2008) covers, among other topics in the psychology of humor, a review of work on humor responses, cognitive processes, motivational processes, study of mood, personality, traits, abilities, character strengths, aesthetics, humor pathology, humor tests, lifespan humor development, heritability and evolution, as well as psychoanalysis. He provides a comprehensive set of references, wide in scope, to research on these topics. For discussion about the therapeutic powers of humor and laughter, the reader is directed to the work of Rod Martin (1996, 2007, 2008) and John Morreall (2008b).

5.0 So What *is* the Contribution of this Book?

Here I return to Wittgenstein. I hope that I have risen to my own challenge to write a serious linguistics book that consists (almost) entirely of jokes. This book is a contribution to that ideal. I am, nonetheless, aware of E.B. White's cautionary advice, which I have ignored.

> Humor can be dissected as a frog can, but the thing dies in the process and the innards are discouraging to any but the pure scientific mind.

Alas, I have been obliged, for reasons of pure science, scholarship and professionalism to do my best to kill the jokes. Commentary and analysis are inevitable companions to the jokes, in a book of this sort, and, for this discouragement, I apologize.

Notes

1 My thinking has been spurred on by the most popular introductory linguistics text, *An Introduction to Language* (Fromkin, Rodman, & Hyams, 2010) and scholarly works of an entertaining and stimulating nature (notably, Pinker, 1994, 1997, 1999, 2002, 2007; Crystal, 2001, *e.g.*).

2 In this work, when I refer to "linguistics", I am well aware that the term is highly contested. When I talk about linguistics, I mean the scientific study of language, within a broadly generative paradigm. I use the notions 'competence' (tacit knowledge of language) and 'performance', in their technical sense, as first defined by Chomsky (1965).

3 Attardo here is talking about puns. I include his remark to make a more general point about language play.

4 I propose a more precise limitation and definition of this class of humor later. For the time being, the reader should understand that the class of data I look at contains jokes that play on some systematic aspect of the language we use.

5 Some time after I wrote this paragraph, I came across a more elegant, and much earlier formulation, by David Crystal.

> We play with language when we manipulate it as a source of enjoyment, either for ourselves or the benefit of others. I mean 'manipulate' literally: we take some linguistic feature—such as a word, a phrase, a sentence, a part of a word, a group of sounds, a series of letters—and make it do things it does not normally do. We are, in effect, bending and breaking the rules of the language. And if someone were to ask why we do it, the answer is simply, for fun.
>
> *(Crystal, 1998, p. 1)*

6 Raskin (1985) refers to these as Verbal Jokes, a subclass of Verbally Expressed Humor (VEH). I discuss this issue further in Section 2.2.

7 Adapted from http://www.hidden-dublin.com/homer/homer01.html, accessed January 23, 2010.

8 Jakobson (1959) uses the term "poetic", as does Hockett (1977).

9 In terms of data collection, my approach has been haphazard with regard to sampling, frequencies and other rigorous data collection methods. I have sought and found jokes

that illustrate particular linguistic points. My sources are joke books, the Internet, commonly heard jokes, childhood memories, my favorite comedians, and my own favorite jokes. I have tried to acknowledge sources wherever I can, the rest of the time, I have stolen jokes when I cannot trace the owner of the intellectual property.

10 In much the same way that the goal of generative linguistics is to explain linguistic competence (or our knowledge of language), the goal of humor theory, according to Raskin, is to describe humor competence.

11 Ritchie's (2004) work, in my view, is the clearest and most precise formulation of the criteria for jokehood.

12 This is not to say there are no onomatopoeic words in a language, but these are notable for their exceptional role in sound-meaning pairs and are, in any event, subject to language-specific phonological rules.

13 For a detailed discussion on the many different senses of "meaning" see Chapter 2 on Pragmatics and Chapter 3 on Semantics.

14 Note, however, that the extent to which the language faculty is an independent module of the mind is an empirical question. For instance, in recent work, some scholars, *e.g.*, Hauser, Chomsky, Fitch (2002) make a proposal for the distinction between Faculty of Language Broad (FLB) and Faculty of Language Narrow (FLN), in which only aspects of syntax are considered to be entirely separate from other modules.

15 This has also been referred to as the "haha moment". I have tried, so far unsuccessfully, to trace the first use of the term. And apparently "ownership" of the phrase "aha moment" itself has been contested: Oprah settles "aha moment" case. http://news.bbc.co.uk/2/hi/8351986.stm

16 Influential research in language processing has shown that all utterances, by their nature, activate a host of associations—phonological, lexical, semantic and extralinguistic—on the part of a hearer. However, as a rule, these never come to consciousness, and are eliminated as part of regular processing. Any use of language, however, that is deliberately or consciously ambiguous, causes a disruption in the automatic flow of processing.

17 A more detailed examination of interlingual jokes can be found in Chapter 7.

18 I discuss this class of jokes in more detail in Chapter 8.

19 A full discussion of cryptic crosswords is to be found in Chapter 9.

20 I do not claim to be the first to suggest that crafted language allows both producer and receiver insight into otherwise unconscious knowledge. I think the insight goes back to Aristotle's views on poetry. I am not sure that the claim has ever been made, however, that appreciation of artistic uses of language necessarily results in an awareness of tacit linguistic knowledge. I'd venture to suggest, though, that in order to get a **joke**, the listener has to consult rules, and that very often, these are tacit.

21 I refer to faithful translation, not translation equivalence.

22 I don't mean to claim that all native users of English find it funny, simply that they can access the necessary linguistic intuitions, whereas many non-native speakers may not be able to do so with quite the same ease.

23 Roeper (2007) is one of the most comprehensive resources for this type of research on child language.

24 Copied from http://www.dreamhaven.org/~data/humor/signs.html accessed 3rd January 2010.

25 This book is not concerned with differentiating between theories of humor. Nevertheless, I point out this difference in response (*i.e.,* feelings of superiority) to a stimulus that manifests similar linguistic features to those that might cause a response of relief, or simple amusement at the incongruity between what is expected and what is produced.

2

PLAYING WITH LINGUISTIC PRAGMATICS

1.0 Introduction

1.1 Theoretical Preliminaries

In this chapter, I discuss jokes that play primarily at the level of pragmatics. Establishing the boundary line between pragmatics and semantics is not simple, since there is ongoing disagreement among scholars as to what belongs on either side of the boundary, and according to any demarcation we may choose, there will always be boundary phenomena. I take the term "pragmatic analysis" to be the analysis of a particular unit of discourse in a context of use. As far as pragmatics *v.* semantics is concerned, I adopt the view that semantics is concerned with the linguistic meaning of sentences, *i.e.*, inasmuch as possible, their invariant or context-free meaning, whereas pragmatics is concerned with utterances in their context of use.

Since in this book I am concerned with what jokes can tell us about tacit knowledge of our language, I present a theoretical position on pragmatic competence that is grounded in an overall theory of language that regards pragmatics as "a central and crucial component" (Stemmer, 1999). According to this view, propounded in various works briefly by Chomsky and elaborated by Kasher,[1] pragmatic competence, or our knowledge of the rules of language use, is part of our linguistic system (Chomsky, 1975, 1978, 1980; Kasher, 1977, 1981, 1991; Stemmer, 1999).[2]

"It could be that one of the systems that develops, either as a distinct module or a component of others, is the kind of 'communicative competence' that enables us to use language coherently and in ways that are appropriate to situations" (Chomsky in Stemmer, 1999). Needless to say, many of the particular instantiations of rules of use are acquired through exposure to a particular cultural context.

However, the claim on which I'll be building regards some principles of language use to be tacit, and many of them to be not immediately available to conscious awareness.[3]

Certainly since the era of the Minimalist Program (Chomsky, 1995), it has been an open question as to the extent to which these principles are specific to the language faculty proper, or *shared* by other cognitive modules. Nevertheless, despite many of his critics' claim to the contrary, Chomsky has always maintained that "[i]t's possible that a form of communicative competence underlies the use of language for communication (one of its many uses)" (Stemmer, 1999).

In some non-Chomskyan frameworks, in relation to the study of pragmatics, the distinction has been made between pragmalinguistics and sociopragmatics (Leech, 1983; Thomas, 1983). This distinction may be described as the difference between illocutionary competence (knowing how to express and understand speech acts appropriately) and the global knowledge of the social context in which particular speech acts are made.[4] Without going into the details of the divisions, nor the extreme theoretical differences between the paradigms of inquiry, I snatch Leech's terminology for my own purposes. I use "pragmalinguistics" to refer to the linguistic knowledge available for understanding and producing speech acts within a context of use. Such resources include pragmatic notions like directness/indirectness, co-operativeness, and knowledge of how these may be encoded in appropriate linguistic forms.

I consider that sociopragmatic knowledge (essentially knowledge about the world in which an interaction is conducted, including non-linguistic context) is generally acquired as part of membership in a culture, and therefore not tacit in quite the way that pragmalinguistic knowledge may be. I take pragmalinguistic knowledge to refer to the rules of utterance use, and I claim that it may be just as difficult for a speaker to articulate the rules of language use as it is for her to articulate the rules of phonological or sentence structure. My claim then, is that pragmatic competence is tacit.

1.2 The Study of Pragmatics in its Different Paradigms

Linguistic pragmatics as a field of inquiry was launched by philosophers of language. The questions they were asking were not necessarily questions about the relationship between language and mind, but rather driven by the impulse to move from formal systems and logic, which considered sentences in terms of truth values, to understanding the way in which language was actually used, that is to say the examination of utterances within their context of use. The later Wittgenstein was the driving force behind this impulse (1953/2001), as was John Austin (Austin, 1962). The study of linguistic pragmatics, thus, is the study of language in its context of use.

The origin and course of the field of pragmatics does not preclude the question that I address here, which is: what is the nature of the knowledge we must have in order to use language appropriately? My particular purpose is to show that, ultimately, pragmatic competence is implicit and the rules are not easily accessible to conscious awareness. In order to answer the theoretical question, we may ultimately have to conduct the inquiry at a degree of abstraction from the phenomena investigated.

1.3 Linguistic Pragmatics and the Philosophers

1.3.1 What do we Mean by Linguistic Pragmatics?

Linguistic Pragmatics is generally regarded to be the study of language in its context of use. Some authors believe it is the study of meaning in interaction (Thomas, 1995). By any of its different definitional guises, certain elements are crucially concerned in the study of pragmatics.

1. The unit of analysis may be bigger or smaller than the sentence.
2. Pragmatic analysis takes place at the discourse level. It requires at least one utterance, considered in its context of use.
3. Thus, in conducting pragmatic analysis of linguistic phenomena, we should consider phenomena within their context of use.
4. Pragmatics, then, is the study of particular linguistic utterances, who is making them, to whom they are being made, where and when the discourse is taking place and the relationship of all these elements to one another, as well as to the structure and conventionalized function of language elements as they have been described. Pragmatic competence is the underlying knowledge of all of the above, required by speakers, in just the same way as syntactic competence is required to produce and understand sentences.

Thus, in the classic example below, we see that in order for speakers and hearers to make sense of what their interlocutors are saying, they need to rely on tacit knowledge about the way in which language is used to do things, *e.g.*, make requests. Naturally, as well, the understanding of A's utterance requires that B know something about the world, *i.e.*, that when it is hot the temperature in a room may be lowered by opening a window.

Example 1

Speaker A: It's hot in here.
Speaker B: Should I open the window?

The fact that B appears to react to A's statement about the temperature with an offer to open the window must lead us to believe that in addition to any world knowledge they both may have, there is something B (at least) knows about how language is used, and that this knowledge is implicit.

1.3.2 The Ordinary Language Philosophers

1.3.2.1 Meaning is Use: Wittgenstein

The study of linguistic pragmatics as it is described here, arises out of Ordinary Language Philosophy. Linguistic Pragmatics as I understand it, draws on Wittgenstein (1953), in tandem with the work of, specifically, Austin (1962), Searle (1969, 1979) and Grice (1957, 1975). The general argument for ordinary language philosophy is that language is not made up of a series of propositions, each of which has a truth-value, *i.e.*, true or false. Wittgenstein (1953) made two major moves from the world of Frege and Russell. The first was to show that the language we use is not a set of logical propositions, each with a truth-value. The second was to argue that meaning is neither an expression's sense or its reference, but in fact, its use. Thus, for Wittgenstein, an expression's use *is* its meaning. This radical view changed the face of linguistic philosophy, and in Anglo-American Philosophy is now the basis of the central debates about meaning.[5] It is, *inter alia*, a view that is instrumental in blurring the distinctions between semantics and pragmatics.

1.3.2.2 Speech Acts: Austin and Searle

John Austin, also a philosopher, was deeply influenced by Wittgenstein. His major theoretical insight was that we use language to do things in the world. The 1962 book in which his lecture notes on this topic are to be found is entitled, *How To Do Things With Words*. In this work, he argues that in using language, we do not simply exchange propositions, rather, we use language to, *e.g.*, request, criticize, praise, vow, demand, deny, apologize and so forth. These uses he termed Speech Acts. He made the distinction between the locutionary act (*i.e.*, an utterance's standard linguistic meaning, as would be understood by means of dictionary definitions) and an utterance's illocutionary force, that is to say, the speaker's intention when making the utterance, in a particular context of use. He made a further distinction between illocutionary force, which is the speaker's intention in making the utterance, and perlocutionary force, which is the effect the utterance is designed to have on a hearer (Austin, 1962).

Searle (1969, 1979) further refined Speech Act Theory by proposing that speech acts are constituted by the rules of language.[6] He articulated the distinction between the propositional content of an utterance and its illocutionary force, a distinction essentially made initially by Austin.

1.3.2.3 The Co-operative Principle: Grice

The philosopher, H.P. Grice, contributed greatly to the field of linguistic pragmatics specifically by proposing a model of human communication, *i.e.*, an analysis of how people understand one another's language acts (Grice, 1957,

1975). He made the distinction between linguistic meaning and speaker meaning, and demonstrated how these interact in human conversational behavior.

Grice made the distinction between the phenomena of natural meaning and non-natural meaning, as follows. Natural meaning is a consequence of certain causes. Thus, "These spots mean measles" (Grice, 1957, pp. 377–8). This phenomenon must, however, be distinguished from non-natural meaning, which is entirely constructed, as in, "Those three rings on the bell mean that the bus is full" (Grice, 1957, pp. 377–8). According to Grice, speaker intention, too, may be accounted for in terms of non-natural meaning. This notion is helpful in analyzing speakers' intentions. When speakers engage in communication, they have intentions, and in expressing their intentions they use language to convey non-natural meanings.[7]

Grice tried to explain, among other things, how it is possible for utterances to be understood (Grice, 1975). He proposed a general co-operative principle to account for human behavior. Note that, for Grice, this principle is not limited to the use of language, and is therefore not a modular and specified competence.

The Co-operative Principle and the Conversational Maxims

Make your conversational contribution such as is required, at the stage at which it occurs, by the accepted purpose or direction of the talk exchange in which you are engaged.

Maxim of Quality
Be Truthful
- Do not say what you believe to be false.
- Do not say that for which you lack adequate evidence.

Maxim of Quantity
Quantity of Information
- Make your contribution as informative as is required (for the current purposes of the exchange).
- Do not make your contribution more informative than is required.

Maxim of Relation
Relevance
- Be relevant.

Maxim of Manner
Be Clear
- Avoid obscurity of expression.
- Avoid ambiguity.
- Be brief (avoid unnecessary prolixity).
- Be orderly.

(Grice, 1975, p. 45)

Essentially, Grice's argument goes as follows. Human behavior is both rational and co-operative. Humans' language behavior is a subset of human behavior, and is thus, both rational and co-operative. Now, for people to understand others' use of language, there needs to be a mechanism that can account for how this understanding happens. The Co-operative Principle (CP), in conjunction with the four maxims of conversation, is postulated as the central engine of the mechanism. The idea is that when we engage in conversation with another person, we expect the interchange to be co-operative (at some deep level at least), *i.e.*, that the participants in a conversational exchange share a commonly understood purpose. Since we are rational, we are guided by the acceptance of this principle, as well as certain maxims, which state, essentially, that unless we have evidence to the contrary, we should understand our interlocutor's utterances to be truthful, appropriate in length and quantity of information, orderly in presentation, and relevant to the interaction at hand. In other words, the utterances should accord with the maxims of quality, quantity, manner and relevance. If we have evidence to the contrary, or reason to think that our interlocutor is not following these maxims, we are entitled to engage in a calculation as to what the interlocutor is really trying to say, *i.e.*, we derive an **implicature** from the discrepancy between what the interlocutor says and what we know about the CP and the maxims. The way we do this is to notice which of the maxims (sometimes it is more than one) is being violated or flouted, and as a result, we are entitled to assume that the interlocutor has a reason for not abiding by the maxim/s. We then engage in a calculation to derive an implicature from the fact that a maxim has not been followed. The implicature is regarded as having been deliberately created by the speaker. This is called conversational implicature.

Here's a standard textbook example of conversational implicature.

Example 2

Mother to teenage son (coat on, about to leave the house): Where are you going?
Son: Out.

In the example above, clearly, the son is not obeying the maxim of quantity, *i.e.*, he is not providing enough information for the matter at hand. The mother can see he is going out. Her question is a request for more information. However, he conveys to her the message that it is none of her business and he is not going to tell her where he is going. The accurate retrieval of the message is due to a conversational implicature being generated and understood as intended.

According to Grice, the Co-operative Principle is a guiding principle that speakers of a language follow, as a way of helping them to navigate conversations. Although most people cannot articulate this principle, Grice claims that it is a description of what people do when they are engaging in conversation. The strength of Grice's proposal of the CP and the maxims lies in the proviso contained in his statement of the CP. This is what allows interlocutors to make judgments as to the appropriateness of a given utterance to the particular context of the conversation. The proviso is contained in the words highlighted in bold below.

> Make your contribution such as it is required, at the stage at which it occurs, **by the accepted purpose or direction of the talk exchange in which you are engaged**.

> *(Grice, 1975, p. 45)*

This proviso requires that interlocutors give as much information as required by the current purpose or direction of the exchange. The rules are difficult to articulate, and are acquired only through immersion in a culture; nevertheless, it is claimed, people follow them.[8]

Many humorous effects are created by the use of conversational implicature and we examine them in more detail as we proceed. Jokes, of course, are the supreme exemplars of what Raskin calls non-*bona fide* (NBF) communication (Raskin, 1985). In terms of the pragmatic rules that we all seem to understand without articulating, conversational participants are given the indication by some clue in the interaction that a joke is coming, or a joke has been made. Often, the indicator is the joke itself, or part of the joke. If the interlocutor does not realize that the conversational partner is playing, or has made a joke, then the interaction is not successful. The primary intention of the speaker in these cases (the illocutionary force) has not been understood. This mismatch in the perceptions of what is expected is often the cause of puzzlement, anger, and misunderstanding between interlocutors.

According to Raskin (1985), non-*bona fide* (*i.e.*, joking or humorous) communication differs from *bona fide* (*i.e.*, earnest, serious, information-conveying) communication in the way it violates one or more of Grice's maxims (Grice, 1975). Raskin makes the interesting observation that violation of the maxims can be either intentional or unintentional; in the one case, the speaker is aware, and in the other case unaware, of the ambiguity she has created (Raskin, 1985, p. 100). This leads to a situation in which, even if the speaker is engaged in *bona fide* communication, the hearer may interpret the utterance as a non-*bona fide* one, if she becomes aware of the ambiguity. This is the sort of occasion in which an acknowledgment of the joke, or a subsequent joking utterance, may be forthcoming, leading to a disruption of the serious conversation that had gone before.

Exploiting ambiguity in the interpretation of illocutionary force is one of the most productive joke-making mechanisms. The recognition of ambiguity (be it pragmatic or otherwise) is in itself an interesting feature of human cognition, which is likely to be innate (Boeckx, 2009).

2.0 Conversational Implicature

As Grice (1975) pointed out, the difference between language use and logic is often to be found in the fact that humans do not feel any compunction to abide by the rules of logic, or if they do, they bend them at will. The following joke shows how in order to communicate a number of different messages simultaneously, people do not feel obliged to follow the conversational maxims in order to operate in conformity with the Co-operative Principle. This is precisely Grice's point. We flout the maxims in order to communicate something other or additional to what we actually say. This is a deep kind of co-operativeness, in which we manage, in some way, to communicate what we intend as well as what we say.

Example 3

Two men, old friends, run into each other at the bowls club.
"I hear that your mother-in law's ill," says the one.
"Yes, she's in the hospital."
"How long has she been there for?"
"In three weeks time, please God, it'll be a month."

(adapted from Minkoff, 2007)

The straightforward, factual answer to the question about the mother-in-law's health is that she has been in hospital for one week. However, a great deal more is communicated by the son-in-law. Firstly, we can gather that he doesn't like his mother-in-law. His speech act, which sounds likes an invocation to God for help, is in fact, a curse. He is creating the implicature that with a little help from some extra agency, such as God, his mother-in-law will remain in hospital for at least another three weeks. He doesn't say any of this: he simply violates the maxim of manner: *be clear*. He could say that she has been in hospital for one week. Instead he makes it obvious by implication that he wishes it were longer. Normally, we use a phrase like *In three weeks time it'll be a month*, when we are certain about an event that has already taken place and we can count ahead from that time, such as in (i) and (ii), but not in (iii).

i. *How long is it since your mother-in-law died?*
    In three weeks time, it'll be a month.
ii. *How long has your brother been overseas?*
    In three weeks time, it'll be a month.
iii. *How long has it taken you to finish painting your house?*
    In three weeks time, it'll be a month.

There is no way that the speaker can know how long his mother-in-law will be in hospital, and much though he would like to rely on his hopes, he can't. So, whereas the speaker's final utterance looks like the response in (iii), it is actually different, because the questioner in (iii) presupposes that in three weeks time the painting job will be over. The man in the joke, however, doesn't want his mother-in-law's time in the hospital to be over yet. His use of *please God* makes him sound as though he is really concerned for her welfare, whereas the implicature is clearly that his *please God* is a plea for her continued hospitalization. This implicature is quite clearly retrievable from his utterance.

Some jokes are based almost entirely on ambiguity in the interpretation of the illocutionary force of one or more of the speakers in the joke. Illocutionary force in an utterance is impossible to discern outside of a context, and is certainly not always reliably derivable from the actual linguistic items used. The classic examples from linguistic pragmatics go along the lines of Examples 4 and 5.

Example 4

Can you pass the salt?
(uttered by a diner to her neighboring diner at the table).

Example 4 looks structurally like a yes/no question, but in terms of speaker intention it may be nothing of the sort. It may have the force of a request, and the force is not derivable from the componentiality of word meanings, nor its syntactic structure as an interrogative.

Example 5

Father: How old are you?
Son: I'm 39, Father
Father: I didn't ask you how old you are, you fool.

(borrowed from Jenny Thomas, 1995)

Clearly, in Example 5, the father's intention is not to find out from the son how old he is. It is not, thus, an information seeking utterance. Rather, it is likely to be intended to rebuke or castigate the son. The son, on the other hand, answers truthfully, because he has not discerned the father's intention in asking the question (or most likely, he has chosen not to understand it). The father, in turn, is annoyed, because the son missed his intention in asking the question. As a result, he defies all logic and says, *I didn't ask you how old you are, you fool*, which is exactly what he did do. This is a good example of how a speaker believes that he is communicating his intention, despite what he actually says.

3.0 Direct and Indirect Speech Acts

3.1 Properties of Speaker Intention

Whereas literal and non-literal uses of language are properties of utterances, *i.e.*, it can be discerned whether the proposition expressed is literal or not,[9] directness and indirectness are properties of speaker intention.[10] Discerning whether a speech act is direct or indirect requires reference not only to knowledge of the language, but also to knowledge of the context in which the utterance is being made, which includes a calculation as to what the speaker might intend. Below is a well-worn example that may serve to illustrate an indirect speech act.

Example 6

Speaker A: It's cold in here.
Speaker B: I'll close the window.

It may or may not be the case that it is cold in the room, especially since the perception of temperature by people is somewhat subjective. However, generally, the hearer is able to decide whether the utterance is literally true or false. Either way, for the purposes of the communication, the hearer needs to decide what the speaker is doing with language here, *i.e.*, is s/he stating a fact, making a request, complaining about the central heating in the building? In this example, the hearer decides that the speaker is making a request for action leading to a change in the temperature in the room. The hearer thus responds as though the illocutionary force of the speaker's utterance is a request, and offers to close the window, which is the perlocutionary consequence of the speaker's utterance.

In terms of Grice's Co-operative Principle and the maxims for conversation, we may say that hearers respond to utterances by first assessing if the utterance obeys the maxims, *i.e.*, is it true, of appropriate length for the situation, orderly in terms of the requirement of the interaction, and relevant to the interaction at hand? The initial point of assessment is to ascertain if the utterance in its propositional form meets the requirements of the maxim of quality, "for the purposes at hand", *i.e.*, is it true or false? In the case above it turns out that the utterance conforms with the facts.

The question for the hearer remains as to what the speaker has in mind in making the utterance (*i.e.*, what is the speaker doing with words?) The speech act might be considered as a request, although nowhere is a request directly made. The hearer responds to the perceived request. The utterance thus functions as an **indirect** speech act. So, Speaker A's utterance above may be regarded as an indirect use of language.

A **direct speech act** is one in which a speaker's illocutionary force is patently derivable from the utterance in a context, *i.e.*, it conforms to the canonical grammatical format for the speech act in question, in this next case, an imperative. Thus, *Please give me a piece of chocolate* has the illocutionary force of a request, particularly with the modification of *Please*. It is a direct speech act, as the inferential chain from the locution to the illocutionary force (in context) is pretty straightforward. *That looks delicious*, on the other hand, when the intention is to express the same request in the same context, is an indirect speech act. The notion of **Indirect Speech Act** was introduced by Searle, in an attempt to further the research agenda of both Austin (Speech Acts) and Grice (the Co-operative Principle). Searle tried to resolve the problem of how hearers derive speakers' intentions, using the CP and the maxims, when the speech act in question is not direct. Searle uses the term "Indirect Speech Act" to refer to an indirect illocutionary act. "In indirect speech acts the speaker communicates to the hearer more than he actually says by way of relying on their mutually shared background information, both linguistic and non-linguistic, together with the general powers of rationality and inference on the part of the hearer" (Searle, 1979, p. 31).

The example below should clarify the distinction between direct and indirect speech acts.

Example 7

A: I want to marry you.
B: Are you crazy?

In this case, B's response is in the interrogative form, *i.e.*, it looks like an information seeking question. If an utterance in an interaction is phrased as an information-seeking question, a hearer might interpret its illocutionary force as being a request for information. In such a case, the utterance would be a direct speech act. Very often, however, in an interaction such as shown in the example above, illocutionary force is independent of grammatical form, and particular grammatical forms are neither necessary nor sufficient in determining illocutionary force. These acts are known as indirect speech acts. In the example above, B's utterance does not have the illocutionary force of a question: it is a refusal. It is thus an indirect speech act.

3.2 Ambiguity in Illocutionary Force Found in Direct Speech Acts

In an interesting twist on an unremarkable idiomatic phrase, Henny Youngman demonstrates how the illocutionary force of an utterance may be altered by the addition of the word *please*. In English, *please* serves many different illocutionary purposes – in this case, it functions to disambiguate illocutionary force.

Example 8

Take my wife ... please

(Henny Youngman, 1906–1998)

Both utterances, *Take my wife* and *Take my wife ... please* are direct speech acts, however in the first the illocutionary force is a gentle imperative, roughly paraphrased as "consider", whereas the use of *please* in the second causes the illocutionary force to be understood as a plea for the speaker's wife to be removed.

3.3 Ambiguity Arising From the Confusion Between Direct and Indirect Speech Acts

The following two jokes are each examples of how a direct speech act and an indirect speech act may be confused.

Example 9

At a rather fancy golf club, a captain of industry found himself unhappy with the quality of attention he was receiving from the drinks staff. The room was full and others seemed to be getting their orders, as he waited, embarrassed in front of his guests, and annoyed at appearing less important than his fellow members. After a few minutes of trying unsuccessfully to get a waiter's attention, he marched up to the manager's area and said, indignantly, "Do you have any idea who I am?" The assistant manager replied, "Honestly, Sir, I've only just been employed here, so I don't know if I can help you myself. But as soon as we get less busy, Sir, I'll ask at the office and get right back to you and let you know."

Example 10

A man went to see a fortuneteller, who said "For $100 I'll read your palm. Not only will I do that, but for the price you'll be allowed to ask three questions."
  "Really," said the man, "questions about what?"
  "Oh, you can ask about anything you like," the fortuneteller replied.
  "Isn't $100 a bit much for that?"
  "It might be. So, what's your last question?"

In the joke about the man at the golf club (a similar joke is discussed by Pinker in *The Language Instinct*), the speaker asks, *Do you have any idea who I am?* As is clear from the context, the desired perlocutionary effect is for the hearer to acknowledge his importance. The speech act is an indirect one, because the club member is not really asking the manager if he has any idea who he (the captain of industry) is, but rather, he is telling him how important he is. The manager takes the utterance at face value, *i.e.*, as a direct speech act, and tells the club member that he has no idea who he is but will enquire at the desk and inform him right away, once he has the answer. Thus, he interprets the club member's self-important rebuke as an information-seeking question (along the lines of *Do you have any idea where we are?*) and helpfully agrees to assist in acquiring the information. It is unlikely that the club member could have intended the utterance as a direct speech act; however, hearers are always entitled to interpret indirect speech acts as direct. Doing so may often not be the most politic way to proceed, but the indirect speech act is always essentially ambiguous, and open to defeasibility.

The joke about the fortuneteller is a simple one, in which the fortuneteller interprets the illocutionary force of *Isn't $100 a bit much for that?* as the second of the three questions the client is allowed to ask. The first one is *Questions about* *what?* So, as we see, the fortuneteller pays attention only to the grammatical form of the utterances, which are both interrogatives. She treats them thus, as direct information-seeking speech acts, whereas the second one, specifically, *Isn't $100 a bit much for that?* is clearly part of the negotiation, and although a direct speech act, serves to express the customer's doubt. Whereas the customer doesn't think he's asked any questions at all, the fortuneteller has already counted two. The customer is thus tricked by the fortuneteller because she is counting the interrogatives, irrespective of the customer's purposes in using those interrogatives. Very often, a literal interpretation of the direct speech act can be relied upon to provide the hearer a defense for pragmatically inappropriate behavior.

As a matter of fact, however, when such questions are interpreted as direct information-seeking speech acts without any examination of their illocutionary force, they tend to reflect on the pragmatic adequacy of the hearer. We may see this demonstrated in one of a series of rather cruel dementia jokes.

Example 11

An elderly gentleman aged in his mid 90s goes to a bar. He smells of fancy cologne and is dressed elegantly in evening wear. Perched on a stool at the bar is an attractive, well-preserved woman in her 80s, sipping a martini. She is expensively dressed and carefully made-up. He approaches her politely and asks, "Do I come here often?"

In Example 11, the joke is playing with the cliché *Do you come here often?* which often functions as a pick-up line. However, in the case of the elderly (read: "senile") interlocutor, the problem is not in his recall of the illocutionary force of the pick-up line, but in his confusion of person. Because he confuses *you* with *I*, the pick-up line loses its illocutionary force although it keeps its interrogative structure.

3.4 Ambiguity in Illocutionary Force Arising from the Confusion of Literal and Non-Literal Utterances

Example 12 serves to show an interaction in which the speaker's utterance is literally true, but her indirect speech act is misunderstood. It turns out, in this example, that an ambiguity in a lexical item, leading to a literal/non-literal confusion, causes the illocutionary force of the utterance to be less clear than was intended.

Example 12

*A man is driving his shiny new car down a road in a semi-rural area. He sees a Stop sign ahead and slows down to stop before turning right. While his car's stopped, another car, somewhat more battered than his, comes screeching around the corner and pulls to a stop alongside him. The woman driving the car gesticulates wildly to him to open his window, and yells, **Pig! Pig!***

He glares at her and snarls, **Bitch! Bitch!**
Slamming his foot on the accelerator, he turns sharply into the street from which her car had emerged, roars down the street, and bumps into a pig.

In this joke, the man does not understand the illocutionary force of the woman's first utterance. The joke plays on the consequent mismatch between the illocutionary force of the utterance that was intended by the speaker, and the force that the hearer understood. This is one of the risks of using indirect speech acts, although it has been proposed that the risks are outweighed by the communal benefits that accrue for the sake of linguistic politeness (*e.g.*, Brown & Levinson, 1978, 1987; Leech, 1983).[11]

Example 12 works in quite a straightforward way. The woman is warning the man that there is a pig in the road. He thinks that she is hurling abuse at him, for some or other reason, and therefore, he responds in kind, by hurling back abuse. So, the illocutionary force of her first speech act is of warning; the illocutionary force of his is insult or abuse. The punch line, of course, turns on the fact that she is using the utterance *pig* literally to warn him that there is a pig in the road. He takes her use of the utterance *pig* to mean that she is calling him a pig, and he responds with immediate aggression by calling her an animal name too.

So, this joke demonstrates that in communication, the hearer's interpretation of speaker intention is the crucial criterion for the success of the speech act. In the joke, the man gets his come-uppance for responding aggressively, rather than reflecting on why the woman was so agitated that she yelled *Pig!*

Because of the lexical ambiguity, which results in literal/non-literal confusion, as well as some blurring of denotative and connotative uses, it turns out that this is a fairly difficult joke to translate.[12] *Pig* is not universally used as an insult, even within the English-speaking world.[13]

3.5 Ambiguity Arising from Non-Literal Uses of Language

In Example 13 below, the brother answering the call starts out using language that is literal, providing his brother with a direct answer to his question about the cat. However, having been rebuked for his insensitivity, he withdraws into using non-literal language to show that he has understood the message that he should be more sensitive. However, his use of non-literal language here is entirely inappropriate.

Example 13

A young man on vacation calls his home, and his brother answers.
"How's the cat?" he asks.
"The cat's dead. He died this morning," replies his brother.

"That's a hell of a way to break it to me. You know how attached I was to him. Couldn't you have broken the news more gently?"

"Like how? How would you have liked me to tell you?"

"How? First you could have said he's on the roof, then the next day, you could have told me you couldn't get him down, then eventually you could have broken it to me that he was dead."

"Ok," says his brother, "I'm sorry."

"Anyway," says the young man, "How's mom?"

"She's on the roof."

(adapted from Poulos, 2001, p. 51)

In the joke, *She's on the roof* is an utterance that is not true, literally or otherwise. It violates the maxim of quality. It also violates the maxim of manner. It is, nevertheless, a direct speech act. It takes the form of an assertion of a certain state of affairs. The implicature it creates, however, is different in many respects from its literal reading.

The idea that a cat could be on the roof is not all that implausible; the idea that the mother is on the roof is somewhat more far-fetched. The point is that the brother showed he had heard the rebuke, and in breaking the news about the mother's death showed that he was capable of using the gentler, less abrupt approach his brother had advocated. This joke demonstrates a more general point about how complex a matter it is to judge context and meet the exquisite requirements of appropriate language use.

3.6 Understanding the Illocutionary Force of an Indirect Speech Act but not its Content

In Example 14, one of the subtlest jokes exploiting illocutionary force I have come across, the confusion is not about the illocutionary force of the utterance *per se* but about the success of the message once the illocutionary force has been discerned.

The joke demonstrates a few different humorous strategies, all of which I discuss in turn. We are shown a situation in which it is clear that a certain utterance is literally true, and is understood as such. However, the utterance is not only literally true, it is also indirect, and although the illocutionary force of the utterance is discerned by the hearer, confusion ensues for other reasons.

The joke is one of the genre of blonde jokes, well known for the underlying premise that the blonde is a woman—she is stupid and interprets all utterances literally. (One might substitute any ethnic stereotype in this genre: Irish, Sikh, and Polish people are often the butt of these sorts of jokes in English). The point of these jokes, generally, is to equate over-literalness of interpretation with stupidity, and use the stereotype as the butt. As a rule, in blonde jokes, we are expected to equate *blonde* with "literal". Here, however, literalness of interpretation is not the problem.

Example 14

A blonde woman walks up to the reference desk in a library. She says to the librarian on duty, "I'd like a double hamburger, a serving of fries and a diet coke, please."
The librarian looks at her in horror, and says, "This is a library!"
Ashamed and apologetic, the blonde woman claps her hand over her mouth, then whispers, "I am so sorry! Please may I have a double hamburger, a serving of fries and a diet coke?"

This joke is particularly sophisticated, since it adds a new twist to the usual misunderstanding of illocutionary force. The librarian's utterance, *This is a library*, is literally true and this fact is accepted by both participants. The blonde, moreover, understands the illocutionary force of the utterance. She gets it that the librarian's intention is to rebuke her, but she doesn't understand the content of the rebuke. Her response shows that she thinks that she is being rebuked for talking loudly in a library, rather than that she understands that she is being reminded that it is inappropriate to order food in a library.

Her behavior is appropriate in the sense that she is following the script of approaching a counter and making a request: she just happens to be making the wrong request. She accepts the reprimand about her behavior and apologizes for what she thinks she has done wrong. The apology is based on the common understanding and unspoken cliché that in libraries we are meant to whisper. The additional twist is that she has missed the most direct and shortest possible interpretation of the librarian's intention: libraries provide books, not fast food.

This is also a joke on librarians, as well as blondes, since it is they who have caused the utterance, "This is a library", to become code for "be quiet".

3.7 Misunderstanding the Illocutionary Force of an Indirect Speech Act

According to Grice, in conversation, if any of the maxims have been violated, consciously or unconsciously, the hearer must seek an interpretation consistent with everything s/he knows about the context. In this view of the world, interlocutors are generally assumed to be in good faith, rational, and, at least underlyingly, co-operative, in that they are assumed to be genuinely trying to communicate some message to each other. The following joke contains a vivid illustration of a hearer trying to seek an interpretation consistent with everything he knows about the world, and the use of language. It's also an example that speaks to the touching faith Grice shows in the underlying co-operativeness and rationality of human beings in interaction.

Example 15 is an old Jewish joke that functions for me as the touchstone demonstration of the indirect speech act in conversational interaction, and provides, I believe, one of the finest examples of mistaken illocutionary force. Naturally, like every joke, example 15 is an example of non-*bona fide* communication.

Additionally, even within the frame of NBF communication, the main character in the joke himself engages in non-*bona fide* communication, for his own purposes.

Example 15

An elderly gentleman has been going to the same restaurant every Wednesday night for the past 30 years. The restaurant has employed the same waiter and same chef for those thirty years. The gentleman always orders the same thing, the soup. One Wednesday evening, as usual, he gets seated in the restaurant, and as always, he orders the soup. The waiter sets the soup in front of him and moves away. The gentleman calls him over.

"Waiter, taste the soup."

The waiter looks worried.

"Mr. Cohen, is there a problem? Something wrong with the soup?"

"Waiter, taste the soup."

"Oh, Mr. Cohen, this is terrible. You are our oldest and most faithful customer. I apologize if the soup is not to your liking tonight. Can I bring you something else?"

"Waiter, taste the soup."

"The chef is going to be devastated. I myself am shattered. This has never happened before. What can I possibly do to make this better?"

"Waiter, taste the soup."

"Look, Mr. Cohen, every one has an off night, and perhaps the chef was careless, or one of the ingredients was not as fresh as it could have been, but we'll make it up to you, I promise. You are our most valued customer. Oh, this is an awful situation. Terrible!"

"Waiter, taste the soup."

"All right, all right, I'll taste it. Right away. Where's the spoon?"

"Aha!"

I want to look in detail at how the humor is created in this particular joke. The dialogue course of the joke is crucial, so that we get a sense of the waiter's anxiety, and of how important to him is the request to taste the soup, given the length and quality of the restaurant's association with the customer. The waiter becomes more and more frantic, and in the telling of this joke, he is often portrayed as wringing his hands, begging and pleading to be allowed a way out of this horrible situation. The customer, on the other hand, is impassive. He simply repeats the same utterance, each time he takes a conversational turn. As audience, we know that the waiter is desperate and that for him the request to taste the soup is enormously important. We also know that the customer is unrelenting. The customer is cast as the powerful participant in this dialogue. At the level of the proposition, the utterance *taste the soup* makes available to the waiter the understanding that the customer wants him to taste the soup. This is the literal content of the proposition. The grammatical form of the utterance is cast in the imperative, and thus the direct speech act might reasonably be taken to be a request or an order. We know, though, that the grammatical form of an utterance very often has nothing to do with its illocutionary force. Thus, although the waiter immediately assumes that he is the recipient of an indirect speech act, he entirely misses the intention of the speaker, as well he might. He understands the customer to be complaining about the soup. He has a fair amount of evidence to think this, given that, generally, when restaurant customers ask waiters to taste the food they have served, the customers usually have something to say about the quality of the food.[14]

The punch line works on different levels and for several reasons. First, we see that the request to taste the soup has, in fact, nothing at all to do with the quality of the soup. So it is not a complaint about the soup, after all, although it is a complaint. Second, we see afterwards, given that it is the customer who wants something that the waiter can give him, the power should actually lie with the waiter and not the customer. It is the waiter who is withholding the means for the customer to eat his soup. However, crucially, the joke turns on the strange behavior of the customer, who might simply have asked for a spoon in the first place. Instead, he allows the waiter to go through the contortions and agonies of guessing what the problem is, and to make futile attempts at reparation. When finally the waiter is brought to his knees and agrees to do as the customer asks, he is forced to ask the relevant question, *Where's the spoon?* Following the CP and the maxims, we might expect the customer to say, in response to *Where's the spoon?* , "I haven't got one". Even if his response were to be indirect, it should be co-operative. In such a world, the customer might then have said, "That's what I want to know," or even, "That's what I've been asking you to notice", but instead he says*, Aha!* And *Aha!* covers a multitude of possible intentions: "at last, you noticed"; "at last, you got there"; "at last you understand my frustration"; "I have taught you something, and at last, you have learnt"; or "at last, you get my meaning". But if the customer had been so keen to get his meaning across and his intention was to get a spoon to eat his soup, surely he should simply have asked for one? Instead he chose to use an extremely roundabout route. He expected the waiter to derive the implicature, "I need a spoon" from *taste the soup*. This is a rather extreme example because the interpretive chain required in order to derive the intention of the speaker is not the obvious one. Further, when the waiter does finally work out what the torturer wants, the customer continues in his indirect vein. *Aha!* What does *Aha!* mean? We don't know what it means, but we know more or less what he intends it to mean, and at this point so does the waiter.

In everything that we know about the use of indirect speech acts, speaker intention is crucial. So what purpose might the speaker have had in not asking directly for the spoon as soon as his soup was delivered? If we were to account for his speech act using Grice's maxims, we could say that he flouted, at least, the maxim of manner, and certainly, in relation to the principle of co-operation, the entire dialogue flies in the face of the maxim of quantity. Here we have to doubt that the motive was politeness (in its technical or non-technical sense). One could argue that face considerations are, in fact, the essence of the joke: in the (facetious) attempt to protect the waiter's negative face, he ends up attacking his positive face rather roundly. But that doesn't entirely account for the humor of the whole joke. If we were to use Relevance Theory (Sperber & Wilson, 1995) to explain the joke, we might say that when the waiter is asked to taste the soup, he jumps to the first relevant conclusion: there is something wrong with the soup. According to common-sense principles the customer should then have steered him in the right direction. It is at this point that the customer begins to torment him. He doesn't answer the waiter's question; instead he continues to insist that the waiter taste the soup. If this weren't a joke, one might say that the customer is not abiding by the rules: it is not clear why he is flouting Grice's maxims, it is not clear why he perpetrates subversive face threatening acts, and his behavior is certainly not predictable in terms of relevance considerations.

As audience, we might draw some conclusions about the personality of the customer. We probably have to do this, because we cannot explain his behavior in terms of any of the pragmatic theories we know. We can usefully describe his behavior using a number of frameworks, but we cannot account for it. We might simply have to say that the customer is playing with the waiter; testing him, tricking him, embarrassing him. Perhaps he is pointing out an accepted state of affairs and asking the waiter to measure up to his job description. Waiters don't taste soup; they bring spoons. He might be making the point to the waiter that it's the waiter's behavior that flouts relevance and appropriateness. As audience, however, we are left wondering how much he wants the spoon. If he wants to ask for it, why doesn't he just ask for it? The answer may simply be because he thinks it's more fun not to. Sometimes we flout the rules of language and language behavior simply to play. So, in some cases, flouts are not intended to create implicatures but just to show that the speaker can flout for the sake of the transgression. Whatever the case, this joke, and many like it, shows that we need to know a rule in order to flout it.

One diagnostic for whether a joke is linguistic or not is translatability. This diagnostic goes back at least as far as Cicero.[15] In thinking about Example 15, I have wondered about its translatability. I have often told this joke to groups of interpreters working between signed and spoken languages and asked them to do a simultaneous interpretation from English into the signed language. Unless one has heard this joke through in its entirety, it is a very difficult joke to interpret into a signed language (and into some other spoken languages too), and this has to do, not with culture, or indirectness, or any aspect of micro or macro-pragmatics. It has to do with the fact that the lexical item used for "taste soup" in signed languages is typically one that incorporates the notion 'spoon'. It's a sign that may be glossed as "USE-SPOON". In simultaneous interpreting, the interpreter is not likely to know the punch line and would probably choose to use the typical sign "USE-SPOON". In this case, the joke is not very funny, or if funny, not nearly as funny. If interpreters were primed ahead of time, they could choose from a number of more general lexical items, such as TRY or FEEL-TASTE.[16]

In terms of translatability, then, Example 15 turns on a very simple, low-level linguistic issue—the choice of lexical item. The relevant notion would work with some equivalent of "try" in terms of translating and retaining the joke. More to the point here, however, is the formulation of the speech act, in terms of both its lexical constituents and its grammatical structure. Even if the joke were to be rephrased for an English telling, the formulation of the imperative *taste the soup*, is very important. There are several indirect ways of asking for a spoon that would not allow the joke its course. For instance, none of these ways listed below would enable the joke to be made.

Could you help me out here?
Could you bring me something to help me?
I can't eat this yet.
There's something missing in here.
The soup's going to get cold.

3.8 Ambiguity in Illocutionary Force Based on the Grammatical Form of the Utterance

Ambiguity in understanding the illocutionary force of certain kinds of speech acts can occur as a result of hearers interpreting the grammatical form of an utterance as its illocutionary force. Thus, if an utterance in an interaction is phrased as an information-seeking question, a hearer might interpret its illocutionary force as being a request for information. This could indeed be the illocutionary force of the utterance, but not necessarily. In some cases, the speaker is actually making an indirect speech act, in addition to the direct speech act, which might be an information-seeking question. Very often, in interaction, illocutionary force is independent of grammatical form, and particular grammatical forms are neither necessary nor sufficient in determining illocutionary force.

Certain linguistic items, particularly verbs, depending on their preferred readings, trigger ambiguous speech act effects. These are verbs like *know, say, call* (verbs of perception/production/cognition). The story that follows illuminates one such case, in which the ambiguity in the use of the word *know* allows the hearer to respond to a different illocutionary force from the one that the speaker intended.

Example 16

A guy walks into a piano bar, looking for a job. He says that he plays the piano, and also, he composes his own music. The manager gives him an audition. He sits down at the piano, and plays brilliantly. He tells the manager that the tune is his own composition and is entitled "Mama, your tits drive me wild". The next tune that trips off his fingers is even more wonderful. He announces that the name of the tune is, "I want to stroke your pussy." The manager gives him a job because he really likes the way this guy plays. After a few nights the manager becomes worried that people will be offended by the song titles. He tells the pianist he can keep his piano playing job but he is forbidden to mention the titles of the tunes he plays. The pianist agrees, although reluctantly. One evening, during the break in the performance, he goes to the bathroom and on his return a member of the audience calls out, "Do you know your dick is hanging out?"

"Know it?" he says. "I wrote it!"

The verb *know* can subcategorize for an NP argument, as in (i) and (ii).

i.   *Do you know the teacher?* or
ii. *Do you know this joke?*

However, *know* can also subcategorize for a sentence, as in (iii) and (iv).

iii. *Do you know (that) the President is on his way out?*
     or
iv. *Do you know how to play the piano?*

For the purposes of this analysis, I ignore (iv). There is a difference in sense between the uses of *know* in (i) and (ii) and the use of *know* in (iii). In the case of (i) the utterance can be paraphrased as (v).

v.   *Are you familiar with the teacher?*

In the case of (ii), *know* has a very similar sense; the utterance can be paraphrased as (vi).

vi. *Are you familiar with this joke?*

On the other hand, in the case of (iii), we can't paraphrase the utterance as (vii).

vii. *★Are you familiar with (that) the President is on his way out?*

Some of the different senses of *know*, then, are "recognize", "be familiar with", "encounter"; it can also mean "be aware of the fact (that)", "be able to".

The joke turns on one of these ambiguities in *know*. The pianist is, in fact, being asked if he is aware of the fact that his fly is open. He, however, thinks he is being asked if he is familiar with a certain song. Because he is presumably still stinging over the fact that he is not permitted to announce the names of his songs and claim their authorship, he responds extremely defensively, feeling somewhat unfairly treated, and claims what is rightfully his. Of course, the joke is triggered by his misunderstanding of the way the word *know* is used by the speaker. His reaction is exacerbated in the misinterpretation of the illocutionary force of the utterance, *Do you know your dick is hanging out?* It is intended to be helpful, to point out to him that his fly is open and he is exposing himself. This is intended as an indirect speech act, *i.e.*, a warning or a friendly nudge. The pianist, however, interprets the utterance as a direct speech act, *i.e.*, an information-seeking question about whether he knows a certain tune or not, preparatory to an implied request that he play it. Thus, he answers accordingly, that he had himself composed the tune being requested. His understanding of the utterance is based on interpreting it as follows: *Do you know "Your dick is hanging out?"* whereas what he was being asked is whether he knew he was exposing himself, *i.e.*, *Do you know (that) your dick is hanging out?*

The play is created by a combination of ambiguity in the argument structure of know, misunderstanding of the illocutionary force of questions like *Do you know?*, and use *v.* mention effects.[17]

4.0 Use and Mention

There's a story about the two philosophers, Morgenbesser and Quine. Quine's writings reflect that he was particularly exercised by the use/mention distinction. Morgenbesser, known to be the source of wonderful linguistic and philosophical jokes, gave Quine a tie as a gift. Quine thanked him. Morgenbesser said, *Don't mention it, use it.*

In studying the linguistics of humor, it is crucial to consider the distinction, made in linguistic philosophy, between "use" and "mention". The understanding of the practice of "mention" in human language use is acquired developmentally. It's not something that children acquire early, because it comes along with socialization, and the learning of cultural appropriateness. Commonly, college students titter nervously when a lecturer announces, "Today we are going to talk about the etymology of the word *fuck*." Even though *fuck* is to be understood as in quotation marks, *i.e.*, it is mentioned rather than used, students might feel it is not quite appropriate to use the word in a lecture theatre. Thus, even within the convention of "mention", charged words often maintain their connotative effect. The famous expression, *Don't mention the War* (courtesy of John Cleese, in the television series, *Fawlty Towers* (1975–9)), is a helpful illustration of how "mention" does not necessarily deactivate connotation.

In the *Fawlty Towers* 1975 episode entitled *The Germans*, Cleese, in his persona as hotel manager Basil Fawlty, attempts to avoid offending the cultural sensibilities of his guests, a group of German tourists. *Don't mention the War!* he reminds everyone around him whenever possible (through clenched teeth). *The War* in question is World War II (which the Germans lost) and Basil seems to believe that it might be hurtful to the tourists if they were reminded of this fact. The effect of the injunction is to continually remind everyone of *the War*, hardly something that anyone had forgotten, and to keep it frontally focussed in every interaction. Among the many absurdities, of course, is the fact that millions died in the war, and worrying about mentioning the war to the German tourists because they might be sensitive about the fact that they lost, hardly seems comparable.

Additionally, since he is so obsessed with not mentioning *the War*, Basil manages, among other vocal and physical tics, to say *Two egg mayonnaise, a prawn* **Goebbels**, *a* **Hermann Göring** *and four* **Colditz** *salads.* When eventually one of the beleaguered guests pleads: *Would you please stop talking about the War?*, he responds, *Me?? You started it!* The guest insists, *We did not start it!*, and Basil, very jittery by now, and mistaking the referent of *it*, overrides his own injunction, and hits back, *Yes you did, you invaded Poland!* Later, giving up any attempt at avoiding the unpleasant reference, he rejoins, *Who won the bloody War anyway? (Fawlty Towers*, 1975. Series 1; episode 6).

So in his attempt not to mention *the War*, and thus keep it far from everyone's consciousness, Basil manages to mention *the War* a great many times, integrating it into his discourse and talking about *the War*, rather than about the term *the War*, which he started out warning everyone not to mention.

As a result of the overwhelming success of the television series *Fawlty Towers*, the expression *Don't mention the War!* has become a part of many English speakers' everyday usage, and is generally used with the intention of warning an interlocutor to keep away from an obvious, controversial and contextually inappropriate topic.

The genre of Johnny and the teacher jokes is ideally suited to making the use/mention distinction, and although these sorts of jokes are regarded as silly, they make very intricate and sophisticated points. Such jokes are easy to understand and laugh at, but the phenomenon they tap is by no means a simple one to explain. On reflection, we see that a good joke demonstrates, in a matter of a minute, what philosophers of language have spent lifetimes trying to explain. Example 17 manages to capture a number of interesting features of the use/mention distinction.

Example 17

Johnny is now in year five, and has stopped using baby words. The teacher is busy teaching the class the basic principles of speaker intention, or illocutionary force.

Teacher: John, could you please give an example of a direct command?
John: Shut up!
Teacher: Very good, John. Could you now repeat the command in indirect speech?
John: I told you to shut up.

This is a good example of a joke that conveys the point it is making by making it. The teacher asks for an example of a direct command. John gives her what she asks for, although the ambiguity of presentation is such that he might simply be telling her to shut up. She cannot fault him, however, because he has given a correct answer, *i.e.*, he has **mentioned** a phrase that meets the requirements of the task. He has, of course, also **used** the utterance, by telling her to shut up, *i.e.*, by issuing a direct command. Let us remember that in most worlds, students are prohibited from telling teachers to shut up. The teacher, unfazed by other possible illocutionary forces (*cf.* section 1.3) of John's answer, continues with her lesson, and asks John to repeat the command in indirect speech. Once again he concurs with her request and correctly completes the task, in a perfect formulation of the indirect speech rule we all learn at school. John appears to be performing a grammatical exercise, turning an utterance in direct speech into one in reported or indirect speech. In the world of the English lesson, he is engaging with exercises involving mention. Of course, if we hear it simply as a discourse between a teacher and a student, the student is behaving in a rude and transgressive manner: in response to the teacher's request to perform another display of rule following, he reminds her that he has already told her to shut up. Thus, the illocutionary force of his final utterance may be understood as being a hostile and impudent reminder to her of his previous utterance, as well as serving as a graphic demonstration of an utterance in indirect speech, which he was asked to provide. To get the joke, we need an appreciation of the difference between use and mention, more difficult to articulate than appreciate.

Example 18, also an example of the use/mention distinction, plays with the ambiguity in the semantic properties of *know*, which in this case is triggered by the illocutionary force of the indirect speech act, *Can you read this?*

Example 18

An immigrant with Polish ancestry goes to the Department of Motor Vehicles to apply for a driver's license. In order to get the license, he has to take an eyesight test. The optometrist shows him a card with the letters 'C Z W I X N O S T A C Z.'

"Can you read this?" the optometrist asks.

"Read it?" the Polish guy replies. "I know the guy!"

In this joke, the optometrist uses an indirect speech act, *Can you read this?* Strictly speaking, *can* questions in English are ambiguous, because they may be understood as *Are you able? Are you willing? Are you allowed?,* thereby requiring an answer of *yes* or *no*. Under those circumstances, *Can you...?* is a direct speech act. Although couched in the grammatical form of a question, the utterance here is intended as a request for the man to read the letters out loud. The immigrant does not respond to either the direct or indirect speech act. Rather, he reads the letters to himself and decides that they make up the name of someone whom he knows. This is, obviously, not the point of the exercise, which is to establish if he can see well enough to read the letters on the chart accurately.[18] However, he misses the illocutionary point of the whole interaction, and much like the pianist in the bar, responds according to his own interpretation of what the conversation requires. Interestingly, his response is not in accord with the Gricean maxims and principles of implicature, in that, rather than answer the direct question or respond to the indirect illocutionary force of request, he provides some information that certainly is neither relevant nor required, and does not create a conversational implicature.

Because of the shortage of librarian jokes, I feel bound to include Example 19. It's about a blonde librarian, and is less sophisticated than the pianist joke in Example 16, but exploits the same sort of ambiguity.

Example 19

A man walks into a library and is greeted by the (blonde) (woman) librarian on duty.
"Do you have 'Great Expectations'?" he asks.
"Well, yes, I do, actually. One day I hope to work as a cataloguer and get a potted plant and my own parking space."

This joke too, exploits a use/mention distinction. Additionally, it exploits the ambiguity potential in the word *have*. The librarian answers his question as though he were asking her about her expectations for the future, *i.e.*, she answers as if she has been asked a literal and direct question. She expresses her professional hopes and dreams. In fact, when the man asks, *Do you have Great Expectations?* he is referring to a particular novel. He is asking a direct question, requiring the answer *yes* or *no*. His intention, expressed indirectly, is to ask for help in finding the book. She fails to make the most obvious interpretation, *i.e.*, that since this is a library, he is asking her, the librarian, whether or not a certain book is in the catalogue. She responds to the fact that his question is a direct one, requiring the answer *yes* or *no*, but answers according to her interpretation of his intention, which she understands to be an expression of interest in her plans for her future which she is happy to share with him. His intention, of course, is either to seek information or indirectly, to ask for help.

According to Grice, interlocutors in a discourse operate by predicting the next utterance in an interaction, and when the utterance is counter to their expectation, they make calculations as to what the intention underlying the speaker's utterance is. There seems to be some evidence from jokes that mistaken illocutionary force can lead to (mis)understandings at lower levels of language than pragmatics, if there is any ambiguity present at those levels.

In Example 20, the use/mention distinction is exploited in an apparently silly, literal response. In this example, mistaken illocutionary force is triggered by the ambiguity in the lexical semantics of *say*.

Example 20

Seagoon: *Do you think they suspect him?*
Moriarty: *That's difficult to say.*
Seagoon: *Do-you-think-they-suspect-him. Hm, it is a bit difficult to say, yes.*
(The Goon Show, *1955. Series 5; episode 17*)

Seagoon asks a question, to which Moriarty replies, *That's difficult to say*. Seagoon picks up a sense of *say* that is different from the one that Moriarty intended, and misunderstands the illocutionary force of Moriarty's reply. Also Seagoon may have interpreted *That* in Moriarty's first response as having a metalinguistic discourse referent, whereas it actually refers to the topic under discussion. Thus, in answer to Seagoon's question, *Do you think they suspect him?* Moriarty intends to communicate that he thinks it is difficult to judge whether or not *they suspect him* (whoever *he* is). He is answering somewhat indirectly, in that he is opting out of answering the direct question that Seagoon has posed. Seagoon interprets this as Moriarty remarking that the utterance, *Do you think they suspect him?* is difficult to utter. Seagoon's next remark is a response to Moriarty's saying that the previous utterance was difficult to utter. Seagoon proceeds as though he doesn't seem to notice that Moriarty has not provided a relevant reply to his initial inquiry about what he thinks. Thus, entirely ignoring the maxim of conversational relevance, Seagoon responds by uttering *Do-you-think-they-suspect-him*. Having tried to utter these words, and succeeded, he nevertheless agrees that the utterance is indeed a bit difficult to say.

This is one way in which conversations regularly get hijacked in *The Goon Show*. Invariably, the shifting sands effect is achieved by a speaker misunderstanding the illocutionary force of an utterance, by applying backgrounded or less preferred interpretations of word and phrase level semantics, and then, as a result, misinterpreting the syntactic structure intended by the interlocutor. The sort of process shown here (although made ridiculous to the extreme by the literalness of the response) is reasonably good evidence to assume that missing the illocutionary force of an utterance may lead hearers to misinterpret other ambiguities to fit in with their mistaken understanding.

5.0 Deixis

As mentioned at the beginning of this chapter, it is extremely difficult to draw a line to demarcate where pragmatics ends and semantics begins. Scholars differ on a number of dimensions: whether or not a distinction should in fact be made; whether or not the content of semantics might be absorbed into syntax and pragmatics; some believe the study of all aspects of meaning belongs entirely to semantics; some claim that semantics is more properly considered as part of the philosophy of language, and there is a range of shades in between.

There is one phenomenon, however, that although crucial for both semantics and syntax, can only seriously be considered within the scope of pragmatics, and that is the phenomenon of deixis. In a broad sense, deixis may be considered as the use of "reference", *i.e.*, *Bedeutung*, in contrast to *Sinn*, "sense" (Frege, 1892/1980).[19]

Shifters, pointers, or deictic markers, as they are sometimes called, are intrinsically context-bound, as their names suggest. The ambiguity of shifter use is always fertile for the creation of humorous effects. In a way, shifters are the visual comedy of verbal humor. Their use enables the confusion of ambiguity and farce. Baldly, we can never know the absolute referents of personal pronouns, locatives, and temporals. That is the wonder of these elements. Their referents shift according to the context of use: they gain their referential meaning dependent on who is speaking to whom, in which particular time and place. They are the true creatures of context.

In Example 21, extracted from the movie, *The Pink Panther Strikes Again* (1976), the joke turns on the referent of *your dog*. This gag has been immortalized by the actor Peter Sellers' particular version of French-English. The *non-bona fide* nature of the communication is enhanced by Sellers' deliberately overplayed French accent in which, in the same movie, he renders *dog* as *derg* and *room* as *rerm*.

Example 21

Clouseau: Does your dog bite?
Hotel Clerk: No.
Clouseau: [bowing down to pet the dog] Nice doggie.
[dog bites Clouseau's hand]
Clouseau: I thought you said your dog did not bite!
Hotel Clerk: That is not my dog.

(The Pink Panther Strikes Again, 1976)

The ambiguity of reference inherent in *your dog* permits the clerk to miss the illocutionary force of the first question. Clouseau's intention is to enquire as to whether the dog he is about to pat is likely to bite him. The hotel clerk chooses instead to answer a question about his own dog, thus exhibiting a fine disregard for the rules of co-operation, specifically that of relevance.

Since the dog does not belong to him, the hotel clerk could be perfectly truthful in the Gricean sense, when he answers *No*. He may well have a dog, and his dog may well not bite. However, he is not following the general idea of the Co-operative Principle since the context should make it clear that the inspector is asking about the dog he is about to pat. Thus, the clerk is ignoring the maxim of quantity, by not saying enough. At that point in the conversation, he is being truthful, but not co-operative. So, he is abiding by the maxim of quality, but violating quantity. In fact, on a number of accounts, he is not abiding by the principle of relevance, either. On both Grice's account and a relevance theoretic account, he is not answering the question by providing a reply that is contextually appropriate.

Nevertheless, he can hide behind the fact that he is being truthful. His final response, *It's not my dog*, would have been more co-operative had he given it in answer to the question, *Does your dog bite?* Instead, choosing to be truthful at the expense of being relevant and providing sufficient information, he provides the information that his dog does not bite. As a result, Clouseau gets bitten. The humorous effect is produced because the viewer knows that *your* is a creature of context. In a situation of *bona fide* communication, the interlocutor would be justified in taking retributive action against such a non-co-operative conversational partner. The defense, *I was only answering your question*, may be correct, but in communication, appeals to appropriateness in context outweigh non-contextual, factual correctness.

The same sort of joke is also to be found in the 1993 movie, *Benny and Joon*, in which Sam says to Joon, *You're out of your tree*, meaning that he thinks she's crazy. She looks up at him, wide-eyed, and replies, *It's not my tree.* This interchange takes the lunacy to new heights, for whereas Inspector Clouseau had been referring to an actual dog, when Sam says *You're out of your tree*, he is using an idiom, with the conventionalized meaning of "quite crazy". Joon responds by treating the idiom literally, and denying the tree is hers, even though there is no tree acting as a referent in this exchange.

Leo Rosten recounts the old and much-loved joke below. It demonstrates the inherently mercurial nature of deictics, and also highlights the engagement in sense-seeking by a too-careful interlocutor.

Example 22

Rabbi Tescher, discovering that he had left his comfortable slippers back in the house, sent a student after them with a note for his wife. The note read: "Send me your slippers with this boy."

*When the student asked why the rabbi had written "**your**" slippers, Rabbi Tescher answered, "Listen, young man. **Think**. If I wrote "my" slippers, my wife would read "my slippers" – and would send me **her** slippers. What can I do with her slippers? So I wrote "your" slippers: she'll read "your" slippers and send me mine.*

(Rosten, 1985)

In this exchange, we see the rabbi second-guessing his wife. Because he and she know each other well, he reckons he knows how she thinks, and how she interprets. In their home context, the wife refers to her husband's slippers as *your slippers*. Clearly, in that context, for her, *your slippers* is no longer a deictic, but a name, or a description of a particular pair of slippers. The rabbi knows this, and knows, by the same logic, that his wife has named her own slippers, *my slippers*. With fine disregard for the use of deictics, or else with great regard for his wife's thought processes, and little regard for her intellect, he sends a message that his wife is to send him *your slippers* when he is referring, in fact, to his slippers. In terms of relevance theory, this is a wonderful demonstration of the great processing effort, and therefore the least positive cognitive effects and lowest relevance to the hearer.

a.   *Other things being equal, the greater the positive cognitive effects achieved by processing an input, the greater the relevance of the input to the individual at that time.*

b. Other things being equal, the greater the processing effort expended, the lower the relevance of the input to the individual at that time.
(Wilson and Sperber, 2005, pp. 607–32)

Jokes based on ambiguity in the use of deictics are legion. Claims have been made (see Akmajian *et al.*, 1995) that indexical use is literal use. The joke about the slippers takes this to new, and entirely unscalable heights.

Another way in which the ambiguity of referents is exploited can be found in the use of English *we*, which contains both an inclusive and exclusive reading. This is not the case in all languages, however. Some languages make a lexical distinction between *we*-inclusive and *we*-exclusive, as well as between *we*-dual as opposed to *we*-plural. As is often the case, Spike Milligan integrates his sensitivity to the ambiguity of English into his sense of the ridiculousness of military and bureaucratic life.

Example 23

We were sitting around at home when a man called Chamberlain who did Prime Minister impressions came on the radio and said we were at war with Germany. I loved that "we".
(Spike Milligan, 1918–2002)

The joke here is obvious: Milligan is asking who this *we* is that is at war with Germany. Chamberlain (who was, in fact, at the time, Prime Minister) had declared war on behalf of Great Britain. Chamberlain's use of *we* is entirely inclusive. Milligan questions Chamberlain's right to declare war on his behalf, by highlighting the ambiguity of the use of *we* in English. *We*, in English, is not only under-determined, in terms of its context of use, but also inherently ambiguous in terms of its reference, even within a context.

The famous line from the 1974 song, *The Lone Ranger*, by Oscar Brown Junior (1926–2005) *What you mean, we, white man?* serves as a wonderful illustration of when *we* may be used to indicate unity and when *we* does not refer to "the two of us." In the song, The Lone Ranger and Tonto were surrounded by a band of Indians. The Lone Ranger turned to Tonto and said, "Our lives are in danger, we got to get away if we can".

The line *What you mean, we, white man?* has become short-hand for reminding people that it is everyone for themselves. We are reminded that English has an exclusive and inclusive *we* and that deictics only ever get their meaning in a context of use.

Deixis, because it is inherently context-bound, and thus pregnant with ambiguity, is the source of any number of jokes. Even within a restricted context—in which speakers share knowledge of the topic, are located in the same place and the conversation is face-to-face—misunderstandings can occur because of the essential ambiguity in the use of deictics. Sometimes these ambiguities can lead to genuine confusion, and they are invariably irresistible to people who discern them, and are in the mood for play. In the following joke, we see how *my wife* is taken to refer, in both its occurrences, to the first speaker's wife.

Example 24

Two clergymen were discussing the sad state of sexual morality. "I didn't sleep with my wife before we were married," one of them declared self-righteously. "Did you?"
"I'm not sure," said the other. "What was her maiden name?"

(adapted from Poulos, 2001, p. 51)

Given the context, one would imagine, as did the first speaker, that the second speaker would understand that the first speaker was referring to his own wife when he said that he didn't sleep with her before they were married, and to the second speaker's wife, in his ellipsis, when he asked, *Did you?* To spell it out, his intention was to ask, *Did you sleep with your wife before you were married?* However, the second speaker was legitimately entitled to understand the question to be, *Did you sleep with my wife before we were married?* What makes it funny is that the first clergyman's opening line was intended to show how upright and moral he was. The second clergyman might be expected to answer that he, too, did not sleep with his own wife before they were married. Instead, he took the opportunity to show exactly the opposite, implying that he had slept with many women before he was married, and would need to know the woman's maiden name before he could answer the question with any certainty. The misunderstanding turns on the ambiguity of *my*. The humor turns, as is often the case, on the (deliberate or perceived) illocutionary and perlocutionary force of the first utterance. The speaker's intention was to show his moral rectitude and to have it affirmed by the other speaker. His expectation was, probably, that the second speaker would confirm that he, too, had not slept with his own wife before they were married. However, the second speaker chose reasonably to understand the illocutionary force of the first utterance as a request for information, and genuinely engaged with the question of whether he had slept with the first speaker's wife before the marriage of the first speaker and his wife. What makes the joke funny, as opposed to simply clever, is that the second speaker is also a clergyman, engaging in a serious discussion of church-based morality, of which he is supposedly an exemplar. His answer puts paid to the high-minded nature of the discussion.

Example 25 parallels this joke, with interesting contextual effects.

Example 25

A man and a woman were having dinner in a fine restaurant. Their waitress, taking an order at another table, noticed that the man was slowly sliding down his chair and under the table, while the woman appeared to be unconcerned. The waitress watched as the man slid out of sight under the table. Still, the woman dining across from him appeared calm and unruffled, apparently unaware that her dining companion had disappeared. After the waitress had finished taking her other order, she came over to the table and said to the woman, "Pardon me, ma'am, but I think your husband just slid under the table." The woman calmly looked up at her and replied firmly, "No, he didn't. He just walked in the door." [20]

Here too, the humor turns on the referential ambiguity of the deictic *your*, as well as a very subtle twist in the illocutionary force of the last utterance. In this case, *your husband* has different referents. In the scenario, the waitress is referring to the dining companion, whereas the woman is referring to the man who just walked in the door. What we are to understand by the end of the joke is that the woman's dining companion is not her husband, and it would not be in either her interest nor that of her dining companion if her husband should see her and her companion dining together.

There are a number of implicit ideas embedded in this joke that need to be understood for the joke to be funny. Baldly: the waitress assumes that a couple dining together, obviously affectionately, are husband and wife; husbands do not like their wives to be out with other men; the fact that the dining companion slips under the table indicates that he knows that his being seen with another man's wife would cause problems for both of them. As it is rather odd for a diner to slip under the table during the course of a meal, the waitress is perhaps within her rights to point it out, although she would no doubt be aware that the woman at the table was cognizant of this strange behavior. The illocutionary force of her utterance when she says, *'Pardon me, ma'am, but I think your husband just slid under the table,'* could be understood as a request for an explanation or as a suggestion to the woman that she do something about it. The woman, who is in possession of additional knowledge, is able to communicate a reply that functions efficiently and briefly as an explanation for her dining companion's strange behavior. Thus, from her point of view, her utterance is relevant, in the technical sense of creating the greatest possible cognitive effect with least effort on the part of the interlocutor.

Example 25 is illuminating in demonstrating to what extent deictics are contextually bound. The woman in the joke knows who her husband is; she may have, by omission, accepted others assigning her dining companion the referential identity of her husband (*your husband*) when it was comfortable for her to have done so, but once the real identity of her husband becomes relevant she is quick to point out that, in a given context, a deictic can pick out only one referent at a time.

Example 26 is another rabbinical joke. We see here that the manipulation of deictics can be part of a canny and skillful use of language.[21]

Example 26

A man stole a rabbi's gold watch and afterwards began to feel guilty about what he did. After a sleepless night, he went to see the rabbi.

"Rabbi, I stole a gold watch," the man confessed.

"But my friend, that's forbidden," replied the Rabbi. "You need to rectify this situation."
"But I don't know what to do."
"Well I think you should give it back to the owner," responded the Rabbi.
"Do you want it?" the man asked.
"No, I said you should give it back to its owner."
"But he doesn't want it," said the man.
"In that case," the Rabbi ruled, "you can keep it."

The joke turns on an interesting distinction: the NP *the owner* can be used extensionally to refer to that particular individual who is the actual owner, or intensionally, so as to mean "whoever owns it". The first, or extensional use, fixes reference; the intensional use does not. The rabbi uses the NP *the owner* in the intensional sense, *i.e.*, "whoever owns it". The man, however, uses the NP *the owner*, extensionally, *i.e.*, referring to the actual owner of the watch, the rabbi. He is entitled to do so in terms of ambiguity in the semantics but not in terms of principles of co-operative behaviour. The man chooses to hear the answer that is most relevant to his personal advantage. Moreover, he may now take the most direct and literal reading of the rabbi's pronouncement. This is another example of how a joke can demonstrate our knowledge of a very tricky ambiguity in referential assignment.

The referents of determiners, such as demonstratives are, of course, in general, entirely context bound. Sometimes the relevant context is in the surrounding linguistic discourse, and sometimes it is in the physical context of the communication. Often, the choice of demonstrative can distinguish the denotation from the connotation of a referent. Example 27, from the 1970s, when Jews were finally allowed to leave the Soviet Union and immigrate to Israel, makes this linguistic point very deftly.

Example 27

An old Jewish man was finally allowed to leave the Soviet Union, to immigrate to Israel. When he was searched at the Moscow airport, the customs official unearthed a bust of Lenin in his luggage.

Customs official: What is that?

Old man: What is that? What is that?! Don't ask, "What is that?", instead ask, "Who is that?" That is Lenin! The genius who thought up this worker's paradise!

The official laughed and let the old man get on to his plane.

The old man arrived at Tel Aviv airport, where an Israeli customs official found the bust of Lenin in his luggage.

Customs official: And what is that?

Old man: What is that? What is that?! Don't ask, "What is that?", ask, "Who is that?" That is Lenin! The sonofabitch! I will put him on display in my toilet to remind me and him of all the years he prevented an old man from coming home.

The official laughed and let the old man go through Customs.
When the old man finally arrived at his daughter's house, his granddaughter watched him unpack the bust of Lenin.
Granddaughter: Who is that?
Old man: Who is that? Who is that? Don't ask, "Who is that?", ask "What is that?" That, my child, is eight pounds of gold.

In this story, the joke turns on the use of *who* and *what*, as well the connotation of the referent *that*. When the old man is leaving the Soviet Union, he sees his chance to smooth talk the official by speaking of Lenin in glowing terms (although for any interlocutor, other than a Soviet official at the time, this utterance could be interpreted as sarcastic). His intention is to take the bust out of the country, without having it confiscated by the Soviet customs official. He gently rebukes the official for referring to the bust of Lenin as a thing, reminding him that he should not ask *what*, but *who* it is. When he succeeds, and arrives in Israel, he has to coax the customs official to let him bring the bust into the country. He knows that he should malign Lenin in the hopes that the customs official will humor an old man who says he has finally come home. In rebuking the Israeli customs official, he points out that the bust is not to be referred to as a thing, reminding him, too, that Lenin was an important person, although an evil one. When he gets to his family, however, and his granddaughter asks *Who is that?* he changes his tune entirely, having outwitted both customs officials.

From the man's answer to his grandchild, we can see that Lenin is entirely incidental to the entire mission, which was to smuggle eight pounds of gold out of the Soviet Union and into the new country. Distracting the officials by highlighting the importance of Lenin as a person, he was able to transport the thing. Thus, he used the personal interrogative demonstrative *who* to focus his listeners on a particular connotation, "Lenin the Soviet leader", and the inanimate interrogative demonstrative *what* to focus his granddaughter on the connotation of eight pounds of gold. In both cases, the denotation is the bust, but the *wh*-words are used very skillfully to create entirely different connotations.

The use of the shifters, *this* and *that*, is the cause of much natural ambiguity, since they are, like all shifters, intrinsically ambiguous with regard to their referents. Groucho Marx captures this in a very deft one-liner, in which he reveals how very tricky referential semantics can be.

Example 28

I've had a perfectly wonderful evening. But this wasn't it.

(*Groucho Marx, 1890–1977*)

As always with Groucho's jokes there is more than just one fancy trick with language at play here. Since the grammatical convention for pronominal use is that a pronominal generally refers to the last NP referent, it is quite legitimate for *this* to refer to *evening*.[22] And indeed, *this* does refer to *this evening*, but not to the perfectly wonderful one he was referring to. The second pronominal *it*, refers to the *perfectly wonderful evening*. So *this* wasn't *it*. *This* refers to *this evening*, and *it* refers to *a perfectly wonderful evening*. Following the grammatical rules of pronominal reference yields a different interpretation than following the rules of pragmatic inference.

The listener expects that when someone says they've had a perfectly wonderful evening they are referring to the evening they've just had. As a listener, one is most likely to process this utterance using the maxim of relevance (Grice, 1975; Sperber and Wilson, 1995). However, Groucho, as speaker, follows the maxim of quality instead — it is true that he has, in the past had a perfectly wonderful evening. He exploits the technically permissible reading that *this* in *this wasn't it* is grammatically co-indexed with the evening he has just spent, but *it* is not. This reading is so dispreferred pragmatically that it is difficult to explicate, yet it is grammatically possible (I suppose). The second part of the joke serves to highlight which maxim he was obeying (quality): and, as always, he is on just the right side of the rule, with grammatical backing. In general, in fact, if we examine Groucho's one-liners, we find that he almost invariably flouts one maxim in favor of a less preferred maxim, for humorous effect.

In the movie, *Young Frankenstein* (1974), directed by Mel Brooks, which is a spoof on the genre of Frankenstein movies, we encounter a character called Igor, who is Dr. Frankenstein's factotum and butler. He happens, as is the case in all the Frankenstein movies, to have a hunchback. In preparation for escorting Frankenstein to his room, he says, *Walk this way*. Frankenstein follows him, imitating his hunchbacked gait.

The comedy is visual, but the misunderstanding is linguistic. Igor intends the newly arrived guest to follow him, *i.e.*, walk in the **direction** in which he is walking. The guest understands him to mean that he should walk in the **manner** in which Igor is walking. Thus the guest imitates the rather peculiar gait of the hunchbacked Igor. This is another example of how the deictic marker can be misunderstood, even within a context of use.

Jokes exploiting deixis of place and time are less common, but do occur. Example 29 is also attributed to Groucho Marx. In this riposte, Groucho plays on the deictic *here*.

Example 29

Woman: I didn't come here to be insulted!
Groucho: Oh, where do you go to be insulted?

(Groucho Marx, 1890–1977)

When the woman says *I didn't come here to be insulted*, she intends the primary sentence stress to be on *insulted*. She means that she did not expect to be insulted (in coming to this place). Groucho, however interprets her as saying, *I didn't come here to be insulted*, pretending that he understands the stress to be on *here*. As a result he asks, *oh, **where do** you go to be insulted?* When we reflect on the joke, we are cast onto our tacit knowledge of the workings of deictics, and may realize how complex they really are. We also realize that what we think of as deictics are not always unambiguously deictic in function. Groucho, as we know, plays with words, and he doesn't discriminate against any of them. The polysemy of words that can be used deictically but also have other uses are part of his stock in trade.

This joke, although it involves deictics is not crucially about deictic issues. The joke plays with two kinds of presuppositions. The woman's statement has two alternative presuppositions. The first is "I came here for some other reason": in this case her statement can be paraphrased as "it is not the case that my reason for coming here was to be insulted", and the negation applies to the reason. The second possible presupposition is "I go elsewhere in order to be insulted".

Deictics of time, too, are shifty creatures. Just as important as the person making the utterance and its place of utterance, is the time of speaking.

Example 30

The last time I was here…—well it's not the last time, this is. But I hope it isn't.
(Paraphrased from Victor Borge, (1909–2000) on stage)

The deictic in question here is *the last time*. Again, we see a subtle interplay between grammatical rules of co-reference and pragmatic inferences. Additionally there is some play between the meanings of *last*, as to whether it is to be interpreted as "most recent", or as "final". There is also a very slippery relationship between naming an event, *the last time*, and referring to that name, either as a name, or to cast doubt on its accuracy as a name, at the time of speaking.

In the first use of *the last time*, Borge is referring to the most recent occasion on which he appeared in the particular location at which he is speaking, at the time of the present utterance. In the second use, he is expressing the idea that since he is in the identical location as on the previous occasion, the previous occasion could not have been his final appearance, as, at the time of speaking, the present occasion must be the final appearance. Up until and including the time of speaking, necessarily, the occasion must be his most recent time of appearance. However, he expresses the hope that the present occasion is not the final time he will be appearing in the location in question.

In summary, we have seen how sophisticated and intricate our understanding of pragmatic rules is. Without a tacit knowledge of the rules of linguistic appropriateness, especially as they pertain to the interaction of rules of sentence structure with rules of use, the jokes analyzed here are very difficult, if not impossible, to comprehend. These rules are not regularly available to consciousness but require some quick introspection in order for the joke to be noticed. Whereas there are arguments in the scholarly literature (within a Chomskyan tradition) about the nature of pragmatic competence, I believe that the analyses presented in this chapter are good evidence for Kasher's claim that there is indeed an implicit knowledge of the rules of language use.

Notes

1   Chomsky (1962) states that a speaker has acquired "an implicit theory of the language that he has mastered, a theory that predicts the grammatical structure of each of an infinite class of potential physical events, and **the conditions for the appropriate use of each of these items**" (p. 528) [my emphasis]. According to Kasher, if we are to talk about a theory of use, the subject matter of pragmatics is the appropriateness conditions of sentences to contexts of utterance. "Appropriateness of use is couched in terms of the relations between intentions and purposes and between linguistic means, of certain forms and meanings, within linguistic institutional settings" (see Chomsky, 1980, pp. 59–60 and 93 and Kasher, 1977).

Proposing the idea of pragmatic competence establishes within the study of linguistic pragmatics the theoretical objectives, scientific methodology and philosophical foundations of Chomskyan Generative Linguistics. "On a par with the major theoretical objective of the generative study of syntax being an understanding of an innate 'Universal Grammar,' the major theoretical objective of a similar study of pragmatics would be an understanding of the invariant or innate constraints of language use. Thus, one would replace mere descriptions and classifications of types of speech act, for example, by much deeper attempts to answer questions such as 'What is a cognitively possible speech act type?....' (Kasher, 1981).

2   Chomsky (1999) makes his position on this clear. "[From this point of view,] 'pragmatics' must be a central component of any linguistic theory that aims to be comprehensive" (Stemmer, 1999).

3   Daniel Barbiero (1997) in asking which aspects of language are plausibly explained by appeal to innate mechanisms and constraints, considers pragmatic knowledge, as well. He says, "One final candidate for an innateness hypothesis merits mention. Following Jackendoff (1995), we might hypothesize an innate faculty specialized for social cognition. This faculty, which is claimed to encode a set of basic, universal cultural parameters, presumably would be responsible for the language user's pragmatic competence. (Interestingly, such a hypothesis would open up a potentially fascinating point of contact between the generative program and Wittgensteinian intuitions regarding forms of life and apparently innate human tendencies to agree)".

4   An earlier distinction is made by Searle (1969, 1979), in which he essentially divides pragmatic competence in the same way, using different terminology, into illocutionary competence, and sociolinguistic competence, as part of his overall critique of Chomsky's notion of man as "syntactical". I mention these divisions here, although, fundamentally, I take a Chomskyan approach to pragmatic competence as argued above.

5   See for example, Kripke, 1972/80.

6   "[t]he semantics of a language can be regarded as a series of systems of constitutive rules and illocutionary acts are performed in accordance with these sets of constitutive rules" (Searle, 1969, p. 380).

7   Of course, this does not suggest that speakers never state propositions that express causality. The central impetus here is to explain language use which is not propositional.

8   The **knowledge** of these sorts of rules, at an entirely different level of abstraction from particular cases, is part of what Chomsky would call a speaker's pragmatic competence.

9   Based both on knowledge of the facts and knowledge of language.

10 It is a somewhat thorny theoretical issue to decide whether literalness and non-literalness belong more properly to the field of semantics or to pragmatics. Some scholars (*e.g.*, Lakoff & Johnson, 1980; Lakoff, 1982) have argued, for instance, that metaphor should properly be considered as semantic and that since pragmatics includes word and sentence meaning as much as speaker meaning, the distinction between pragmatics and semantics is a false one. Others (*e.g.*, Lyons, 1977; Akmajian, Demers, Farmer, & Harnish, 1995) have argued for a clear distinction between semantics and pragmatics, claiming that literalness is a property of utterance or sentence meaning and not of speaker meaning, and therefore properly part of the field of semantics and not pragmatics. For my purposes here, although I want to make clear the distinction between the literalness and directness axis, it makes little difference if literalness is a part of semantics or of pragmatics.

11 The close relationship between indirectness and politeness as a universal phenomenon has been robustly challenged, however, especially by Blum–Kulka (1987).

12 See Chapter 3 for a more extensive discussion of denotation and connotation.

13 In discussions with native speakers of English, as well as translators and interpreters, it has emerged that "pig" has a range of different connotations, in English, including the slang word for police (in this case, there is a scope for a different, but related joke). It was pointed out to me that were the joke to be translated into French, "pig" would retain the illocutionary force of insult, but the connotation would be "glutton". This wouldn't help the joke along much in translation.

There are ways around translating this joke. It would be necessary to find an animal equivalent that also corresponds to an insult in a particular language. If that were possible, the translation of the joke is probably reasonably straightforward. What remains is the issue of gender friction. It is possible that parts of this joke would work if both characters were men, or both women. However, there is a stereotype built into this joke too, and that is the one in which men are quick on the offensive and ready to attack, whereas women are more kindly and helpful. Playing with the stereotype provides an additional dimension.

14 In fact, *taste the (soup)* may be argued to be conventionally indirect in these contexts and be taken to mean *this is a complaint, there is something wrong with it*.

15 Cicero made the distinction between jokes that are *de re* and those that are *de dicto*. Jokes that are *de re* (about things) are in principle translatable; jokes that are *de dicto* (about the words) are not (Cicero, 2001). See Chapter 1 for a brief discussion of *de re* and *de dicto* jokes.

16 The capital letters represent a simplified gloss of signs from American Sign Language.

17 This joke is as much an example of ambiguity in syntax and semantics as it is of pragmatic ambiguity. Other related jokes are to be found in Chapter 3 and Chapter 5. Another joke exploiting the semantic ambiguity in *know* is to be found later in this chapter.

18 His answer, strictly, might be rephrased as, "Not only can I read it (this name) but I know the guy whose name it is".

19 For further discussion of issues relating to meaning, see Chapter 3, on Semantics.

20 Adapted from http://www.emmitsburg.net/humor/archives/marriage/marriage_10. htm, accessed October 21, 2010.

21 I would not be the first to suggest that the tradition of *pilpul*, *i.e.*, exegetical analysis of sacred texts in the Judaic tradition, leads to a fascination with "meaning" in many of its forms.

22 Naturally, if this weren't a joke, the deictic reading of *this* would probably be more basic.

3
PLAYING WITH SEMANTICS

1.0 The Linguistics of Meaning

1.1 Meaning and Its Meanings

The understanding of the term "meaning" has been a major source of debate in the philosophy of language (*cf.*, for instance, from different traditions, Hume, Locke, Berkeley; Frege, Russell, Wittgenstein; Strawson, Burge; Putnam, Kripke; Peirce). Additionally, within the tradition of Linguistic Pragmatics (see Chapter 2) conceptions of "meaning" have perhaps been more vigorously and endlessly debated, than almost any other problems. A brief consideration of some potentially equivalent terms will serve to illustrate the problems involved in how we are to understand the term "meaning." In no particular order, we might say that a word or expression's "meaning" =

its sense
its reference
its intension
its extension
its definition
its denotation
its connotation
the intention that its speaker has in using it
the understanding that its hearer has in receiving it
its use
its interpretation
its significance
what it represents or stands for

A history of the discussion related to these terms, and the debates they encapsulate, is a good part of the history of analytic philosophy[1]; the search for "meaning" in continental philosophy is beyond the scope of this chapter.

1.2 Linguistic Semantics

Linguistic Semantics is regarded as the subfield of linguistics that is given over to the study of linguistic meaning. As noted above, this covers a multitude of interpretations, and although there are many different theoretical approaches, not all semanticists recognize the work of other semanticists as legitimate areas of inquiry. This should give us some idea of the immensity of the subfield, as well as the range of approaches that have been taken.

In this chapter, I consider semantics as the study of meaning focussing on the features and properties of linguistic units (words, phrases and sentences) and their interpretation. In other words, I look at the foundational components of "meaning" (a term yet to be teased apart and defined for our purposes). I use jokes to explore the relations among different semantic units: with particular reference to lexical relations such as homonymy, synonymy, antonymy, and polysemy. Additionally, I use jokes to examine compositional semantics, in other words, how meaning is assigned to chunks of language, sometimes as the result of composition from smaller units of meaning. I also investigate what jokes reveal about the relationship between language and logic. Naturally, the jokes that I look at include the distinction between "sense" and "reference"; thematic roles; and the relationship (however construed) of semantics to syntax. Thus, the analysis of jokes in this chapter focusses on lexical semantics, compositional semantics, and the somewhat blurry interface between semantics and pragmatics.

2.0 Lexical Relations: Sameness and Difference

2.1 Sameness

In linguistic jokes involving lexical semantics, the phenomena of synonymy (sameness of sense), referential equivalence (sameness of referent), homonymy (sameness of signifier, difference in sense and reference) and polysemy (same signifier, multiple related senses and references) in human languages lead inevitably to the exercise of wit and humor. Jokes exploiting these phenomena abound, potentially making us conscious that very few words have true synonyms—words that are equivalent in sense in every way. As can be seen, some of these sorts of jokes lead to interesting questions about the coverage the concepts synonymy and antonymy really have. The borderline between semantics and pragmatics is rather permeable in this respect, particularly with respect to connotation.

2.1.1 Sameness of Sense: What Counts?

In this section, I use the term "synonymy" to refer to "sameness of sense." In the genre of *little boy and the teacher* jokes, a very easy genre to use in order to make clear the importance of word choice, we find a few illustrative gems.

These inevitably involve the naïf, a child, who tells it like it is.

Example 1

The children in the second grade have returned from their annual vacation. The teacher starts off by asking them one at a time how they spent their holidays.

Mary says, "We went to the seaside and everyday I went for a ride on my father's new brrm-brrm."

The teacher says, "Now that you are in Grade Two, I'd like you to use grown-up words. Don't call it a brrm-brrm, call it a motorbike." Mary is duly chastened.

Jimmy says, "I went to my uncle's farm, and saw the clippity-clops."

The teacher reminds them again that they are now in Grade Two, and she expects them to set aside their childish words.

"Ok, Johnny, and what did you do?"

"I stayed home and read a book."

"That's good, Johnny. What book did you read?"

"Winnie-the-Shit."

The joke here is that the teacher gets more than she bargained for when she asks the class to use adult words. Johnny very swiftly generalizes a rule he thinks he understands. If, in adult language, a *brrm-brrm* is a *motorbike*, and a *clippity-clop* is a *horse*, then a *pooh* is a *shit*. The joke works, because *pooh* (or *poo*) may be a baby word, and *shit* may be an adult word, but *shit* is not only an adult word, it is in some uses, transgressive. It is, especially for children, somewhat taboo. *Shit* is, of course, denotatively accurate in referring to feces, and in common use, but it is not an adult word in the same way that *motorbike* is. The teacher has a long way to go to explain that not all adult words are equivalent in terms of their register. Once words are in use, their connotations are all-important. Although the joke hinges on synonymy, or the lack thereof, once use is invoked, pragmatics, too, is implicated. Users make informed choices: children may not yet have acquired the system of adult register.

The joke illustrates this particular distinction between denotation and connotation very neatly. Denotatively, and outside of a context of use, both *pooh/poo* and *shit* refer to "excrement". Neither is neutral in that both are loaded with connotations, *poo* of childish use and *shit* of adult, often vulgar, use.[2] The additional dimension of the joke, that raises it above the level of simply showing how crude the advice to use adult words is, is that *Winnie-the-Pooh* is a name. It is, first, the name of a character (who happens to be a teddy bear) but second, the name of a book by A.A. Milne (1926) about that teddy bear. Now, we live by an unwritten rule that says we can't change given names out of some kind of squeamishness about the way they sound. The joke demonstrates how that rule can be broken.

For the characters in the joke, *pooh/poo* refers to excrement. The major linguistic point that the joke illustrates is that there is a very real distinction between "use" and "mention".[3] When a child says *I made a poo*, he is using *poo* to refer to the product of his bowels. When a child says *I read a book called **Winnie-the-Pooh***, he is mentioning a name, and names belong to things. The function of "mention" is to seal off a term, set it in quotation marks, and then to use it in its impermeable entirety. It then becomes a special kind of item, not subject to internal changes. It is, as Wittgenstein might say, a fact. And for us to get some kind of a handle on the concepts of denotation, connotation and other synonymy-related issues, we need to keep in mind the crucial distinction between "use" and "mention".[4] Jokes that play on this distinction are legion, and in their appreciation, raise interesting and subtle linguistic and philosophical points. The distinction between use and mention may be difficult for a joke consumer to articulate, but it is one s/he is forced to consider in appreciating these sorts of jokes. For children, particularly, mentioning a transgressive word in a context they perceive to be innocent, licenses its use.

The notion of the analytic proposition and its application to the real world of language users is frequently given the lie in jokes. An analytic proposition is one that is true by definition. For example, the proposition, "A triangle has three sides" is analytic. Real language use, however, somewhat restricts the applicability of these sorts of propositions. We can say whatever we choose, and it does not have to make logical sense, because language use, we discover, is not bound by the rules of logic. Woody Allen is a specialist in this kind of humor, demonstrating that word meaning is a very supple sort of a concept. The following joke is typical of his style.

Example 2

I don't want to achieve immortality through my work. I want to achieve it through not dying.
                                                            (Woody Allen, 1939–)

Woody Allen, a great comedian, surely does want to be immortalized through his work lasting beyond his death. However, in this remark, he takes the more strictly definitional view of the term "immortality". He says he wants to achieve immortality by not dying. So he wants to not die by not dying. This is, of course, true by definition, being *immortal* necessitates not dying. The absurdity is patent: it is part of the minimum requirements of being a human being that one dies eventually, so he cannot possibly not die. Allen does, however, in this remark, capture the limitations of human life. Is there a point in our work living on if we are not there to see it? Here Allen explicitly rejects the only kind of immortality available him, instead picking up on the total absurdity of humans bargaining their way out of mortality.

Of course it's a joke, but the joke is deeply embedded in the way we use language. Uncontroversially, meaning is created in a context of use, and in the context of a legacy of work, immortality may well invoke the notion of unforgettability. However, although "immortality" has, as one of its meanings, "unforgettability", this is not its most literal meaning. "Immortality" is denotatively equivalent to "not dying". Speaking as though he has the choice, he says he doesn't have any desire to be unforgettable; he simply wants the biologically impossible alternative, to live forever. These sorts of linguistic maneuvers make it clear that language use is not a straightforward business, and that if we willingly and obediently follow the impeccable logic of the comic, we see that language use and logic do not necessarily co-exist. This is the central point of *Ordinary Language Philosophy* (*cf.*, the later Wittgenstein, Austin, *inter alia*) and Woody Allen is one of the experts in helping these ideas along.[5]

Spike Milligan, in contrast with Allen, was more accepting of his mortality.

Example 3

I don't mind dying, I just don't want to be there when it happens.

(*Spike Milligan, 1918–2002*)

Of course, we don't know what happens when we die, but it is generally assumed by those who take a scientific view of the world that when you die, you are no longer present. In other words, you no longer exist. If that is the case, given Aristotle's law of excluded middle, you cannot both exist and not exist at the same time. Milligan taps into the anxiety about dying that many mortals have. They fear dying because they are frightened it will be an unpleasant experience. If you're not there, then the experience can't be unpleasant. But, let us remember, it is you who are in the process of dying. So you've got to be there, at least till it's over. Thereafter, it's not likely that you'll be there any longer. Another, more abstruse interpretation is that the speaker might be saying, "I don't mind the **concept** of 'dying', I just don't want to be around when it happens to other people, and, of course, I don't want it to happen to me." The central issue the joke highlights, however, remains that language use and logic do not follow the same rules.

2.1.2 Difference in Sense: What Counts?

Oppositeness in sense is sometimes called antonymy, or in the case of a unit bigger than a word, antonymic paraphrase. Antonymy is a slippery concept, as we see through an examination of some jokes exploiting techniques of opposition, contradiction and negation. Antonymy also, of course, involves sameness, as well as oppositeness. Oppositions and contrasts between two entities can be set up in many different ways but all of them require that some features be consistent across both entities in order for a contrast to be drawn. This is the basic notion of the minimal pair.

Spike Milligan played on accepted antonyms or antonymic paraphrases to great effect.

Example 4

Seagoon: We can't stand around here doing nothing. People will think we're workmen!
(The Goon Show, 1959. Series 9; episode 4)

The linguistically definitional notion is that workmen work. Milligan is referring to the widely held perception that workmen in the UK at the time spent their lives standing around doing nothing. Analyzing Seagoon's statement logically, at the purely linguistic level of the utterance, we face a contradiction: workmen work, and working is not equivalent to doing nothing. We have to resort to a different level of sense-making to understand the joke. There are people who think that workmen do nothing. Thus, if the characters stand around doing nothing, people will mistake them for workmen. Milligan plays with this perception, and in so doing points out several facts. The first is a non-linguistic one, which is that it is generally perceived to be the case among "people" (unspecified) that workmen stand around doing nothing.[6] The relevant semantic point is that words have a connotative life of their own, and a workman is not necessarily one who does any work. To understand the humor in Seagoon's remark, we have to become aware that the semantic consequences of morphological compounding are not simply a matter of adding together the senses of the two independent morphemes.[7]

Oppositeness in sense can be more complex than simple antonymy (such as seen in *alive* v. *dead*, or *opaque* v. *transparent*). Winston Churchill is said to have engaged in the following exchange of insults in conversation with Bessie Braddock, a British Labour politician, at an important social function. It is likely that Churchill had imbibed enough whisky to lift some of his very few social inhibitions.

Example 5

Bessie Braddock (to Winston Churchill): Winston, you're drunk.
Churchill: Bessie, you're ugly. But tomorrow I shall be sober.[8]

Churchill's remark exploits the differences between different types of adjectives and their antonyms. Drunkenness is not an essential property of a person, whereas ugliness might well be. Braddock is commenting on Churchill being in a state disgusting to her, *i.e.*, drunk. He is quick to insult her in return, and point out that he will no longer necessarily be in that state the next day, whereas she will be just as ugly, a state which is not as transient as drunkenness. He thus wins the exchange of insults, because his jibe will still hold true the next day, as there is little that she can do to change her ugliness. He, on the other hand, will be as drunk or as sober as he wishes. From this little piece of repartee, it can be observed, that although we are taught in school that many adjectives have antonyms, these do not all have the same status in terms of type.

This is a very good example of the 'stage-level' *v.* 'individual-level' distinction, first proposed by Carlson and expanded by Kratzer (Carlson, 1980; Kratzer, 1988, 1995). A stage-level predicate, *e.g.*, *drunk*, is one that is true of a temporal stage in its subject. An individual-level predicate, however, such as *ugly*, is true throughout the existence of an individual. We don't need to know as much as Carlson and Kratzer do to get this joke. Our tacit knowledge of English is adequate.

Woody Allen, a master at turning antonymic paraphrase to humorous advantage, demonstrates that the drawing of equivalences is a way that leads to madness. The following remark demonstrates complementary antonymy, at the same time as exploiting the semantics of scope.

Example 6

Most of the time I don't have much fun. The rest of the time I don't have any fun at all.
(Woody Allen, 1939–)

He sets it up by saying that most of the time he doesn't have much fun. The expectation is that he will say *The rest of the time I do* (have some fun). This is equivalent to

i.   *Most of the time I don't have much luck; the rest of the time I do have some* (luck).

The parallelism in (i) is between the complementary terms *most of the time* and *the rest of the time*, and also between the terms *much X* and *some X*. This parallelism is created probably because the implicit connector in (i) is understood to be *but*. So the expected format that is set up is:

ii.   *Most of the time I don't have much X, but the rest of the time I do have some X.*

Allen turns this inside out, however. He sets up his own parallelism, quite logically legitimate, between *much X* and *no X*. This goes along the lines of the following examples.

iii.   *I don't have much **and/but** he has none*
      or
iv.   *I don't have much **and/but** he has even less.*

The connector in (iii) and (iv) could well be *and* or *but*, whereas the preferred and expected reading in the original example seems to be as shown in (ii) repeated below.

ii. *Most of the time I don't have much X,* **but** *the rest of the time I do have some X.*

In this template, understanding *but* as the connector works much better than understanding *and* as the connector, as in (v).

v. *Most of the time I don't have much luck* **and** *the rest of the time I do have some.*

This is not interesting news, whereas in (ii) the use of *but* tells us that there is a contrast, and some interesting claim will follow. We can illustrate this with a simple example:

(a) *She is rich and happy*
   v.
(b) *She is rich but happy*

The *but* in (b) alerts us to the fact that a contrast is coming.

Thus, in contrastive parallelisms like the one Allen has set up, until we hear *I don't have any fun at all* we consider that the implicit connector is *but*. Then *I don't have any fun at all* trips us up and defeats our expectations. This occurs because Allen's remark works with the implicit reading of the connector as *and*. We are hoping for good news and expecting a *but*: we want poor Woody to have some fun sometimes. Instead we are told that the situation is generally bad and sometimes it is worse.

Another way of analyzing the humor comes from the ambiguity of readings available in *don't have much fun*. Here we might be inclined to take *much* as essentially equivalent to *any*. For social reasons we sometimes say *not much* when we mean *no*—for instance, *Did you like the play? Not much.* This then sets up a linguistic scale, on which the only other options are positive quantities of fun. So of course we then anticipate that the next remark will be *the rest of the time I have lots of fun/some fun.* The humor then, comes from the fact that Allen intends the original *much fun* not as a Negative Polarity Item (see section 4.1) but as introducing a positive quantity of *fun*.

This joke works by defeating our linguistic expectations. Given the complexity of the semantic mechanisms at work here, the joke must surely tap tacit intuitions in the listener.

Using parallelism to set up expectations is one of Woody Allen's common tricks. The listener is primed to expect a certain word or phrase and in the case below, this is undercut, by use of an antonym, to humorous effect.

Example 7

For the first year of marriage I had basically a bad attitude. I tended to place my wife under a pedestal.

(Woody Allen, 1939–)

To place someone on a pedestal is an idiomatic way of expressing the idea that one person idolizes another. Idols, in statue form, are placed on pedestals. When we hear *I tended to place my wife*, the expectation is very strong that the next phrase will be *on a pedestal*. Instead, Allen plays with the preposition and substitutes *under* for *on*; these prepositions are logical opposites for some class of events. It is a common cliché to say that someone who idolizes his wife places her on a pedestal. It is logical, therefore, to say that someone who does not idolize his wife places her under a pedestal. The picture is amusing: the idea of a person underneath a pedestal is quite ridiculous, although if one unfreezes the metaphor, the cliché of someone perched on a pedestal is not much less absurd. Allen unfreezes the metaphor for the sake of the joke. The action of putting someone under a pedestal may be considered to be abusive (especially if the pedestal is heavy), the sign of something a little worse than a bad attitude. All Allen has done is substitute one preposition for the other to create a picture that plays with the staleness of the cliché and at the same time, the logical absurdity of language use.

In another example, attributed to Henny Youngman, the same principle is exploited, with a similar humorous effect.

Example 8

A man goes to see a psychoanalyst.
The psychoanalyst asks, "So, what do you do?"
"I'm an auto mechanic," says the man.
"Right," says the psychoanalyst, "Get under the couch."

To get this joke, we need to know that analysands lie on psychoanalysts' couches. We also need to know that auto mechanics spend a lot of their time under cars. Mechanics fix cars: psychoanalysts (so they say) fix people. Who is fixing who or what here?

Linguistically, all we need to know is that for some class of events, *on* and *under* function antonymically. For other classes, such antonymic use is just ridiculous. The joke makes us aware of how ridiculous our communication can be if we follow what we think are linguistic rules.

In humorous uses of language, lexical or semantic parallelism can be highlighted or created by the use of some forms of antonymy. For instance, in humorous cases, parallelism can be created by the identification of a spurious shared property that is contrasted. There's a context in which I've heard people dismissed as *hard of thinking*. This is not intended to be an insult to people who are actually mentally impaired, but rather as a way of referring to people who the speaker thinks are rather stupid. The obvious parallelism employed here is with the term *hard of hearing*. This term is itself a euphemism used to describe people who are deaf. The person who coined the witty expression *hard of thinking* was clearly playing on the euphemism and extending it more generally. *Hard of hearing* is a supposedly gentle way of saying that people have difficulty hearing. By analogy, *hard of thinking* refers to people who the speaker thinks have difficulty thinking. The semantic contrast is between thinking and hearing. It is of course an illegitimate one, as thinking is not a sense in the way that hearing is, but they are both psych verbs,[9] and English certainly allows the contrast.[10]

In the following example, Woody Allen exploits a potential morphological parallel between two words describing two processes, and employs an implicit parallelism between the two processes. In so doing, he highlights the traps of paying too much attention to the surface parallelism that abounds in language use.

Example 9

I don't tan, I stroke.

(Woody Allen, 1939–)

In order to catch the humor of this one-liner, we need to recognize that by *tan*, Allen means "suntan". Although it's more usual to use *tan* to describe the process, it is possible to use the compound, *suntan*, as a verb, as well, as follows:

   i.   *I like to go to the beach so that I can suntan all day.*

We should note that, more usually, *suntan* is regularly used as a noun, originally a compound made of *sun+tan*. We should also note that along with getting a suntan, from sunning oneself all day, one might also get sunstroke. The noun *sunstroke* is also a compound, made of *sun+stroke*. Sunstroke (insolation) is a condition caused by excessive exposure to the sun, usually accompanied by a fever, delirium and other unpleasant symptoms. The (somewhat spurious) parallelism is between *suntan*, a tan you get from the sun, and *sunstroke*, not precisely a stroke you get from the sun, but a compound of sun+stroke: *stroke* being a noun derived from the verb stem *strike*, meaning "to deliver a blow". More accurately, we could say that *sunstroke* has the meaning "struck by the sun". Grammatically, thus, there is not a true parallelism between *tan* and *stroke* in *suntan* and *sunstroke*. Although one can say (i), one cannot say (ii) on the reading proposed.

   i.   *I tan*
        "I get a tan"
   ii. *★I stroke,*
        "I get a stroke".

The utterance in (ii) is illegitimate, because stroke can't be used in the middle alternation (*cf.* Levin & Rappoport Hovav, 2005).

This does not stop Woody Allen. Paraphrasing prosaically and unhumorously, we could assume he intends to say *If I spend time in the sun, I don't get a suntan, I get sunstroke*. Notice, one cannot say *a sunstroke*, so even here the parallelism is not exact.[11] The apparent parallelism, however, probably looks too tempting to leave alone, and the entire observation is condensed as *I don't tan, I stroke.*

Thus, we can more or less track the derivation process he uses, and work backwards to see how he makes this flagrantly grammatically incorrect and lexically inaccurate claim. It's intended to be a joke: Allen surely does not really want us to think that he strokes, rather, that he is struck. The joke asks us to notice the similarity between *suntan* and *sunstroke*, and to remark that if one can tan, one can therefore also stroke.[12]

Groucho Marx also uses an aspect of semantic feature opposition to create his particular brand of slippery slope humor.

Example 10

I was married by a judge. I should have asked for a jury.

(Groucho Marx, 1890–1977)

The underlying implication in this remark is that marriage is a jail sentence.

The element of surprise is what activates this joke. The joke works in an interesting way. The terms *judge* and *jury* are in obvious collocation. A judge is not a jury and a jury is not a judge: they differ by one crucial semantic feature, in a certain context. For this joke we need to know that the term "judge" is used to refer to a marriage officer, in the event of a marriage, and there is no legal case which s/he is to adjudicate.

Justices of the peace do not adjudicate in trials—legally qualified judges are given this responsibility. The jury is a group of people chosen to provide a verdict on a trial in a court of law. The participation of a jury does not preclude the participation of a judge, but is complementary to it. In the USA, in a trial in which there is a judge but no jury, a trialist can ask for a jury.

However, a marriage is not a court case, but an official solemnization of a contract. It is not the same in kind as a legal trial, although Groucho draws the parallel.

The semantic parallelism here is, of course, a false one. Although *judge* and *jury* are collocations, they are collocations in a specific context. Not all situations that involve a judge require a jury, or *vice versa*. The concept of getting married may indeed be associated with a judge: Groucho's association of the event with a jury creates the strong suggestion that marriage is a jail sentence

Consistent with maintaining his nerdy image, Woody Allen is responsible for the following claim:

Example 11

I am at two with nature.

(Woody Allen, 1939–)

This remark, too, exploits a cliché: *I am at one with nature*, which means something like "I am perfectly comfortable in the physical world of natural phenomena and all living things". It is a term generally associated with people who disdain the comforts of civilization. As a rule, the expression is used with positive connotations:

someone who is at one with nature is to be admired. However, Allen distances himself from nature, moving away from the romanticism and transcendentalism of nature lovers, and makes it clear that not only does he not feel at one with nature, but that he feels entirely not a part of it at all. This is of course, logically ridiculous: as we are all living beings, we are, by definition, a part of nature. But, on the other hand, from the logical and linguistic point of view, if you can be *at one* with something, why not *at two*?[13] Of course, *at one* is an idiom chunk, and can't easily be interfered with to make meaning changes. If Allen really wanted to make a claim opposite to *I am at one with nature*, he could have said *I am not at one with nature*. However, he chose to express it a different way, using a logically legitimate generalization. As it happens, Allen is making the claim in order to create certain implications: we are intended to understand that he considers himself entirely separate from nature. The implication is that he considers himself to be a non-natural being, uncomfortable and at odds with the outdoors. All Allen has actually done is change one word for another of the same class. He has substituted *two* for *one*. He has also shown the essential redundancy of the cliché and by making this claim he has demonstrated that he considers himself not only to be detached from the world of nature, but also able to determine his relationship with it, another patent absurdity. He doesn't say *I feel*, but rather, *I am*, as though this is a fact about the world. And indeed, he has as much right, linguistically and philosophically, to say *I am at two with nature* as anyone has to say *I am at one with nature*.

The late, lamented stand-up comedian, Lenny Bruce, maintained a fine and biting line in humorous patter. In this example, he too exploits the technique of exchanging one lexical item for another, apparently syntactically parallel, and differing semantically by one feature. This exchange creates a significant difference in meaning.

Example 12

I won't say ours was a tough school, but we had our own coroner. We used to write essays like, "What I'm going to be if I grow up."

(Lenny Bruce, 1925–66)

What I'm going to be when I grow up is a standard topic for junior school essays. In such essays, students are supposed to discuss their dreams and hopes for the future. Bruce starts off by saying he won't say that he went to a tough school. He then undercuts this remark by saying, *but we had our own coroner*, implying that there were so many deaths at the school that it was worth their while to have their own coroner. Bruce then begins to provide examples to enhance his implication about how dangerous his school was. Having made the point that they had their own coroner, he then goes on to mention the kinds of essay topics they were assigned. Simply substituting *if* for *when* entirely changes the meaning of the essay topic, and adds further depth to the implication that his school was mortally dangerous. *If* is a subordinating conjunction (a complementizer in the terminology of Generative Grammar) that introduces a clause whose truth-value is unknown.[14]

If I grow up suggests that there is only a possibility that the person will grow up, and conversely, there is also a strong possibility that the person will not reach adulthood, *i.e.*, that he will be quite likely to die (at school). So, Bruce doesn't actually say that his school was dangerous. However, tampering with the essay topic by simply substituting one subordinating conjunction with another that apparently fits the resultant sentence just as well, he produces a subtle but pointed reminder that, although it can be generally assumed by schoolteachers and other adults that students have a future to look forward to, in the case of his school, this was by no means to be expected.

Spike Milligan had a particular knack of exploiting aspects of antonymy/ synonymy in language that demonstrates that meaning really does reside in the way we use words, rather than being found in their inherent semantic features.[15] He, too, used frozen clichéd expressions and defrosted them in order to set their semantics free. The following remark is typical of his style.

Example 13

Are you going to come quietly or do I have to use earplugs.
                    (The Goon Show, *1958*. Vintage Goons *series; episode 8)*

The semantic feature that is being exploited here is +/− noise. We use earplugs to silence the noise we hear. When Milligan asks, *Are you going to come quietly?*, he is picking up on a stereotypical utterance made by police officers when they arrest someone. This is normally followed by something of the order of *or do I have to X?*, *e.g.*, *do I have to use violence, do I have to bring in the reinforcements?* or some other kind of threat. Milligan says, *or do I have to use earplugs?* If the utterance were to be understood simply according to its surface level semantics, this would not be absurd. If someone is making a noise, we can stop our auditory perception of the noise by using earplugs. This is certainly not going to make the person stop making the noise, but it will solve the problem of our hearing the noise. However, the illocutionary force of the standard utterance (as made by police officers and the like) is threat, and Milligan's version certainly is not going to serve to threaten or warn any person, screaming and struggling, that the hearer is going to use earplugs to protect himself from the noise.

In its conventional pragmatic usage then, the grammatical question about whether or not the person is going to come quietly, is not a question about whether the person is going to turn down the volume, but a threat that if they don't co-operate some new and terrible thing will happen to make them co-operate. Milligan picks up on the more literal meaning of *come quietly*, and reduces his threat to a question equivalent in illocutionary status to *Is it going to stop raining or do I have to bring a raincoat?* There's no threat here, simply a request for information followed by a question as to what he might find it necessary to do based on the information he will receive. The joke then, is based on play with semantic features and properties, but also on play with illocutionary force. It is presented here to highlight the semantic play, but it serves as well as a very good example of mistaken illocutionary force, a pragmatic notion.

As we can see through the analysis of the jokes that exploit sameness and difference in sense, the claim of synonymy or sense equivalence in language is wide open to attack. And, indeed, proposals about word meaning have been contested from different perspectives by almost everyone who cares about "meaning" (clearly an inadequate term for the multiple phenomena): philosophers of language, rhetoreticians, semanticists, semioticians, systemicists, functionalists, postmodernists and their friends and enemies.

Analyticity, too, has been given a rough ride through the fields of philosophy of language. We know the status of a proposition like *A triangle has three sides.* This is analytic *a priori*. Establishing the denotation of specific terms as close to identical, however, does not help to make certain analytic propositions sensible.

In the next example, we see how Groucho Marx, by setting up two definitionally similar terms and using syntactic parallelism to set up the expectation of a potential contrast (similar to the technique in Example 6), manages to reveal that the syntax tells one story; the semantics another.

Example 14

I worked myself up from nothing to a state of extreme poverty.

(*Groucho Marx, from* Monkey Business)

There's not much to choose between the state of having nothing (or being nothing) and being in a state of extreme poverty. In both cases, we might say that the person is exceptionally deprived of material possessions and money. However, Groucho phrases it in such a way that we are led to believe that the state of having nothing is lower than the state of extreme poverty. He achieves this by using the structure *worked myself up from X to Y*. In this way, the syntax already sets up the skeleton of the proposition. If we did not know what either *nothing* or *a state of extreme poverty* referred to, we would still be able to speculate that the person worked himself from an extremely bad situation to one that was less bad. However, the semantics tell a different story. Groucho is actually saying that although it looked like he worked very hard and improved his position, in effect, there was no great change in his material circumstances.

In fact, Dorothy Parker exploited the same sort of structure when she commented on Katharine Hepburn's performance in a 1934 play, *The Lake*.[16]

Example 15

Miss Hepburn runs the gamut of emotions from A to B.

(*Dorothy Parker, 1893–1967*)

In this case, the structure is set up by use of the phrase *runs the gamut of*. To *run the gamut of something* is to span the entire range of it. For instance, a *gamut* often refers to a whole series of musical notes from the lowest to the highest. The implication inherent in the use of *gamut* is that there is a large range to be explored. Had Dorothy Parker said that Hepburn run the entire range of emotions from A to Z, without our knowing what A and Z referred to, we would know that her performance encompassed an extensive emotional range. However, this sort of idea is pithily undercut by the use of *from A to B*. The implicit contrast is between *from A to Z* and *from A to B*. In other words, although *gamut* sets us up to expect a wide ranging repertoire of emotions, *from A to B* tells us that the range she achieved was actually so narrow as not to be seriously called a *gamut* at all.

The device of using synonymous expressions in an overtly contrastive manner, activated by the choice of syntactic frame is a favorite of Milligan's, and examples are legion throughout the Goon Show scripts.

Example 16

Seagoon: Rather than surrender we gave ourselves up.

(The Goon Show, 1957. Series 8; episode 14)

The meaning is set up by the syntactic frame *rather than*. *Rather than X* primes us for *we did Y*, where X and Y are in some way contrastive. However, what we get here is the use of two synonymous expressions, *surrender* and *give ourselves up*. Yet again we are faced with two different messages, one from the syntax and another from the semantics. The message from the syntax is that *give ourselves up* is an alternative to *surrender*. The message from the semantics is that the terms are synonymous. Which are we to believe?

Another example of Milligan's tricks is to play with paradoxes and paraphrases. In order to achieve the humorous effects, he works simultaneously with syntax and semantics, creating logical absurdity.

Example 17

Seagoon: As I swam ashore, I dried myself to save time.

(The Goon Show, 1954. Series 5; episode 3)

The compositional semantics of swim involve a feature [+in water]. It is therefore impossible to dry oneself whilst swimming. The syntax here does not allow for a reading involving consecutive action, such as *First I swam and then I dried myself* or *after I swam I dried myself*. Instead, it stipulates simultaneous action. *As I swam ashore, I dried myself to save time*. Whereas it seems very efficient to dry oneself simultaneously with some other activity to save time, as the syntax would suggest, in fact, it is not possible to dry oneself while swimming. Nevertheless, by his own account, Seagoon sounds, on first hearing, like an efficient and focused hero. This is part of the way Milligan sets up ridiculous scenarios that sound epic and bold, whereas, in fact, they are normally about cardboard-cutout boy scouts and pieces of string.

Another variation on the principle of exploiting apparently shared semantic features to create logical absurdity, is the following, also from the Goon Show.

Example 18

Seagoon: We tried using a candle, but it wasn't very bright and we daren't light it.
(The Goon Show, *1954. Series 5; episode 3)*

Generally speaking, the main function of a candle (other than for decorative purposes) is to provide light. This would be our assumption if we heard *We tried using a candle, but it wasn't very bright*. However, this is undercut by *and we daren't light it*. If that had been the case, it wouldn't be surprising that the candle wasn't very bright, given that it was unlit. The semantic features of *candle* include [emits light] and certainly one of the semantic features of *bright* is [+light]. However, once we hear that Seagoon didn't dare light the candle, we realize that the semantic features we have been focusing on are entirely irrelevant in the case of an unlit candle. One of the semantic features of *unlit* candle is certainly [-light]. Not lighting a candle and expecting it to provide light is simply silly. However, the idea of someone using an unlit candle and being surprised that it provides no light is the cause of the humor. There's merit in talking about lighting a candle, rather than simply talking about using one. *Using* is a more general term than *lighting* and it lends itself to some ambiguity, which, of course, Milligan exploits.

Thus, so far in this chapter, having examined notions of antonymy, opposition, contrast, and antonymic paraphrase, we find that these are by no means easy notions to apply or understand. The whole is not always equal to the sum of its parts; true antonymy is rare, different kinds of contrast, syntactic parallelism, semantic oppositions, literal and non-literal uses of language, all work together and against one another to complicate the linguistic phenomena. Yet it is not at all difficult for any native speaker to get the jokes presented in this section. It is the description and analysis that is tricky: the knowledge is easily available to users of the language.

2.2 Homophony

The use of puns (or paronomasia) is often regarded as capturing the essence of linguistic humor. This is much too narrow an application of the many ways in which humor that exploits the formal and functional nature of language can be understood. Nevertheless, a discussion of puns is in order. In my view, the choicest puns are those that involve a reanalysis of the sound sequence so that a larger structural disturbance is caused. These sorts of puns are discussed in the chapters dealing with phonological, morphological and syntactic reanalysis. Here, however, I look only at whole lexical items and the deliberate way in which people play with them.

Simple puns are based on the principle of homophony, *i.e.*, when there are two or more lexical entries that sound similar, but have different meanings, jokes can be made that deliberately exploit the confusion among the different meanings. A pun is the result of a deliberate decision to play with aspects of sound and meaning in language. Unintended confusion of two or more similar sounding words is not generally regarded as punning behavior, although when it is recognized, linguistic insight is triggered.

Spike Milligan's puns are sophisticated examples of the type. This one is pulled from the context of an ongoing dialogue.

Example 19

Neddy Seagoon: Now, where's the rent?
Grytpype-Thynne: In my trousers.

(The Goon Show, 1959. Series 9; episode 12)

This is a sophisticated pun, because rent is homonymous, and in this case it works in a linguistic context with both the selected senses of *rent* remaining intact. On one reading, *rent* may be read as referring to a tenant's payment to a landlord. When the response to the question is that the rent is in the speaker's trousers, we are meant to assume that the money to pay the landlord is in the speaker's trouser pockets. On the other reading, *rent* may be read as referring to a tear or a rip. On this reading, we understand the speaker to be saying that the tear is in his trousers, *i.e.*, that he has torn his trousers. This response is rather snappy, being perfectly appropriate on both readings of *rent*, correct in grammatical contexts, and evoking two different real world contexts.

Milligan's touch is very light. His puns exploit the duality of meaning very deftly, so that the twist is seamless. Here too, he puns on a polysemous word *draw* without losing either of the selected senses.

Example 20

Here's a pencil. Go and draw the blinds!

(The Goon Show, 1958. Series 9; episode 3)

When we hear *Here's a pencil. Go and draw the*, we expect that the object will be something that may be drawn with a pencil. Indeed, one may draw a picture of the blinds, although it's not clear why one might want to do so, but it is not immediately obvious to think of the action of drawing the blinds closed being achieved by means of a pencil.[17] The play is on *draw*, *i.e.*, sketch and *draw*, *i.e.*, close (the blinds). The first kind of drawing is done by means of using the pencil as instrument, in contrast to the second kind of drawing, which is not done by means of anything, but by human agency (unless a hook or stick of some sort is used as an instrument). The humor is achieved by the smoothness of the transition from one kind of drawing to the other, and the ludicrousness of the image created. As always with Milligan, the utterance sounds so fitting to the ongoing register of a particular saga that its content catches the listener unawares.

As part of one of the Monty Python Flying Circus sketches about World War II, the British are trying to design a joke to get the Germans to die laughing. However the Germans, too, have in their armory, a joke, designed for the same purpose. In the sketch, the joke is told by Hitler, with very little success (probably because of the way he tells it).

Example 21

Hitler: My dog has no nose.
Crowd: How does it smell?
Hitler: Terrible.

The joke is embedded in a broader comic context, with Hitler bellowing it at a full stadium of people, who bark obediently back at him. This creates a fair bit of the comedy in any event. The linguistic joke itself is a fairly simple pun on the English word *smell* and two of its senses: as a verb "to detect something by means of nerves in the nose" and "to produce an odor", in conjunction with the ambiguous syntactic structure triggered both by these sense differences, and the wh-word *how*, which turns out to be ambiguous as well.

How does it smell? then, can be interpreted as,

i. "If it has no nose, how is it able to engage in the act of distinguishing odors?" or it can be interpreted as
ii. "What is the nature of the odor your dog gives off?"

So, this joke works, firstly, because of the polysemy of *smell* in *x smells*—between the interpretation where 'x' is the source of the odor, as opposed to where 'x' is undergoing an olfactory experience. One would expect this to be translatable in a language where there is a similar ambiguity between the experiencer *smell* and the stative *smell*.

Strictly, applying either Grice or Relevance Theory (see Chapter 2), the preferred answer should be to the interpretation in (i) although it is perfectly legitimate to ask a question about the sort of odor a dog produces if we believe we are hearing a series of statements describing a particular dog. The joke works by exploiting the reading in (ii): the odor the dog produces is terrible.

The idea of a dog without a nose is reasonably funny to some people, to start off with, and the question as to how it is able to smell (iii) is a fairly obvious one.

iii.   *How does it smell?*

The expected answer to (i) would be something like:

iv.   "It can't smell."

Thus the answer to (iii) in the reading as in (i) then, involves sentence negation.
The response for the purposes of the joke, however is an answer to the reading
in (ii), as seen in (v).

v.   *Terrible!*

The answer provided in (v) is simply a predicate adjective. This ambiguity is
to be found in the polysemy of *how*. *How* is a wh-word that (a) can question the
manner in which something is done, but also (b) can question what the state of
being is that is predicated of some subject.

2.3 Homophony and Polysemy: The Case of Modals

Among other examples of homophony leading to semantic ambiguity, we find
the particular case of modals. Modals in English are polysemous.
Example 22 is generally considered to be a quintessentially Jewish joke,
although its humorous effect is to found in ambiguity of language use that does
not depend on any particular cultural knowledge. Some cultural knowledge
might intensify the enjoyment of the joke, but this knowledge is not necessary for
the understanding of the linguistic aspects that it exploits.

Example 22

A Frenchman, a German and a Jewish person are trudging across the Sahara desert.
The Frenchman says, "I'm so thirsty. I must have wine!"
The German says, "I'm so thirsty. I must have beer!"
The Jewish person cries out, "I'm so thirsty! I must have diabetes!"

The joke hinges on the semantics of *must have*. When the Frenchman and
the German say they *must have* they mean that it is essential for them to have
a drink (in this case the stereotyped national favorite). So they use *must* in its
deontic reading. In this context, they use *have* with the reading "drink", *i.e.*,
"I must drink x".
In contrast, the Jewish person uses *must* with the reading, "it seems obvious
that", or "the only conclusion to be drawn is that", thus in its epistemic use. In
this context, he uses *have* with the reading "suffer from", *i.e.*, "suffer from
diabetes". So, in the last line of the joke, the meaning of *must have* is twisted from

the previously established reading, "I've got to have a drink" to "It's obvious that I'm very ill".

The joke relies on a fine distinction between the expression of deontic and epistemic readings of modals, as well as some play with the very general uses of *have*. Syntactically, the utterances of all three speakers are identical. Pragmatically, the first two utterances express the speakers' need; the last expresses the speaker's inexorable self-diagnosis.

The humor of the joke is also intensified by the play on the stereotyped national characteristics: the French crave wine, the Germans crave beer, and Jews are catastrophic and hypochondriacal (and crave attention). The full humorous effect of the joke is achieved by combining the ambiguity inherent in the English modal system with a semantically very adaptable word, *have* (also polysemous) to form a witty observation, recognizable to many in the group that has been stereotyped. This is not a racist joke, in my view, since in order to be funny it requires listeners to recognize themselves. Diabetes is a condition well-known among older Jewish people with a certain lifestyle and is recognizable as a stereotypical Jewish disease in a way that cirrhosis of the liver is not (for similarly stereotypical reasons).

The ambiguity present in the use of modals in English is a fruitful source of humor. Example 23 dates back to the 1960s. In order to appreciate it, we need to know that the USSR was the most powerful superpower in the Communist Bloc in Eastern and Central Europe, with its officials controlling other Communist countries in the region, one of which was Czechoslovakia. Leonid Brezhnev was the General Secretary of the Communist Party of the USSR and Fidel Castro was the President of Cuba, also a powerful Communist country.

Example 23

Castro visits Moscow and is taken on a tour by Brezhnev. First they go for a drink, and Castro praises the beer. "Yes, it was provided by our good friends from Czechoslovakia."

Next they go for a ride in a car, and Castro admires the car. "Yes, these cars are provided by our good friends from Czechoslovakia."

They drive to an exhibition of beautiful cut glass, which Castro greatly admires. "Yes, this glass is provided by our good friends from Czechoslovakia."

"They must be very good friends," says Castro. "Yes, they must," says Brezhnev.

The joke here turns on the modal *must*. Castro's remark is probably intended to mean that since he could see that the Czechs were so generous as to give all these expensive gifts to the USSR, he could deduce that the Czechs were indeed very good friends of the USSR. Brezhnev's retort can be read as a confirmation of this deduction, *i.e.*, that he recognizes and acknowledges that Castro's use of *must* is epistemic. However, Brezhnev's *must* can also be understood as "obliged to", and is, therefore, deontic. His reply then may be understood as a wry statement of fact: the Czechs do not have a choice, they are obliged to be very good friends to the USSR.

On the deontic reading, our knowledge of the semantic properties of *friends* enables us to see that there is a contradiction in saying, "they are forced/obliged/ have to be very good friends". Friendship is a voluntary relationship: people cannot be forced to be good friends with each other. This tips us off to the fact that Brezhnev's response should be understood to mean that the Czechs have no option but to be good friends. However, it is clear, then, that they are not good friends, but are forced to provide the USSR with gifts. Castro's attribution of generosity to the Czechs is thus unwarranted. It is possible to understand the humor here without knowing the relationship between the USSR and the people of Czechoslovakia, but if one does know about the relationship and that Czechoslovakia functioned as a mandatory handmaiden to the USSR, the humor is sharper and the joke more bitter.

English modals, because of their polysemic nature, form the crux of many English linguistic jokes. The fact, as well, that they are generally monosyllabic, and homophonic with other words in English is another crucial factor in the significance of their contribution to such jokes. Thus, for example, consider *must*, in its epistemic and deontic uses, as well as its lexical entry as a noun, meaning, *inter alia*, unfermented grape juice, the state of an elephant in heat, or the cause of mustiness (*i.e.*, staleness) in a room. Similar sorts of versatility are found in the uses of *can*, *will*, *would*, *may*, and *might*.[18]

3.0 Literal and Non-Literal Uses of Language and their Semantic Collision

The distinction between literal and non-literal interpretations of expressions has always been the source of misunderstanding and humor. All the human languages we know contain sentences that are both literal and non-literal. In language use there is a fine line between literal and non-literal truth, and this is because pragmatic factors always tend to overwhelm and dwarf compositional semantics (Recanati, 2004). See Example 13 in this chapter, for an illustration of this claim.

Spike Milligan, apparently, found it irresistible to take the literal interpretation of a non-literal expression, especially one that had become clichéd. This famous example is also his.

Example 24

Moriarty: My nerves are strained to breaking point!
Fx:[Boing!]
Moriarty: There goes one now

(The Goon Show, 1955. Series 6; episode 15)

Moriarty uses a well-worn expression to describe the state of his nerves. He is suffering from emotional strain. However, he presents strained nerves as a physical condition. The metaphor he employs is that his nerves are tautly stretched strings, much like those on a stringed instrument. He threatens his interlocutor that his nerves might not hold out, since they are so severely strained. *Boing!* (in some versions *Twang!*) is the sound that a snapping string might make. When someone says their nerves are stretched to breaking point they are not suggesting that they expect them literally to snap. However, in the sound effects we hear, Moriarty's nerves do just that. He hears it too, and makes sure his interlocutors are informed that the sound they hear is his nerve snapping. As far as we know, nerves do not physically break through emotional strain. However, Milligan, through one short sound effect, shows how easy it is to make literal and non-literal expressions collide.[19]

The inverse of this process is also very common in the creation of humorous effects. In this exchange from the movie *Young Frankenstein* (1976), Dr. Frankenstein asks his factotum, Igor, to help him with the guests' luggage.

Example 25

Dr. Frederick Frankenstein: Igor, would you give me a hand with the bags?
Igor: Certainly, you take the blonde and I'll take the one in the turban.

This exchange is a tribute to Groucho Marx.[20] In the movie, *Young Frankenstein*, there are two women guests, who have arrived with their luggage. One of the guests has blonde hair and the other is wearing a turban. Igor (deliberately or otherwise) mistakes Frankenstein's literal use of the term *bags*, referring to the guests' luggage, and instead understands him to be asking for a hand with the women, "bags" being a rather disrespectful term for older women. So, here we see the non-literal interpretation of a literal use of *bags*. It's left to the imagination as to how exactly he proposes to give Frankenstein a hand with these bags.

Dorothy Parker (1893–1967), who in her career as a reviewer was the source of many great one-liners, also used parallelism of syntactic structure to set up expectations, which she then undercut with some semantic surprises, many of them exploiting a literal/non-literal distinction. In this case, Parker makes use of unexpected contrastive focus, and it is on this that the joke turns.

Example 26

This is not a novel to be tossed aside lightly. It should be thrown with great force.
                    (Dorothy Parker (1893–1967) in her review of Mussolini's
                    The Cardinal's Mistress)[21]

She sets up the joke by saying what should not happen to a novel such as the one under discussion. She uses a cliché, *not to be tossed aside lightly.*[22] As a rule, pragmatically, this expression means that the topic, whatever it is, should be taken seriously. The next sentence begins *It should be.* The expectation set up is that the sentence that follows will be something along the lines of

i. *It should be read with great concentration*
   or
ii. *It should be treated with immense gravity.*
   Instead, Parker picks up on the literal meaning of the phrase
iii. *(not a novel) to be tossed aside lightly*
   and contrasts it with an equally literal direction as to how it should be treated, *i.e.*,
iv. *thrown with great force.*

Thus, although Parker might be understood to be saying at first that the novel should not be dismissed, (tossed aside lightly) and setting up the implication that it should be taken seriously, she continues to say that tossing it aside lightly is too gentle a treatment for a piece of work as bad as this novel is, and the more appropriate treatment would be to throw it with great force to show the full extent of one's disgust.

Her opening sentence, however, given our usual expectations of a book review and the kind of remarks that are made in that genre, really does not prepare us for the way in which the second sentence is used to exploit the literal, and less expected, reading of the first. Instead of focussing on the non-literal meaning of (iii) she focusses more narrowly on the notion of 'throwing', and specifically on ways of throwing, *i.e.*, *tossing lightly* v. *hurling with great force*. The effect of this utterance is to create a very strong implicature that not only is the book not worth taking seriously, it is so bad it should be rejected violently. Her focus on the literal reading of toss allows us to draw the obvious conclusion of her non-literal (and intended) meaning.

Example 26 above also highlights another aspect of semantics. The joke provides a good illustration of the different ways in which any noun (in this case, *book*) can be interpreted – what Pustejovsky calls logical polysemy (Pustejovsky, 1995). He talks about the *qualia* roles of nouns (analogous to the *thematic* roles of verbs). At least two different *qualia* roles of *book* are activated here: book as physical object or book as readable item.

A version of the following joke was voted in an Internet poll to be the funniest joke in the English-speaking world.[23] The joke appears to have been originated by Milligan and used in 1951. It, too, plays on both the interpretation of meanings as strictly literal and the misunderstanding of speech acts. Milligan's original, which dates from 1951, is reproduced below.

Example 27

Bentine: I just came in and found him lying on the carpet there.
Sellers: Oh, is he dead?
Bentine: I think so.

Sellers: Hadn't you better make sure?
Bentine: Alright. Just a minute.
Sound of two gun shots.
Bentine: He's dead.

The joke here turns on the question, *Hadn't you better make sure?* The intention of the questioner is to confirm the certainty of the claim that the person is actually dead. This is because any further decisions or actions would need to be made based on that certainty. However, owing to the fact that *make sure* is semantically ambiguous, and additionally, that the appropriate understanding of illocutionary force requires some common sense (and in this case relies on good judgment), by the end of the story there is no doubt whatsoever that the person with whom we are all concerned is now well and truly dead.

Make sure here can mean "be absolutely certain that the claim you are making is correct". In this case, there are at least two ways of doing so. One is to check that the claim that the person is dead is, in fact, correct. This is equivalent to

    i. *Make sure that the meeting you plan to attend is really scheduled for Tuesday.*

The other way to make sure is to let there be no doubt that the person is actually dead, even if this means taking some irrevocable action to ensure that this is the case. This is equivalent to

    ii. *Make sure that the door is locked before you leave the house.*

Anyone uttering (ii) does not mean that the interlocutor should find out whether the door is locked or not and then leave the house. The speech act is in fact an instruction or a request to lock the door. Thus the speaker's intention in (i) is to remind the hearer to check that something is the case, whereas the speaker's intention in (ii) is an instruction to do something that will ensure that a state of affairs comes into being. In the joke, the speech act *Make sure he's dead* is intended as a suggestion to the hearer to be conscientious and cautious (as in (i)), but is taken up as an instruction to kill the person, if need be (as in (ii)).

Literal and non-literal uses of languages may be considered, as here, as part of the semantic interpretation of language. Very often, however, we rely on our knowledge of linguistic pragmatics to separate out the semantic ambiguities. A much deeper discussion of linguistic pragmatics is to be found in Chapter 2.

4.0 Ambiguity

4.1 Logical Ambiguity/Scope Ambiguity

The use of logical ambiguity in language is a well-known device for creating humorous effects. In order to disambiguate different readings on the basis of semantic scope, one generally has to resort to the context in which the utterance is made. It is possible to rephrase such utterances to remove the logical ambiguity, but this would also remove the humor. To understand these jokes, then, the hearer has to be aware of at least two possible readings.

The next few examples demonstrate some ambiguities that are inherent in the structure of the specific sorts of sentence highlighted. The elements that allow the ambiguity in these cases are what are known as Polarity Items, in tandem with potential scope ambiguities.

Many of these sorts of jokes are due to the presence of polarity items, such as *any, somewhat, ever*. A polarity item is an expression, such as **any** *wool* which, when used in a sentence, has to have its polarity triggered by the presence of another expression, *i.e.*, in this case a question or a negative expression.

So, we can say

   i.   I don't have *any wool*.
   ii. Do you have *any wool*?

But we cannot say

  iii. *I have *any wool*.

We can consider *any* to be a negative polarity item, because it is licensed by a negative expression.

Similarly, some expressions can be anti-licensed by the presence of a negative expression. One such expression is *somewhat*. *Somewhat* is a positive polarity item, as it is ungrammatical in a sentence that contains a negative expression.

So, we can say

  iv. I enjoyed the play *somewhat*

But not

  v. *I didn't enjoy the play *somewhat*

The triggering expressions, thus, are regarded as licensing (or anti-licensing) expressions. Essentially, the licensing expression is a trigger for the polarity item.[24]

The polarity items discussed here are sensitive to negation. A way of thinking about polarity items is to sort them into polarity items that must co-occur with a "somehow negative" expression—these are called Negative Polarity Items (NPI); and those that cannot co-occur with a "somehow negative" expression—these are called Positive Polarity Items (PPI). NPIs are licensed by negative expressions; PPIs are anti-licensed by negative expressions. Similarly, NPIs are licensed by questions, and PPIs are not.

Some examples of negative polarity items in English are *any, ever, at all.* Examples of positive polarity items in English are *somewhat, some, rather, already.*[25]

As Paul Portner puts it, "[t]he world of language contains a very strange species known as negative polarity items (NPIs). These creatures like the shade of negative sentences, those containing words like *not* or *nobody*, and dislike the full sun of positive sentences" (Portner, 2005, p. 122). This strange species is exploited to marvelous effect in jokes that play with NPIs in conjunction with scope ambiguities.

Example 28

A self-righteous clergyman is reported to have said the following whilst condemning the evils of city life, and publicly declaring his piety.
    "There are a dozen brothels in this town and I haven't visited one of them".

His statement can be understood in at least two different ways. On one reading, the clergyman is saying that

  i. He has indeed visited eleven of the twelve brothels in the town.

On the other reading, he is saying that

  ii. He has not visited any of the twelve brothels in the town.

Of course, we know that it is highly unlikely that a clergyman would publicly confess to having visited **a** brothel, let alone eleven of them. On the other hand, the reading in (i) is available, and can only be discarded on the basis of what we know about the world, and the person involved. The ambiguity works on the basis of the scope relations created by *haven't* and *one.*

In the case of (i), the scope of *n't* (not) is over *visited.* This yields "not visited", *i.e., I have* [*not* [*visited*]] *one of them*. On this reading, therefore, he is saying (iii).

  iii. "There is one of them that I have not visited".

In the case of (ii), the scope of *n't* (not) is over the NP [*one of them*]. This yields "not one" or "none", *i.e.,* the reading in (iv).

  iv. "I have visited not one of them", or "I have visited none of them".

The propositions in (iv) are equivalent to the preferred unmarked way of expressing the intention in (ii), by means of a sentence involving the NPI *any* as in (v).

  v. "I haven't visited any of them".

The fact that the clergyman chose not to use the unmarked expression as in (v) is what allows the ambiguity.

Scope relations are tricky: using semantic scope properly is difficult to learn, and the rules governing the semantic scope of operators are difficult to articulate consciously, even for linguists. Native users of a language can be made conscious of scope rules through this sort of joke, and as a result, may realize how fraught the communication of intended meaning can be, particularly in the case of scope readings.

There are lots of jokes, many of them for children that exploit the term *nothing*. This has something to do with the way *nothing* takes its scope. I remember, as a child, musing over *Nothing washes better than Omo, so use nothing*. The following joke is an adult version of the same phenomenon.

Example 29

A man was ruminating about his relationship with his wife. He turned to his friend, and said, "There's nothing I wouldn't do for my wife, and there's nothing my wife wouldn't do for me. And that's how we go through life—doing nothing for each other."

There's nothing I wouldn't do for my wife can be interpreted as meaning

   i.   "I would do anything for my wife."

This reading is achieved by understanding the double negative as a positive, *i.e.*, as (ii).

   ii.   "There's nothing I wouldn't do for my wife."

(although this version is not entirely grammatical as phrased here, but fine as phrased in (i)).

The other reading, as in (iii), however, is not a logical one, but is achieved by sleight of hand. Logically, in order to derive

   iii.   *Doing nothing for each other*

he should have said

   iv.   *There's nothing I would do for my wife and there's nothing she would do for me.*

This could be rephrased using the NPI *anything*.

   v.   "There isn't anything I would do for my wife and there isn't anything she would do for me".

However, in the joke, it's the word *nothing* that is salient, and the speaker slides into what appears to be a logical derivation as shown in (iii) which is quite the opposite of what he says in the first part of the utterance, *There's nothing I wouldn't do for my wife, and there's nothing my wife wouldn't do for me.* The speaker is not using logic; he is playing with the content of the phrase, *I'd /she'd do nothing for her/me.* It's possible to show what's wrong in the argumentation, but it's not worth it, since the joke is based on the sleight of hand, and not the detail of the logical exercise.

A major source of logical ambiguity in English is the use of definite and indefinite articles. The indefinite article is the source of confusion in this utterance.

Example 30

Every 15 minutes in New York City a man gets mugged. If I were him, I'd leave.

The ambiguity here is in the use of the indefinite article, the determiner *a*.

There are two logical readings of the first sentence in this utterance. On the one reading, we might conclude that

  i. In New York City, every fifteen minutes, someone or other gets mugged.

On the other reading, we might conclude that

  ii. In New York City, one poor man (let's call him Jim), gets mugged every fifteen minutes of his life.

In the first case, we are quite entitled to claim that New York is a very dangerous city and everyone who frequents it is at risk of being mugged, because muggings are so common that they occur every fifteen minutes. In the second case, we are justified in suggesting that poor Jim leave New York City, because he appears to get mugged every fifteen minutes and his life must be a misery.

The problem is that in ordinary English usage, we use the indefinite article to signal a number of subtle semantic and pragmatic differences. The rules governing the use of *a/an* are extremely complicated and native speakers are not generally conscious of them.

There are two particular rules that are activated in the joke about New York City. One is a rule that states that the indefinite article *a/an* is used generically, as in

  iii. *A man must know his limitations.*

The article in (iii) does not refer to a specific man, but to men in general. On the other hand, the indefinite article can also be used to refer to a particular man, as in (iv).

iv. *As I arrived, a man approached me.*

Although we do not know anything about this man in (iv), we know that the entity being referred to is specific, not general.[26]

The opening line of a famous English novel, demonstrates some of the uses of the indefinite article.

Example 31

It is ***a*** *truth universally acknowledged, that* ***a*** *single man in possession of* ***a*** *good fortune, must be in want of* ***a*** *wife.*

(Austen, 1813)

In this case, ***a*** *single man* and ***a*** *wife* are used extensionally, to mean any single man or any wife. On the other hand, ***a*** *truth universally acknowledged*, refers intensionally to a particular truth, which is about to be spelled out. It is clear that ***a*** *good fortune* is used intensionally here; it refers not to a particular good fortune but to whatever good fortune the single man in question owns.

In a feminist slogan from the late 1960s, the question was posed:

Example 32

If they can put ***a*** *man on the moon, why can't they put them* ***all*** *there?*

In the slogan, the connection is made between "a man" and "all men". The expression *a man*, in this instance is, in itself, ambiguous as to whether it refers intensionally to a particular man (Neil Armstrong, in this case) or extensionally, to any member of the human race, particularly of the male variety. We never find out who *they* are, but that's part of the joke, since certainly they (or at least some of them) are men. The expression *them all* certainly refers to all men. The implication is that if they are so powerful that they can put any **one** man on the moon, they should be able to put **all** the men in the world on the moon. The generalization thus is drawn from "a/one man" to "all men", from singular to plural. On the semantic level, there is an ambiguity between the extensional and intensional use of *a*. However, at the pragmatic level, there are a number of clearly laid out inferences to be drawn. The questioner is creating the implicature that it would be a good idea if all the men (contrasted here with *women*) were to be put on the moon. The logic starts to wear thin, past this point: if *they* are men, then they'd have to put themselves there.

Another joke, which plays very cleverly on the use of the indefinite article *a*, as well as confusion about reference, shows how the use of *a* can cause the hearer to attribute specific rather than general reference.

Example 33

A man and an acquaintance of his are walking down a street one afternoon. The man spots his wife and his mistress talking in a café and amusedly remarks, "Imagine a mistress spending the morning with her lover and then having a friendly chat with his wife that afternoon". The acquaintance, a pale shocked look on his face, responds, "How did you find out?"

(Poulos 2001, p. 51)

The man who says, *Imagine a mistress spending the morning with her lover and then having a friendly chat with his wife that afternoon*, is observing his wife and his mistress having a friendly chat. We know that he had spent the morning with his mistress. The other man observes the same two women, noticing that one is his own wife and the other his mistress. He recalls spending time with his mistress that very morning. However, he does not know that his wife is the first man's mistress, nor does he know that his mistress is the first man's wife. The first man, similarly, does not know that his own wife is the other man's mistress, nor that his mistress is the other man's wife. The first man is rather self-satisfied and amused, until the second man goes pale, and asks, *How did you find out?* Then we are left to imagine that the first man is either not as self-satisfied as when he made his observation or that he realizes that he must now keep his smugness to himself and act injured instead. In any event, the two acquaintances are now in the same boat *a propos* of their wives and mistresses having a friendly chat. It is no longer clear, who, if anyone, besides the joke's audience, is amused. The ambiguity hinges on the use of the determiner *a*, and the way in which it is intended by its user to refer covertly (*i.e.*, intensionally) to a particular woman, and overtly (*i.e.*, extensionally) to *a mistress* more generally. The joke is that the second man hears *a* as referring to his own mistress, although the referent is, in fact different. Essentially, the first man's mistress, referent of *a mistress*, is the second man's wife; and the second man's mistress, referent of *a mistress*, is the first man's wife.

Woody Allen put paid to some of the confusion about the use of indefinite articles with the following remark.

Example 34

The great roe is a mythological beast with the head of a lion and the body of a lion, though not the same lion.

(Allen, 1986)

So much for the indefinite article.

4.2 Quantifiers: Somebody Anybody Nobody Nothing

Formally speaking, a quantifier binds a variable over a domain of discourse. Quantifiers in English can quantify over the domains of person/thing, time and place. Examples of quantifier phrases in English are *for all, for some, anybody, somebody, nobody, nothing, many, few, a lot,* and *no; sometime, never, somewhere, anywhere, nowhere.* [27] Quantifiers can be described in formal logic, using Predicate Calculus, as being universal or existential, *i.e.*, ($\forall$x) "all x" and ($\exists$x) "there exists an x". These are the quantifiers; x is the variable. We say that a quantifier has scope over a specific domain if it binds a variable in that domain. A variable x is free if it is not within the scope of a quantification for that variable. [28]

The use of quantification is very seldom available to consciousness, unless it is being studied by linguists, philosophers or mathematicians. However, jokes that play with quantification reveal the complexity of the phenomenon, and trying to understand why the joke works can lead to an awareness of the difficulty in articulating the rules involved in apparently easy and effortless production. These jokes provide very good examples of the complexity of the phenomenon, and further evidence that the knowledge of such rules must be implicit and not easily available to conscious scrutiny.

I have sampled fairly randomly among the many jokes that play with quantifier scope.

Example 35

When I was a boy I was told that anybody could become president. I'm beginning to believe it.
(reportedly said by Clarence Darrow)

There is a complex play on *anybody* and *could*, here. We might interpret the first part of the utterance as meaning that Darrow thought that the opportunity to become president was available to everybody. The second part of the utterance, however, undercuts this noble statement of the American Dream. Having been taught (and having believed) that anybody and everybody had the opportunity to become president, as a result of seeing who actually has become president, he must conclude that it is not only possible, but that it has, in fact, become the case, that a person who might be described as nobody special, *i.e.*, just "anybody", has achieved this position. *Anybody* in the second part of the utterance refers to someone who is nobody special. In fact, it refers to someone who is of no particular importance, but could be an arbitrary choice of someone who would be interchangeable with any other person. When he says that he now believes that "just anybody" might find be found in this high office, he reveals his disdain for the recent incumbents. Part of the way this complex ambiguity is achieved is because *anybody* functions in conjunction with *could*, in the first part of utterance. *Could* is also subject to an ambiguous reading, in that it may mean "had the opportunity to" but also "was able to". No comment is made on the ways and means that might have been employed to enable someone to become president, but Darrow implies that the provision of opportunity left it open to all and any sorts of people to become president. Clearly, the presidents he has encountered have disappointed him; the implication is that democracy makes it possible for those who are not worthy of the role of president, to achieve it nevertheless. In the joke, being someone is taken to be not only a necessary, but also a sufficient condition of being eligible for the job of president.

In the example below, the comedian, Lily Tomlin plays around with the ambiguity of *somebody*.

Example 36

I always wanted to be somebody, but now I realize I should have been more specific.

(Lily Tomlin, 1939–)

She plays here with the ambiguity of *somebody* in its different meanings of *somebody special* as opposed to *anybody*. Essentially, this joke points out the differences in usage between *somebody* in its intensive and extensive readings. She should have said that she wanted to be somebody specific, rather than anybody. Everybody is somebody; she didn't want to be just anybody.

Somebody does not have quantificational scope in Example 36. However in Example 37, we see a different kind of picture.

Example 37

I always wondered why somebody doesn't do something about that. Then I realized I was somebody.

(Lily Tomlin, 1939–)

In this case, the joke is about the identity between *somebody* and *I*. Here *somebody* is working as a quantifier, but also as a referring term (I). Example 37 provides an interesting contrast with Example 36, also, in that *somebody* in Example 36 is a description of a kind of person, whereas *somebody* in Example 37 is a quantifier in the first sentence and a peculiar referent (identical to I) in the second sentence. Example 37 provides a nice puzzle for semanticists; for the joke-hearer it may simply cause bafflement and amusement because the rules of language are so difficult to think about and yet so simple to use. We should remind ourselves of Pylyshyn's remark that "most of what goes on when we act intelligently is not available to conscious inspection." (Pylyshyn, 1984, p. 19).

Subtle and unexpected ambiguities in English may be caused by different (and unexpected interpretations) of scope, and thus of focus. In the following joke, the play occurs between the two readings of the utterance following the conditional *if*, as shown in Example 38.

Example 38

A couple had just got married. On their way to their honeymoon, the husband said to his new wife, "Would you have married me if my father hadn't left me a fortune?"

She replied, "Darling, I would have married you no matter who had left you a fortune."

According to the reading in (i), the man is asking if his wife would have married him if X had not been the case, where X= (my father left me a fortune).

i.   *if my father had not left me a fortune*
     if not (my father had left me a fortune)
     if not (X)

However, according to the reading in (ii), the man is asking his wife if she would have married him if Q had not left him a fortune, (where Q = my father).

ii. *if my father had not left me a fortune*
     if (not my father) had left me a fortune
     if (~Q) had left me a fortune

The husband intends to ask the question corresponding to the reading in (i) *i.e.*, would the woman have married him if someone had not left him a fortune? This is an appropriate question, although a little late in their relationship. The wife's answer corresponds to reading of the question as in (ii), *i.e.*, she would have married him irrespective of who had left him a fortune. Now, of course, the answer he wants is that she would have married him irrespective of whether he had been left a fortune or not. His worry is clearly that she married him for his money. She does nothing to reassure him by answering that she would have married him as long as he was in possession of a fortune.

Another way we might phrase this a little formally is as follows:

Husband's reasoning: if and only if there exists a fortune, such that X gave husband
the fortune, then wife would marry husband.

Wife's reasoning: if it's not the case that there exists a fortune, then wife would
not marry husband.

The joke illuminates one of a host of ambiguities, which are rather common in our daily use of language. The joke also highlights, for linguists, the difference between pragmatics and semantics. Semantically, the utterance in Example 38 bears at least two different readings, and there is no formal reason to prefer one above the other. Pragmatically, on the other hand, given the context of the previous part of the story, and our stereotypical knowledge of the world, listeners would have the expectation, like the husband, that her answer would be *Yes*. And indeed, her answer is *Yes*, but her answer is relevant in the context that she is marrying him for his money, irrespective of who left it to him. Thus, the husband would be justified in drawing the implicature that her real answer to his intended question is *No*. Logically, there are other possibilities, because she doesn't say she wouldn't have married him if he had not inherited money. Nevertheless, it would seem that pragmatic considerations outweigh semantic analyses, in a situation like the one in the joke.

In non-humorous spoken language use, it would be easy enough to disambiguate the two readings by use of focal stress. The reading in (ii) would be preferred if *my father* were stressed, whereas the reading in (i) requires sentence stress on *left me*. It's also possible to analyze Example 38 so that there is focal stress on *me*, as in (iii) or on *fortune* as in (iv), although there's no reason to do it for the purpose of the joke. I point it out to show, that among others, this part of the utterance might have many different interpretations, depending on sentence stress as well as other formal features.[29]

iii. *if my father had not left* **me** *a fortune*
      contrast with *if my father had left* **my brother** *a fortune*

iv. *if my father had not left me a* **fortune**
      contrast with *if my father had not left me a* **debt**

4.3 Language Use and Logic are Not the Same

Logic and language intersect in an unexpected way in the following joke. The humor is created by a play on implied connectors. Depending on which connector we understand to be implied, we can get very different readings.

Example 39

Wife: "You'll be sorry—I'm going to leave you."
Husband: "Make up your mind—which one is it going to be?"

Uncontroversially, the illocutionary force of the wife's utterance in Example 39 is that of a threat.

i. *I'm going to leave you*
ii. *You'll be sorry*

Preparatory to threatening him, she warns him that he is going to be sorry. The actual threat is *I'm going to leave you*. The implied connector between (ii) and (i) is *because*, i.e., she is saying *You'll be sorry because I'm going to leave you*, or perhaps, *You'll be sorry when I leave you*.

The way the husband interprets it, however, is that the wife is presenting him with an option: either he can be sorry or she can leave him. He goes for an exclusive reading of *or*, either one thing can happen, or the other thing can happen. Telling her to choose, he sets up the binary opposition, so that we understand that, from his point of view, if she leaves him he will not be sorry, and moreover, he will be sorry if she doesn't leave him. Thus, whereas she sees his being sorry as a consequence of her leaving him, he sees her not leaving as the cause of his being sorry, or her leaving as a cause of his not being sorry. He forces this interpretation by saying *Make up your mind—which is it to be?* Thus, whereas the illocutionary force of her utterance is warning, followed by threat, he calls her bluff by interpreting one of her implied propositions as a threat and one as a promise. We are left in no doubt that for him the threat is that she will not leave (and he will be sorry) and the promise is that she will leave (and he will not be sorry).

In this chapter, I have touched on some of the many complex, finely wrought and hard won insights of linguistic semantics. The jokes I have chosen display aspects of semantic knowledge that are easy to use but not to explain. Getting these jokes might give us cause to reflect on how complicated a business it is to make meaning from language.

Notes

1 The history of "presupposition" and implication is probably the rest.
2 The orthography may be crucial here. Once the child has learned to read: *poo(h)* and *Pooh* may be lexicalized differently, in that only the former has the "excrement" interpretation. However, for the purposes of the joke, the words have the same phonetic representation, irrespective of the spelling.
3 See Chapter 2, section 4 for a discussion of the use/mention distinction.
4 For philosophers, this distinction is an important part of semantics. For linguists, who are a little more prickly on the distinction between semantics and pragmatics, it is relevant to both the study of pragmatics and semantics. The phenomena are difficult to separate, since once an utterance is in use, it is by definition, subject to pragmatic principles. See Chapter 2 section 4, as well as Chapter 9 on Cryptic Crosswords.
5 See Chapter 2, section 1.3.2 for a discussion of Ordinary Language Philosophy.
6 See also *The Goon Show*, 1957. Series 8; episode 14.
Major Spon: Did you say work?
Commandant: Ja.
Major Spon: But we're English.
7 Textbook cases of this are, e.g., *blackboard* which in some cases is neither black nor a board; *Blackberry* which is a smartphone, (not black, not a berry, and not an apple); *sweetbreads*, which are neither sweet nor bread, but offal; *dogleg*, which is neither a dog nor a leg and so on.
8 Sources vary on the exact wording of the exchange, and also on whether it took place between Churchill and Braddock, or Churchill and Nancy Astor.
9 *Psych* verbs describe a psychological event or state.
10 Not all languages make this contrast of course. For instance, in some languages, the ear is conceptualised as the location of intelligence (see Evans & Wilkins, 2000). A translation into a language in which this is the case would render this joke completely incoherent.
11 I can't say it in my dialect; I'm not ruling it out for others.
12 Interestingly, although stroke (v), meaning "caress" is a potential reading, it is entirely dispreferred as a result of the set up of the joke. Nevertheless, the implication that he strokes something or somebody is activated.
13 See the discussion in Chapter 4, section 2.2.4 on linguistic inflation.
14 Huddleston and Pullum (chapter 8, §14) analyze *if* as a preposition. "The prototypical conditional adjunct consists of a PP with *if* as head and a content clause as complement" (Huddleston & Pullum, 2002, p.738). It's not crucial in terms of this example to choose one analysis of *if* above the other. The main point is the contrast with *when*.

15 The point has been made in various different formulations that antonymy involves both similarity and difference. Usually antonymy results from a difference in one semantic feature between two words. Humorous play can exploit both the similarity and the difference in interesting ways, as in this tricky example.

16 The play *The Lake* was written by Dorothy Massingham and Murray Macdonald, premiered in 1933, and was regarded as a flop.

17 Of course, it's possible to imagine closing the blinds by hooking a pencil through the handle, but I'm not persuaded that this is the preferred suggestion here.

18 Obviously not all modals have the same range of nominal polysemies.

19 Etymologically 'nerve' could also mean 'sinew, tendon, bowstring'. These are things that literally can snap. In this case, however, the snapping is part of extending the metaphor.

20 The line is delivered in Groucho Marx style in the stereotypical Brooklyn/Bronx accent.

21 The quote is from a *Constant Reader* review in *The New Yorker*, September 15, 1928.

22 *not to be tossed aside lightly* is a negative polarity item. See the discussion on NPIs later in this chapter.

23 According to the results of a project conducted on behalf of the British Association for the Advancement of Science by Dr. Richard Wiseman (2001–2002). This is not considered to be a scholarly study.

24 NPIs have been found in a number of languages. The distribution of NPIs is subject to considerable variation crosslinguistically and this continues to be a live topic for semanticists.

25 Licensing contexts are *inter alia*, the scope of negative particles and negative quantifiers, questions, the antecedent of conditionals, the restrictor of universal quantifiers, also negative conjunctions, comparatives and superlatives, non-affirmative verbs, adversative predicates, *too*-phrases, negative predicates, a subset of subjunctive complements, some disjunctions, imperatives.

26 See the discussion about intension/extension in Chapter 2, section 5 following the joke about the man who stole the rabbi's watch.

27 Note that many of these are NPIs and subject to a host of strange forces.

28 Quantification is a major topic in Formal Semantics and far beyond the scope of this chapter. Readers are directed to detailed and helpful discussions in Cruse, 2004; Kearns, 2000; Portner, 2005; Riemer, 2010; Saeed, 2003.

29 And naturally, this is the case for almost any sentence we can utter, varying the sentence stress.

4

PLAYING WITH MORPHOLOGY AND PHONOLOGY

1.0 Introduction

In this chapter I look at jokes that exploit morphological and phonological aspects of language, tapping tacit knowledge. I start with morphological play and show how such play evokes implicit knowledge of the rules of morphological structure, and then go on to phonological play, in order to show, as well, how this play evokes implicit knowledge of phonological rules. In many jokes, these phenomena involve knowledge of more than one level of representation, and my decision about where to locate some of these jokes is a fairly intuitive one.

2.0 Morphological Play

In this section I consider jokes that are based on morphology, *i.e.*, those structural meaning based units that either stand alone or may be combined with other morphemes to make new words. I focus almost entirely on English morphology in this chapter, although I use the morphology of other languages now and then to show that what may be a morpheme in one language is simply a meaningless phonological string in another.

2.1 The Difference Between a Morpheme and a Syllable

The following remarkable graffito was found sometime in the early 1980s, in London. I saw it on a bumper sticker that read:

Example 1

My karma ran over my dogma.

In analyzing this, we discover that this joke hinges on the componentiality of certain English lexical items, *karma* and *dogma*. In the English word *dogma*, (meaning a religious belief) *ma* is a syllable. It is non-morphemic in the context of this particular word. In the word *karma*, (meaning something like destiny or fate) now a borrowed lexical item in English, but originating in Hindi, *ma*, too, is simply a syllable. The native user of English will quickly discern that there is a trick here: on the most immediate reading, the semantics are anomalous: *karma* cannot run anything over, and *dogma* is not something that is run over. There are thus two ways to proceed: the one is to consider the meaning of this potential metaphor; the other is to notice that there is something strange about two words ending with the syllable *ma* occurring in the same short sentence. This is particularly noticeable since the occurrence of *ma* as a final string in a word is not massively frequent, nor is it all that likely that it should occur twice in near succession in an ordinary everyday utterance.

It would not be unusual for a speaker of English to notice that if the syllable *ma* were removed from each of the items, the sentence would read *My kar ran over my dog*, and thus, would sound like, "My car ran over my dog".

It can easily be seen that the syllable *ma* is simply attached to the end of each of the two nouns in the example, to yield a witty result—meaningful, targeted, sharp and entirely separate in meaning from the likely input sentence, "My car ran over my dog", a simple, predictably familiar English sentence, with no particularly obvious communicative force as a bumper sticker.

The knowledge required both to produce and comprehend this joke is the knowledge that spelling is not uniquely matched with phonology; syllables can attach (*inter alia*) to the ends of words; and, there is no requirement that the phonological unit, syllable, has any morphemic status. Crucially, as well as accessing this knowledge, the listener needs to recognize that the addition of this syllable in two separate places entirely affects the meaning of the input sentence, even though the addition of the syllable is not a morphological process. It is also necessary to know the usual meanings of both *karma* and *dogma*, and realize that there is no morphological way in which *karma* is related to *car*, or *dogma* to *dog*. The humor is activated by the ingenuity of the sloganeer in noting all of the above, as well as the relationship in certain language games between *karma* and *dogma*, although there is not much of a relationship between *car* and *dog*.

We might try a quick set of minimal pair exercises, to test whether *ma* is rule-governed with respect to its potential use as a suffix.

i.   My karma ran over my **dogma**
ii. My karma ran over my **catma**
iii. My **karma** ran over my dogma
iv. My **vanma** ran over my dogma
v.   My karma ran over my dogma
vi. My **vanma** ran over my **catma**

The results of these exercises are clearly ridiculous, and odd, but not particularly funny. There is no skill or wit in the operation, the exercise simply yields bizarre products that don't go anywhere, or mean anything. Finally, it is the great triumph of this slogan that it makes sense at a philosophical level: my fate is more important than, and overrides, what I believe in.

I wouldn't claim that most people seeing or hearing this slogan have a conscious knowledge of all the requisite rules listed above. Yet, getting the joke is reasonably effortless, requiring that the tacit knowledge all fluent speakers of English possess is evoked. It is, in fact, the joke that evokes this knowledge.

As must be obvious, there is no way that a translation could be effected that retains the humor of the original. I have no doubt that an equivalent example could be created in another language, but no translation could replicate this joke. The joke is language-specific in this sense, because of the arbitrary relationship between a signifier and a signified in the sense of Saussure, and all the claims that follow from this (Saussure, 1916/1993).

Another joke exploiting the knowledge that morphemes and syllables are different in kind, is found in Example 2. This kind of joke is rather more productive than Example 1, for the obvious reason that morpheme affixation is by definition productive, whereas syllable or phoneme "affixation" is *ad hoc*.[1]

Example 2

Boy: Do you like Kipling?
Girl: Don't know, you naughty boy, I've never kippled.
(Donald Fraser Gould McGill, 1875–1962)

As you might know, Rudyard Kipling was a British author, who lived in the late 19th and early 20th century. Clearly the questioner is trying to ascertain whether the interlocutor likes the work of the author. *Kipling* is one meaning unit; it is simply the name of a particular person, picked out by the use of that name. The interlocutor reanalyzes the word *kipling* into two morphemes, *kipple* (verb) + *-ing*. The joke turns on this misanalysis. It is probably made additionally funny by the particular sound of *kipple*. Somehow, *Don't know, I've never browned*, in answer to the question, *Do you like Browning?* doesn't work as well.

Similar kinds of jokes may be found exploiting other suffixes in English. The name of the cognitive scientist and linguist, Steven Pinker, was the source of inspiration for this one.

Example 3

Librarian: Do you want to borrow the Pinker?
Student: No, I'd rather get the Pinkest.[2]

This example works on the same principle as Example 2. The word *pinker* is reanalyzed into adjective stem *pink* plus suffix *-er* thus forming a comparative adjective.

2.2 Componentiality

2.2.1 Multimorphemic Forms

English is not replete with separable verbs (and participial forms that function adjectivally) in the way that some Germanic languages are. However it does have a number of multimorphemic forms such as *outwit, outdo,* and *inbreed* that invite play. The composition of these terms is not always obvious, except in the language play of children, where misanalyses are frequently made. For instance, in their chapter on Morphology, Fromkin *et al.* use a *Dennis the Menace* cartoon to illustrate an incorrect, but believable and understandable analysis of *behave.* In this case, Dennis understands *behave* as *be have* (be + adjective) [bi heɪv], and thus says he is being *have* (*contra* he is *behaving*). He analyzes the instructions by analogy with a directive such as *be brave,* and answers by analogy with *I am being brave.*

Example 4

You told me to behave; I am being have.

In real conversation, outside comic strips and textbooks, Dorothy Parker, the mistress of repartee, exploiting a genuine ambiguity in an English morphological construction, produced a very swift comeback, when told she was outspoken.

Example 5

By whom?

(*Dorothy Parker, 1893–1967*)

The humor in this case works in the following way. *Outspoken* (adjective) is generally understood to describe the frank, fearless and direct expression of opinions. Dorothy Parker was well known for such behavior. However, when told she was outspoken, she chose to interpret the term *outspoken* as meaning that she was defeated in a speaking contest, presumably by someone who spoke better, faster or more. Thus, when she asked, *by whom?* she chose to play on the sense, "Who is it that speaks better, faster or more than I do?" The humor of this comeback rests not only in the fact that, given her reputation, it would have been hard to defeat Dorothy Parker in such a contest, but also in the dispreferred reading of *outspoken* that she seized upon. She exploited the reading of *out* as found in *outclassed* or *outwitted,* counterposing it with the reading to be found in *outgoing* or *outstanding.* In two words, as well as demonstrating some warranted self-awareness, she produces a pithy comment on an ambiguous English morphological structure. We learn, simultaneously, something about the structure of English, and something about how hard it might be to outspeak Dorothy Parker.

The television program, *The Simpsons,* is a source of much humor involving morphological misanalysis. The linguist, Heidi Harley, has an entire section of her website devoted to Simpson language jokes, and I have helped myself to a few, for the purposes of this discussion.[3] Clearly, the writers of *The Simpsons* are very aware of the ambiguities of English structure and use, and they introduce a number of jokes that play on these sorts of ambiguities into the flow of the comedy.

Example 6

Otto says: *They call them fingers but I never see them fing.*

(The Simpsons, *episode 1316)*

This is a backformation or clipping, by analogy with *singers*, who *sing.* The morphological relationship between *singer* and *sing*, is real, however, and is not a backformation. Backformations are a result of the process through which a new word is formed by removing a morpheme, or something that looks like a morpheme, from a legal word. In cases in which what is removed is not a real morpheme, nonetheless, very often new words are formed and used. For instance, the verb *edit* results from a backformation of *editor*, and the verb *peddle* is a backformation from *pedlar*. These new words are formed by removing, respectively, *-or*, and *-ar*, from *editor* and *pedlar*, although neither is a suffix.

The suffix *-er* is very productive in English (functioning morphologically as an agentive, as well as a comparative). When added to a verb, *-er* generally yields a form that means someone or something that verbs. However, despite the fact that *bringer, stinger, ringer, winger,* and *springer* in English each derives from a verb, and notwithstanding the existence of *finger,* there is no verb *fing* in English. And indeed, one feels, there really should be such a word. We should note, however, that the pronunciation of the /g/ in *finger* does actually give us a clue that /ɪŋɡə/ is not the same kind of sound pattern as in found in *ringer, stinger* etc., /ɪŋə/, but for the purposes of the joke, the observation is a sharp one. If a singer sings, why shouldn't a finger fing? Or more accurately, why shouldn't a finger [fɪŋɡ]?

In another episode, Homer Simpson says he is a rageaholic.

Example 7

I'm a rageaholic! I am addicted to rageahol!

(The Simpsons, *episode 287)*

This new word formation is based on a mistaken use of productive derivational morphology. The source of the mistake is the term *alcoholic,* which is used to describe someone who is addicted to alcohol, or more specifically someone who suffers from a condition induced by alcohol. This requires the suffix *-ic* to be attached to the noun *alcohol.* Similar types of suffixes are used to describe people who suffer from medical conditions, *e.g.,* from the condition of *rheumatism* → *rheumat* + *-ic; diabetes* → *diabet* + *-ic; dyslexia* → *dyslex* + *-ic.*

The term *workaholic* is now used to refer to someone who is addicted to work, and can't stop themselves from working all the time. This requires the new pseudo-suffix *-aholic* (meaning, presumably, "addicted to") to be added to *work*. The process has been extended to describing people who are addicted to chocolate. They call themselves *chocoholics*, formed by adding *-holic* to *choco*. This is a strange and mistaken use of *–holic*, which although not a morphological suffix in *alcoholic* is reanalyzed as meaning something like "a person who is addicted to stem X". In the *rageaholic* case, Homer misanalyzes *alcoholic* in such a way that he first assumes that *-aholic* is the suffix morpheme for "addict, or sufferer from". We may also assume that for Homer, *-aholic* and *-oholic* are allo-pseudomorphemes.

Thus Homer claims to be a *rageaholic*. He then engages in a little backformation, or clipping, and says he is addicted to *rageahol*, by analogy with alcoholics being addicted to alcohol. *Rageahol* is yet another novel creation, clipped from his previously illegally formed creation, *rageaholic*. This is all so swift, and seems in its Simpsonesque way to make so much sense, that it is not immediately obvious that two misanalyses have been done here, in order for Homer to say that he is both a *rageaholic* and addicted to *rageahol*.

More generally, this phenomenon may be considered as part of new word formation, in English. This is a particular example of the process of blending. The classic case is that of *smog*, which is a blend of *smoke* and *fog*. However, the phenomenon shown in the *-aholic* case is an example of a productive process that has spawned an expanding set of new "morphemes", for instance *infotainment*; *edutainment* (based on *entertainment*) *funorama*, *cardorama* (based on *panorama*), all sound sequences that appear have gained a morphemic status on the basis of (illegitimate) generalization.[4]

2.2.2 Morphological Generalization

When people become conscious of the word formation rules of their language, it is very tempting to overgeneralize these rules. This is something that children do when they are learning their first language, without any consciousness that what they are doing happens to be blocked by the actual lexical items of their language. Thus, children may say *speaked* as the past tense of *speak*, by analogy with *walk* and its past tense *walked*. There are a number of clever jokes that exploit the principle of overgeneralization. For instance,

Example 8

Q: If a vegetarian is someone who eats only vegetables, what does a humanitarian eat?

Example 9

Q: Do adults get as much fun out of adultery as infants do out of infancy?

The principle here is very simple. The word formation rule by which *vegetarian* is formed from *vegetable* is to add *-arian* to the stem *veget-*. *-arian* is a common suffix in English, found in words like *sectarian, agrarian, octogenarian, egalitarian*. Its meaning is not completely fixed, but clear enough. As we can see, a *sectarian* is someone who is a member of a sect, an *egalitarian* is someone who believes in equality, an *agrarian* is someone who works the land, an *octogenarian* is a person in their eighties. So the suffix *-arian* seems to mean something like "person who is somehow involved with the noun".

Example 8 works simply on matching the equivalence in the sound pattern— *etarian* (from *vegetarian*, rather than *-arian*, which it should be, morphologically). The logic of the joke is inexorable, too. Follow the pattern: if someone who eats only vegetables is a vegetarian, then a humanitarian is someone who eats only humans. Of course, this is nonsense, since a humanitarian is one who is committed to working for the good of all humans, and would thus be unlikely in most cases to eat them. The trick is in the syllable, *-et/it*, [ət] or [It] in any event. The originator of the joke asks us to analyze the syllable *-et* in *vegetarian* and *-it* in *humanitarian* as the first part of a new, invented suffix, *-etarian*. Anything that comes before the suffix *-etarian/-itarian*, according to the logic of the joke, is the thing that is eaten. Of course, the sources for the *-et* and *-it* are different formal units; *-it* is part of a suffix in *human-ity*, whereas *-et* is part of the stem *veget-*.

It doesn't pay to get too involved in the real world implications of the linguistic play: some humanitarians are vegetarian; many vegetarians consider themselves to be humanitarian in that they are concerned with the wellbeing of all living beings, not only humans.

A similar principle is at work in the joke about adults and adultery. The parallelism is set up between infants and adults. The abstract noun formed from *infant* is *infancy*. When we hunt around for an abstract noun formed from *adult*, we get *adulthood*. However, there is another candidate that suggests itself: *adultery*, a perfectly good English word, which appears to have the stem *adult*. The fact is that the word *adult* and the word *adultery* come from different Latin roots: in the case of *adult*, as a participle of the verb *adolescere*, meaning "to grow up", and in the case of *adultery* from the Latin *adulterare* meaning "to corrupt, spoil or foul", (*cf., adulterate*). So *adultery* is seen as corrupting, or spoiling, the marriage vows. This is the linguistic source of the joke. Of course, infancy is a time of innocence (apparently, unless we think Freud wasn't joking) and adultery, a sexual relationship outside of marriage, engaged in by adults, is far away indeed from innocence, corruption being regarded as the opposite condition. The joke might be suggesting that sometimes more fun is to be had in being an adult, doing what adults do. However, it is probably the coincidental linguistic parallel between *infant/adult* and *infancy/adultery* that is most amusing, when it is brought to our attention that language has rules and that either following them or ignoring them can yield quirky results.

2.2.3 Cranberry Morphemes

English has a number of examples of apparent antonyms, exhibiting what look like common English prefixes bound to stems, that do not, however, have corresponding present day forms that consist simply of the unbound stems. Normally, we expect a certain class of antonyms to be formed by adding a prefix, such as *dis-* or *un-*, to a freestanding stem. Thus, in a typical example of this process, we are able to see that the antonymic form *dislike* is derived from *like*, and *unhappy* is derived from *happy*.

Affixes have regular selectional properties, and in general, speakers know these tacitly. Thus, in English, for example, speakers know that *un-* attaches to adjectives and participle bases to form antonyms ("not", or "the opposite of"), and to a small class of verbs to form verbs meaning "to reverse the action", or "to release from" or "deprive of". These selectional restrictions on prefix attachments distinguish between allomorphic prefixes, usually on the basis of phonological restrictions, or due to historical accident. There are cases when tacit knowledge of rules fails in production, so speakers may stumble occasionally with *dis-* and *mis-*. For accidental reasons, in certain cases the process of prefixation cannot be legitimately reversed to derive a free-standing base form.[5]

However, an example of an atypical and strange phenomenon may be found in the word *disgruntled*, which should, logically, have as its stem **gruntled*. This is an application of a similar process found in the relationship between *dislike* and *like*. When these apparent prefixes are removed from certain lexical items that are apparent antonyms, the resultant forms are generally illegitimate, or are simply lexical gaps in the existing lexicon of the language. These are versions of cranberry-morphemes, and some are actually creeping into legitimate, unhumorous usage. Cranberry-morphemes are the source of some debate among linguists, who, frankly, don't know what to do with these messy cases. Often, we resort simply to saying that historically there must have been two morphemes in words of this sort, but these days, one of the erstwhile morphemes has become inert, or unproductive. Some of the words in the examples that follow are cranberry morphemes, and the others may be described simply as unpaired words, *i.e.*, they do not have a matched root antonym.

Playing with unpaired words by removing the prefixes and using the bare roots can be amusing, because as users of English, we know the word in its prefixed form, and because we know the particular morphological rule of antonym formation, we know how to reverse the process, to yield the root. However, we also know that these examples of potential root morphemes are not in current usage as free morphemes. Users of English play with these supposedly freestanding forms to various extents depending on how amusing they find them. The most complete set of unpaired words and cranberry morphemes I have found is this piece, entitled, *How I met my wife*, written by Jack Winter (*The New Yorker*, July 25,

1994) that has been described as a *pareil* tale of *bridled* passion. I have indicated all the relevant cases in bold, as well as inserting ø in the cases where an idiom only exists in the negative and sounds peculiar in the positive.

Example 10

*It had been a rough day, so when I walked into the party I was very **chalant**, despite my efforts to appear **gruntled** and **consolate**.*

*I was **furling** my **wieldy** umbrella for the coat check when I saw her standing alone in a corner. She was a **descript** person, a woman in a state of total **array**. Her hair was **kempt**, her clothing **shevelled**, and she moved in a **gainly** way. I wanted desperately to meet her, but I knew I'd have to make ø bones about it since I was travelling **cognito**.*

***Beknownst** to me, the hostess, whom I could see **both hide and hair of**, was very proper, so it would be ø skin off my nose if anything bad happened. And even though I had only **swerving** loyalty to her, my manners couldn't be **peccable**.*

*Only **toward** and **heard-of** behaviour would do. Fortunately, the embarrassment that my **maculate** appearance might cause was **evitable**. There were ø two ways about it, but the chances that someone as **flappable** as I would be **ept** enough to become **persona grata** or a **sung** hero were slim.*

*I was, after all, **something** to sneeze at, someone you could ø easily hold a candle to, someone who usually aroused **bridled** passion. So I decided not to risk it.*

*But then, all at once, for **some** apparent reason, she looked in my direction and smiled in a way that I could ø make heads and tails of. I was **plussed**. It was **concerting** to see that she was **communicado**, and it **nerved** me that she was interested in a **pareil** like me, sight **seen**.*

*Normally, I had a **domitable** spirit, but, being **corrigible**, I felt **capacitated** as if this were something I was ø great shakes at, and forgot that I had succeeded in situations like this only a **told** number of times.*

*So, after a **terminable** delay, I acted with **mitigated** gall and made my way through the **ruly** crowd with strong **givings**. Nevertheless, since this was all **new hat** to me and I had no time to prepare a **promptu** speech, I was **petuous**.*

*Wanting to make only **called-for** remarks, I started talking about the hors d'oeuvres, trying to **abuse** her of the notion that I was **sipid**, and perhaps even **bunk** a few myths about myself. She responded well, and I was **mayed** that she considered me a **savoury** character who was up to **some** good. She told me who she was. "What a perfect **nomer**," I said **advertently**.*

*The conversation became more and more **choate**, and we spoke at length to **much avail**. But I was **defatigable**, so I had to leave at a **godly** hour. I asked if she wanted to come with me. To my delight, she was **committal**.*

We left the party together and have been together ever since. I have given her my love, and she has requited it.

Jack Winter (The New Yorker, July 25, 1994)

Each of the words shown in the table is a cranberry-morpheme or an illegitimately paired word stemming from the original. In the case of phrases, these are idioms that in common use occur in the negative polarity only.

This piece of prose deftly and wittily demonstrates that English speakers know there are rules for the formation of antonyms from freestanding roots, in English. At the same time, it exploits the fact that there are obviously lexical gaps and places where we would expect a rule to be applied, and are surprised to find that it isn't.

TABLE 4.1 Cranberry morphemes, lexical gaps, non-paired antonyms

Column 1	Column 2	Column 1	Column 2
chalant	nonchalant	bridled passion	unbridled passion
gruntled	disgruntled	some apparent reason	no apparent reason
consolate	disconsolate	plussed	nonplussed
furling	unfurling	concerting	disconcerting
wieldy	unwieldy	communicado	incommunicado
descript	nondescript	nerved	unnerved
array	disarray	pareil	non pareil
kempt	unkempt	sight seen	sight unseen
shevelled	dishevelled	domitable	indomitable
gainly	ungainly	corrigible	incorrigible
make bones	make no bones	capacitated	incapacitated
cognito	incognito	great shakes at	no great shakes at
beknownst	unbeknownst	a told number	an untold number
skin off my nose	no skin off my nose	terminable	interminable
swerving	unswerving	mitigated gall	unmitigated gall
peccable	impeccable	ruly	unruly
toward	untoward	givings	misgivings
heard-of	unheard-of	all new hat	all old hat
maculate	immaculate	promptu	impromptu
evitable	inevitable	petuous	impetuous
two ways about it	no two ways about it	easily hold a candle	not easily hold a handle
flappable	unflappable	make heads or tails of	not make heads or tails of
ept	inept	both hide and hair of	neither hide nor hair of
abuse	disabuse	up to some good	up to no good
sipid	insipid	choate	inchoate
called-for remarks	uncalled-for remarks	commital	noncommital
nomer	misnomer	a godly hour	an ungodly hour
advertently	inadvertently	defatigable	indefatigable
bunk	debunk	to much avail	to no avail
persona grata	persona non grata	something to sneeze at	nothing to sneeze at
a sung hero	an unsung hero		

Additionally, we might note that many of the idioms are lexicalized phrases—and are not necessarily subject to regular rules—similar to the failure of morphosyntactic rules to apply to at least some idioms. Thus, when we try to passivize some idioms the results are not successful in retaining their idiomatic status. For instance, *he kicked the bucket* v. *the bucket was kicked* and *she let the cat out of the bag* v. *the cat was let out of the bag*. We see a similar phenomenon of un-idiomatization if we try to interfere with the internal structure of *e.g., no two ways about it, an unsung hero* or *an ungodly hour*. These phrases are lexicalized and then sealed off from further morphological processes.

People are quick to create an antonym from an existing word, if they have to, and they follow rules for doing so. The rules for prefixation are easy to apply, even though the reasons for choosing a particular prefix are not terribly easy to articulate. Similarly, when people want to create an antonym from an existing prefixed multisyllabic word, it is simple to remove the prefix. However, in some cases the prefix is not a prefix at all, simply a sound sequence that is homophonous with a prefix, such as the *un* in *understand*. In other cases, such as many listed above, the unprefixed form simply does not exist as a separate word in English, or may mean something entirely unrelated to the prefixed form. Thus, *awry* is not the antonymic form of *wry* (as it would be by analogy with *atheistic/theistic*).

In most of the cases listed above, the words or phrases in column 1 simply do not exist, and there is no obvious technical account for why that should be so. Why should this be an example of humor? In these cases, considering a word that appears to be antonymic with a potential pair-mate, our expectations may be defeated. Reflecting on the oddness of the forms in Column 2, we are likely to realize that some rule is being followed to create a bizarre effect. Once conscious of the play, we are likely to be tickled. In reading Winter's piece, we may be surprised at how many examples there are in which the rule has failed us, and also to marvel at the keenness of the author's observations and at his ingenuity in assembling them as he has.

2.2.4 Morphological Reanalysis

Victor Borge (1909–2000), the late lamented Danish humorist and pianist (also known as the Clown Prince of Denmark) invented what is now known as inflationary language. Here he explains it in his own words.

Example 11

Many years ago in Denmark we had inflation, and you are familiar with that problem. In inflation, we have numbers rising. Prices go up. Anything that has to do with money goes up... except the language. See, we have hidden numbers in the words like "wonderful", "before", "create", "tenderly". All these numbers can be inflated and meet the economy, you know, by rising to the occasion. I suggest we add one to each of these numbers to be prepared.

For example "wonderful" would be "two-derful". Before would be be-five. Create, cre-nine. Tenderly should be eleven-derly. A Lieutenant would be a Lieut-eleven-ant. A sentence like, "I ate a tenderloin with my fork" would be "I nine an elevenderloin with my five-k". And so on and so fifth.[...] I have a story here that I would like to read to you so that you can get an idea of Inflationary Language.

Twice upon a time, there lived in Sunny Califivenia a young man named Bob. He was a third leiutelevenant in the US Air Fiveces. Bob had been fond of Anna, his one-and-a-half sister, ever since she saw the light of day for the second time. And all three of them were proud of the fact that two of his fivefathers had been among the crenineders of the US Constithreetion.

They were dining on the terrace. "Anna," he said as he took a bite of a marininded herring, "You look twoderful threenight. You never looked that lovely befive." Anna looked twoderful, despite the illness from which she had not yet recupernineded. "Yes," repeated Bob, "You look twoderful threenight...but you have three of the saddest eyes I have ever seen."

The table was tastefully decorninded with Anna's favorite flowers: Threelips. They were now talking about Ann's asiten husband, from whom she was sepeninded. While on the radio, an Irish elevenor sang "Tea Five Three." It was midnight; a clock in the distance struck thirteen. And suddenly, there in the moonlight stood her husband Don Two, obviously intoxicnineded.

"Anna," he said, "Fivegive me. I am only young twice and you are my two and only." Bob jumped to his feet, "Get out of here, you three-faced triplecrosser!" But Anna warned, "Watch out, Bob. He is an officer." "Yes, he is two. But I am two three!"

Anytwo five elevennis?

"All right," said Don Two as he wiped his fivehead. He then left and when he was one-and-a-halfway through the revolving door, he muttered, "I'll go back to Elevennessee and be double again. Farewell, Anna. Three-de-loo, three-de-loo."

(Victor Borge, 1909–2000)

The principle of inflationary language, as Borge explains it, is simple: to every number, add one. This exploits the phonological fact that words or parts of words may sound the same as others, even though they have different meanings. The homophone is of course, the source of many jokes in English (see, for instance, section 2.2.6 in this chapter, and Chapter 3, section 2.2). However, Borge does several different tricks with the homophone. Firstly, he applies the principle across the board, so that every word or part of a word that sounds like an English number is inflated by one. Secondly, he works only with the phonological sequence, specifically targeting syllables that are homophonous with numbers. Thus, *anyone for tennis* turns into *anytwo five elevennis*. For larger chunks of language, such as the phrase, sentence or paragraph, this systematic rule application yields what sounds like a code. In fact, this is precisely what it is, for he has treated language entirely formally, and has substituted accordingly as do those who encrypt codes. In order to crack the code, we need to know the counting system of English; the sound system of English; and how to reconstitute the code into the original sound patterns and reassign the appropriate morphology to the set of reconstituted syllables. We also need to know the trick—inflate everything that sounds like a number by one. Borge performs this piece as a spoken presentation. He recites it quickly, which is masterful, and we have to listen and perform the decoding quickly, otherwise it passes us by, as gibberish. This system is productive and the game can be played and understood by any child who has knowledge of English, each time yielding fresh and comic results.

A particular type of morphological reanalysis is the phenomenon now known as the eggcorn. The term "eggcorn" was coined by the linguist Geoffrey Pullum, to describe words that are mis-heard or mis-parsed and given a new and different life. The interesting feature of these new coinages is that although different from the original, the new word or phrase is plausible in the same context. The term "eggcorn" itself is the first example of these to be described as such. The original case was discussed by Mark Liberman, on *Language Log* in 2003.[6] Apparently, a woman wrote in to say that she had always used the word *eggcorn* to refer to an acorn. This is clearly the way she heard the word. In certain dialects of English *eggcorn* and *acorn* are not dissimilar in pronunciation. Since acorns are egg-shaped and seed-like, her misanalysis was based on the human desire for sense-making and the application of logical processes to understand the compound she heard, and used. There is now a database of eggcorns, some of them wonderfully accurate and funny, all testament to the human ability for morphological reanalysis and the belief that language use makes sense. Some examples from the database: *all goes well* as an eggcorn for *augurs well*; *girdle one's loins* for *gird one's loins*; *French benefits* for *fringe benefits*.[7] The eggcorn phenomenon finds its musical sister in the mondegreen, discussed in section 2.2.6 below.

2.2.5 Morphological Reanalysis between Languages

The fact that a sequence of sounds may constitute a morpheme in one language and simply a sound sequence (sometimes one or more syllables) in another is a rich source of linguistic humor for people who know at least two languages.[8] Often the humor arises only as a secondary consequence of a new analysis or re-analysis of the word or phrase coined. The following example demonstrates how a sound sequence from one language may be reanalyzed as a morpheme in another language.

In East Africa, specifically in Tanzania and Kenya, former British colonies, a traffic circle or roundabout is known as a *keepy lefty*. This is derived from the rule of the road in these countries, which is that once in a traffic circle, the driver should keep the car to the left edge of the circular road. So, *keepy lefty* is an English term, meaning something like "the thing which you keep left of". However, this term appears to have been reanalyzed as Swahili, and hence obeys Swahili morphological rules. The plural form *of keepy lefty* (traffic circle) is now regularly produced as *vipilefti*. The process of reanalysis is as follows.

In Swahili, a Bantu language, which is the lingua franca of much of East Africa, nouns are prefixed by a classifier morpheme, which varies according to the class membership of the noun. Additionally, each class has a morpheme prefix for singular and another for plural. For example, noun classes 7 and 8 (7 is the singular, 8 is the plural) include terms for everyday objects, animals, body parts, persons, diminutives, and languages. The prefix for nominals in class 7 is *ki-* and the prefix for their plurals, in class 8, is *vi-*. Thus, the Swahili word for "book" is *kitabu* (one book) and for "books" is *vitabu* (more than one book).

In the *keepy lefty* example, the term seems to have been perceived by its users to be a Swahili word, pronounced *kipilefti*. Since the first syllable is in all respects analyzable as a class 7 noun prefix, and since the item in question is an everyday object, it is reasonable for a Swahili speaker to assume (along analogous lines with *kitaba—vitaba*) that the plural of *kipilefti* is *vipilefti*. This is indeed what has happened. And it is, naturally, a source of some amusement to linguists, and anyone who knows both English and Swahili.

In fact, the reanalysis of a non-morphemic sound sequence in one language as a morpheme in another is a process that is quite common in English as well. The most well known example is that of *hamburger*. The term *hamburger* comes from the name of the German town, Hamburg. A *Hamburg + -er*, in English then, would be someone who comes from the town of Hamburg (*pace, London— Londoner*). From round about the end of the 18th century, many immigrants to the USA from Germany and Austria brought with them knowledge of food (usually sausage meat of various kinds), which began to be made and eaten more generally. Thus, people from Frankfurt (known as *Frankfurt + -ers*) made a type of sausage, which became known as a *frankfurter*, and the sausage made or eaten by people who came from Wien (Vienna) became known as *wieners*.

Thus a certain kind of meat mixture became known as *hamburger*. However, since the hamburger as it is currently known, contains meat, the term seems, at least for advertising and marketing purposes, to have been reanalyzed by English ears as *ham+burger*, such that ham refers to the meat filling, irrespective of whether this is ham or not. Generally speaking, it is beef, as it happens. We have evidence for the sound sequence *ham-* in *hamburger* being assigned morphological status from the new terms that have been coined for different sorts of hamburger-like things, i.e., **beef**-*burger*, **veggie**-*burger*, **chicken**-*burger*, **turkey**-*burger* and so on.

Sometimes, however, *burger* is used as a clipping for *hamburger*. At the same places we can now buy *veggie-burgers*, we can also buy *cheese-burgers*. A *cheese-burger* is a hamburger (meat, bun etc.), with the addition of cheese. A *bacon-burger* is a hamburger with the addition of bacon. These forms, then, pick out different kinds of items than do the *veggie-burger, turkey-burger, chicken-burger* forms. A *veggie-burger* is a bun, in which a vegetable filling has been substituted for the meat part; a *chicken-burger* is one in which chicken is substituted for the regular beef, and so on. In contrast a *cheese-burger* is a regular hamburger, plus cheese. An *Aussie-burger* is a hamburger with all the trimmings, plus a slice of canned beetroot, but without an Australian either as the filling or the trimmings.[9] In this last usage, then, *-burger* is a hamburger (bun, meat, etc.) with the addition of other ingredients.

Additionally, *burger* itself now has a new morphological status in parts of the English-speaking world, meaning something like "the bun part of a filled bun sandwich", as we can see in these terms as well as terms such as *burger bar*, a place where one can buy burgers.[10]

2.2.6 Morphology and Homophony

When it comes to morphological reanalysis, the use of puns (more technically, we should probably call them plays on homophones) to create new and humorous meanings is at its most fruitful. There are all sorts of jokes that involve punning on some sound sequence, morpheme or word part. The sound of English words lends itself well to morphological reanalysis, allowing the play of puns to be made on any sound sequence. This apocryphal reminder from the electricity company is a simple but effective example.

Example 12

The Electric Company: We would be delighted if you send in your bill. However, if you don't, you will be.

The play is on the sound sequence *delighted*. The standard meaning of this participial adjective is something like "very pleased". The Electric Company has sent out a reminder to customers to pay their bill, saying that they would be very pleased to receive the payment. The speech act is dressed up as a friendly reminder to pay the bill. However, the threat follows: if customers don't pay the bill, their electricity supply will be cut off. The wittiness is to be found in the play on *delighted*, which in the reading shown above, has only one root morpheme: *delight* and a participial suffix *-ed*. Note, however, that in the second part of the utterance, the Electric Company's notice reads, *if you don't, you will be*. The joke is not heavy-handed: the notice leaves it to the reader to do the work. For the purposes of exposition, I'll spell out the ellipses: If you don't (pay your bill), you will be (delighted). This is clearly paradoxical. Why should the Electric Company be delighted if customers pay their bill, but, at the same time, tell customers that they are in for a pleasant surprise if they don't pay their bills? If we look further, to make some sense of this utterance, we see that under a certain reading, *delighted* might be analyzed as *de-* + *lighted*. Strictly speaking, *de-lighted* is not acceptable in English, with the reading "remove the light", by analogy with *defrocked*, and *defrosted*. This is because *defrock* and *defrost* each consist of two morphemes, *de-*

and verb root. *De-frost* means to remove the frost, *de-frock* means to remove the frock (metaphorical use for stripping a priest of the priesthood). On the other hand, although it should be possible in English to use this rule productively with other nouns, (and in fact, a recent American use, *deplane,* has started to be more widespread) *de-lighted* is possible only in a joke.[11] *De-lighted* in this context means, "your light will be removed", *i.e.*, your electricity supply will be cut off, if you do not pay your bill. Note that the notice itself doesn't actually say that customers will be *delighted*, but leaves us with no option but to come to that conclusion, and then to work out what the intention behind this strange elliptical utterance could have been.

Clever punning is a technique that simultaneously cuts across several levels of the grammar. In this example from Groucho Marx, the joke requires recognition of a well known dialect of casual fast New York speech of the 1930s. The example serves well to illustrate reanalysis of a sound sequence into a new morphological structure.

Example 13

Love goes out the door when money comes innuendo.
(Groucho Marx, from the movie, Duck Soup, 1934)

There is a parallelism set up here between *out the door* and *in the window*. The pun is based on the phrase *in the window*. Love is contrasted with money: love goes out the door when money comes in the window. However, he doesn't clearly articulate the phrase, *in the window,* he says [ɪnʊˈɛndəʊ]. An innuendo is an indirect remark or insinuation that can carry the suggestion of some impropriety, precisely what this statement actually is. Much of Groucho's humor actually works by innuendo. In this case, he is reanalyzing the sound of *in the window* so that it is equivalent to *innuendo,* which in his New York fast speech rules it probably resembles. Thus he has taken the sound sequence of the prepositional phrase and reanalyzed it as one word, *innuendo.* This statement is indeed an innuendo—when money is involved, love vanishes.[12]

Groucho has used the prepositional phrase *in the window* as one phonological word, *innuendo,* although the phrase actually contains three grammatical words. Here we may discern a good example of the distinction between the phonological word and the grammatical word. These can be formally characterized in terms of prosodic domains, *e.g.*, for stress assignment.[13]

Masses of jokes are based on the principle of punning on one sound sequence and then assigning it new morphological and syntactic analyses. As a rule, such jokes require a certain narrative structure to be constructed in order to set the pun in a context that will make the whole reanalysis yield a humorous and clever outcome. A fairly clear example may be found in the following, not very sensitive or politically correct, joke. Note also that this joke has among its properties the frequently found homophony between modals and some open class words, discussed in Chapter 3.

Example 14

A young woman who is disabled with a hunchback has had enormous difficulty finding suitors. She finally joins a singles' club that caters to other people with physical disabilities and is invited to a dance. A young man, who wears a strange but useful contraption, a wooden eye, to assist him to see, shyly asks her if she would like to dance.

"Would I? Would I?" she responds eagerly.

"Hunchback, hunchback," he snarls.

The joke exploits a number of strategies. Centrally, it concerns the word *would*, which is played upon by the homophone, *wood*. *I* is played upon by its homophone, *eye*. *Would I* thus is reanalyzed by the young man as *wood eye*. *Would* is a modal auxiliary and *I* is a pronominal. The original utterance is structurally a polar question and the illocutionary force it is intended to convey is probably relief and gratitude. The joke turns on the reassignment of morphological and syntactic categories, but also on a misunderstanding of the illocutionary force, as a result. The young man interprets *wood* in this instance as an adjective, or possibly, the first part of a noun compound; he also hears the nominal *eye*. The unfortunate young man hears *Wood eye* and this conditions his understanding of the speech act. He believes he is being insulted, and his disability is being used to shame and reject him. He hits back by reciprocal name-calling: if she calls him *wood eye*, he will call her *hunchback*. There is of course, a degree of implausibility in the joke, but no more so than in most jokes of this nature, such as those in which strings can talk and say, *I'm not a string, I'm a frayed knot.*

Spike Milligan, the comic genius who didn't have to construct a narrative to make linguistic jokes, simply used dialogue that evoked enough context to make the jokes funny.

Example 15

Bloodnok: Admit it, you're a German spy.

Krupp: I'm not a spy, I'm a shepherd.

Bloodnok: Aha! A shepherd-spy!

(The Case of the Mukkinese Battle Horn, *1956*)

Milligan's humor very often works through association, sometimes of sound, sometimes of sense, but regularly through ambiguity. He had a very fine sense of the speech act (see Chapter 2 for an extensive discussion of Speech Acts). In this joke, which turns on a sound reanalysis, he maintains the illocutionary force of Bloodnok's original speech act, which is accusation. Here he yokes together shepherds and spies, which have nothing in common other than that they are occupations, and then deftly turns the sound structure of both into a third term, which describes a type of pie, well-known as a culinary delight. *Shepherd* and *spy* are thus reanalyzed as *shepherd's pie*. An entirely new free morpheme, *pie*, is created as a result. The punchline enables the expression of the concepts *shepherd+spy* as well as *shepherd's pie*. The joke is particularly clever and unusual in that one might expect the punchline to be a pun on *shepherd* or on *spy*, but in fact it is in the creation of the new term, aided by the clever addition of the possessive *'s* to *shepherd*, that the joke rests.

Ogden Nash has a series of silly jokes in English about eggs, that reveal similar processes. In the book, the narrator and the character Billy are discussing different types of food (all as it turns out, different types and forms of eggs—zeggs, seggs, and yeggs, for instance.

Example 16

"Turkey yeggs?" I said.
"Duck seggs?" I said.
"I'm fonder of zeggs, hen zeggs," I said.
*"Some **girl** told you," said Billy.*

(Girls are Silly, *1962, Ogden Nash*)

Thus, *yeggs* (turkey eggs), *seggs* (ducks' eggs), *zeggs* (hen's eggs) are all new linguistic creations, referring to different kinds of eggs. This is quite productive. Other forms suggest themselves—*cheggs* (ostrich eggs), *leggs* (crocodile eggs), *neggs* (ham 'n eggs), *sheggs* (fish eggs), *keggs* (duck eggs), *deggs* (boiled eggs), *teggs* (poached eggs) and so on. The principle is simple: The last sound of the previous word adjacent to *eggs* is reanalyzed as the first sound of the new item. This is good for a long car journey with children, but pales if the journey stretches into adulthood.

The fact, of course, is that as native speakers of a language we fluently, and usually correctly, analyze strings of sounds into meaningful units all the time. Occasionally we misanalyze: this causes either misunderstanding, or a joke. Such misanalysis is so frequent in processing the words of poems and songs that a special term was coined to describe this mis-parsing. The term "mondegreen" (Wright, 1954) was invented (perhaps discovered) by Sylvia Wright, who explains how, as a child she had believed the last two lines of a poem her mother regularly recited to her, were

They hae slain the Earl O' Moray,
And Lady Mondegreen.

Wright (1954) points out that the original line is "*And laid him on the green.*" In naming these sorts of misinterpretations, she notes, "The point about what I shall hereafter call mondegreens, since no one else has thought up a word for them, is that they are better than the original."

It also happens now and then that we hear a snatch of one language and analyze it into another (usually our own). Spike Milligan is responsible for this remarkable reanalysis that occurs in the flow of dialogue through one of the Goon Shows.

Example 17

Toulouse: *I'm Toulouse-Lautrec.*
Gauguin: *Oh? And where are you going to lose him?*
(The Goon Show, *Tales of Montmartre, 1956*)

As is commonly known, Henri Toulouse-Lautrec was a French post-Impressionist painter. Milligan doesn't really need to set up much narrative although this snatch is embedded into a grandiose tale of adventure and skulduggery. The joke is created by simply reanalyzing the sound sequence of *Toulouse-Lautrec* into *to lose Lautrec*. It takes a skilful scriptwriter to make the joke work in a couple of words, by ensuring the correct phrase structure fits the perfect retort.

In order to demonstrate how very economical Milligan is as a jokesmith, I provide the next joke for contrast. It exploits very similar principles but is not as neat, swift or witty as Milligan's. It also requires a narrative frame to work effectively.

Example 18

Recently a guy in Paris nearly got away with stealing several paintings from the Louvre. However, after planning the crime, getting in and out past security, he was captured only 2 blocks away when his Econoline ran out of gas. When asked how he could mastermind such a crime and then make such an obvious error, he replied: "I had no Monet to buy Degas to make the Van Gogh."
[...] *and you think I didn't have de Gaulle to put this in the paper.*
(Peter FitzSimons in the SunHerald, *Australia July 1, 2007*)

The joke here depends on reanalyzing the names of the artists (all Noun Phrases, as names are) so that they sound like English phrases, spoken with a stereotyped French accent. Thus, *Monet* is to be heard as *money*, *Degas* as *the gas*, and *van Gogh* as *van go*. *Money* remains a NP (or a DP depending on the analysis you choose), *the gas* is a DP, and *van go* is part of a more complex Verb Phrase.[14] De Gaulle, of course, was a famous French president, and his name is easily reanalyzed in English as *the gall*. In order to understand the joke, one must have some recognition of the stereotyped French accent in English, in which *the* may be pronounced as *de*. This sort of joke technique is very productive and no doubt there are many more of the same type. The Toulouse-Lautrec gag, in my opinion, is more sophisticated in terms of its linguistic complexity, and a better, more economical joke.

The following is even more egregiously contrived than the joke about Monet and his fellow Impressionists. It plays on the way in which Anglophone speakers who are scared to pronounce the sounds of German and French, are wont to say the names of well known composers. It also exploits the minimalist pidgin structures that are stereotypically associated with foreigner (and animal) talk.

Example 19

Two dogs and a cat go to a symphony concert, and having relished the music, they decide they want to go backstage to meet the orchestra. The guard on duty refuses to let them in: "You're animals. You can't come in here! What do you know about music?" The first dog says: "I Bach," the second one says, "I Offenbach," and the cat says, "And I'm Debussy." [15]

For those who pronounce these names *Bach*, *Offenbach* and *Debussy* authentically, I translate the relevant utterances.

"I bark."

"I often bark."

"And I am the pussy".

The joke is slightly untidy in that the cat clearly uses more elaborated syntactic structure than do the dogs. It is nevertheless clear that speakers of one language are always prepared to process sound strings from another language into their own linguistic frame, and to experience some delight when a happy coincidence is found. The tacit knowledge of the sound systems of all the languages involved is evoked, and the listener is made aware of the ubiquitous arbitrariness and multicategoriality of language.

3.0 Phonology

3.1 Introduction

In this section I focus on jokes that exploit facts about the phonological system of English in order to create humorous effects. I'll use the term "phonology" to refer to [the representations of] the sounds of language and the rules by which they are combined.[16]

Naturally, here, I dwell on the duality of patterning, *i.e.*, the basic fact that phonemes are meaningless units, and gain their meaning only in combination with other meaningless units in allowable combinations in a particular language.

3.2 Sound Sequences

A friend of mine, on hearing that a woman called Pippa would be marrying a Mr. Perkins, immediately said,

Example 20

Oh, Pippa Perkins, the stutterer.

In this instance, he was (for the purpose of the joke) analyzing the series of [pə] syllables as a stutter, and thus denying all but the first their status as different syllables. Arguably, the humor in this derives from the joker noticing a structural fact, a coincidental series of repeated syllables and yoking that together with the knowledge that this series is similar to the unfortunate production of someone who stutters. This sort of perspective on language in use entails paying attention to the sound only, and not to the sense at all, and brings into question how we know when a series of sounds is meaningful and when what we are hearing is a speech disorder. The human ability to distinguish between noise and language has been extensively discussed by linguists as well as cognitive scientists, highlighted of course, by Chomsky's claim that our knowledge of language is abstracted away from false starts, hesitations and stutters and other performance variables (Chomsky, 1957).

Repeated sounds in sequence in a sound string seem to encourage this sort of humorous play. It is as though there is something rather marked about the sound of identical repeated consonant vowel clusters in English that triggers certain kinds of jokes.

A *kikoi* is a cotton wrap, originating in Kenya, used variously as a skirt, a beach wrap, a beach mat, or a sarong, among other things. The word is Swahili. *Kikoi* is pronounced [kəkɔɪ], at least as it is used in English. One day, as I joined a friend who was sitting on the beach, she said,

Example 21

Put your c-carcass on the kikoi.

All this joke requires in the production and reception is the application of a rule. Of course, there is no rule. It is accidental that the word *kikoi* has a repetition of the first consonant sound (making it sound something like a stutter). My friend noticed this repetition and generalized it to another [k] sound, in this case the [k] in carcass. This game of reduplicating [k] sounds could, of course, go on endlessly, (I c-can't) but is probably only really funny in the context that the word *kikoi* is present in the immediate discourse.[17]

Noticing the recurrences of certain syllables and playing with them is the source of a particular kind of joke that points out the regularities and lack of regularities in the English sound and spelling system. English is notorious for the lack of regularities between its orthography and its pronunciation, and this irregularity (and the search for regularity) is to be found among native as well as non-native speakers and readers of English. Ethnic stereotypes have a particular currency in these "naïve idiot" jokes. I reproduce this one as is, from whence I have borrowed it. The joke could just as well be about any "naïve idiot". In this instance, it is the stereotype of the Sikh in India.

Example 22

A Sikh walked into a travel agency in New Delhi, and said to an agent, "I wish to purchase an airline ticket to the Netherlands. I must go to the Haig-you."

"Oh, you foolish Sikh. Not Haig-you, you mean 'The Hague'."

"I am the customer and you are the clerk," replied the Sikh, "Do as I ask and hold your tung-you."

"My, my, you really are quite illiterate," laughed the agent. "It is not 'tung-you'. It is 'tongue'."

"Just sell me the ticket, you cheeky fellow. I am not here to arg."

(from Cohen, 1999)

In this case, the joke hinges on the fact that the words *Hague* and *tongue* are spelt with *–gue* endings, but that the *–ue* component of those endings is not pronounced. The Sikh is obviously pronouncing the words according to a grapheme-phoneme mapping that says "pronounce *-gue* as *gyoo*". As the customer, he is irritated by the agent's superior attitude, and indicates this irritation, but he does, at the same time, take note of what the agent has said and accordingly changes the rule he is following. Consequently, he produces the word *arg*, following the new rule. The joke, of course, nestles in the fact that the pronunciation of *argue* does not follow the new rule, but is in accord with his old rule.[18] Hypercorrection (over-correcting to produce an ungrammatical form) is well documented especially in cases where speakers are known to feel insecure about their language use for sociolinguistic reasons. Yet again, the Sikh in the joke is seen to be foolish. The ethnic stereotype is not necessary for the success of the joke, but it is possible that there is a layer of meaning that Sikhs might perceive that would make this joke funnier for them, if it were told by a Sikh, as is the case in a number of Jewish jokes made by Jews about themselves. This depends entirely on who is making and telling the joke, a discussion of which is beyond the scope of this book.[19]

Those who do have some form of speech or language disorder are often the butt of jokes. The production of spoken language often supplies the fodder for jokes. Usually these jokes are of the same category as jokes that mock others for their obvious physical defects. Many jokes play on the revenge of the person suffering from the disorder. However, others reflect a certain knee-jerk response sometimes found in people who have long been the victims of oppressive and unfair systems. The example below offers a comment on some people's perception of their own linguistic performance.

Example 23

On a plane, a passenger found himself seated next to a young man with a terrible stutter. When they got talking, the young man informed him that he was on his way to a job interview, in fact, an audition to be an announcer for Vatican Radio.

"What do you reckon your chances are?" asked the passenger.

"N-n—not t-t-t-too g-g-g-ood," the young man replied. "They will p-p-probab-b-bly g-give it t-t-t-tto s-s-s-om-m-me b-b-b-bloody Ca-ca-ca-tholic."

The content of the joke here is, among other things, about discrimination. The young man thinks his chances of getting the job are slim, because he is not a Catholic. The fact that he is not competent to do the job, given that he stutters and that a radio announcer should, among other qualities, have a smooth delivery, does not seem to affect this belief. It should be perfectly obvious to anyone who hears him speak that he will not get the job: on some level, it is even obvious to him. He is either deluded or setting up the excuse for his failure in advance. However, he will not acknowledge that it is anything about his abilities that would lose him the job. He prefers to blame his certain failure on religious discrimination. It's an interesting joke, because it is true that he will be discriminated against. However, the discrimination will be on the basis of his disability, as this is directly relevant to whether or not he can do the job. He, however, wants to believe that he will be the target of unjustifiable discrimination.

Some of these sorts of jokes, though, make a different point; just as a person might say, *You have a great face for radio*, and create the implicature that the person is not physically very beautiful, and therefore not destined for a career in television or film, a person interviewing for a job might be forgiven for believing that they have been discriminated against for some or other reason, of a more or less obvious nature.

3.3 Phoneme Replacement

The Monty Python's Flying Circus team's repertoire of jokes is replete with extreme sensitivity to the componentiality of language. One of their most salient techniques for creating humor is to focus on one aspect of the conventionalized system that is language and apply a new rule to this aspect, creating strange and humorous effects. In the case below, they have seized on the phoneme /k/ and decided to replace all occurrences of the sound [k] with [b]. Since their talent is not only for language play, but for creating generally surrealistic experiences out of the mundane, it is not terribly surprising that they have chosen to set this one in a travel agency.

Example 24

Bounder   *Anyway, you're interested in one of our adventure holidays, eh?*
Tourist   *Yes. I saw your advert in the bolour supplement.*
Bounder   *The what?*
Tourist   *The bolour supplement.*
Bounder   *The colour supplement?*
Tourist   *Yes. I'm sorry I can't say the letter 'B'.*
Bounder   *C?*

Tourist	*Yes that's right. It's all due to a trauma I suffered when I was a sboolboy. I was attacked by a bat.*
Bounder	*A cat?*
Tourist	*No a bat.*
Bounder	*Can you say the letter 'K'?*
Tourist	*Oh yes, Khaki, king, kettle, Kuwait, Keble Bollege Oxford.*
Bounder	*Why don't you say the letter 'K' instead of the letter 'C'?*
Tourist	*What you mean... ... .spell bolour with a K?*
Bounder	*Yes.*
Tourist	*Kolour. Oh that's very good, I never thought of that.*

(Monty Python's Flying Circus, Just the Words, episode 31)

The basic joke turns on the problem that the Tourist has in pronouncing the sound [k]. Or as he puts it, the letter B; (he means C). In fact, what he really means is that when he perceives the word he is pronouncing to contain the phoneme /k/, he can't do it. Thus, he produces both a nonsense word, *bolour*, which does follow the legitimate sound pattern for English, and a nonsense word, *sboolboy*, which doesn't. Then he produces *bat*, which, now following the rule, his interlocutor interprets as "cat". But like every novice linguistics student, he discovers that phonological rules can take the form: /k/ is realized as [b] but /b/ is realized as [b] too. So, he discovers that the tourist was actually attacked by a bat.

Bounder is helpful. He asks Tourist whether he is able to pronounce the letter k (meaning the sound [k]), and Tourist immediately reels off a string of words genuinely spelt with the letter k, but reminds us that he still can't pronounce c words, hence, *Kebble Bollege*. Bounder suggests that Tourist simply spell words that use the letter c with k, instead. This reminds us that the English spelling system is not transparent with regard to mapping between grapheme and phoneme. As is often reasoned, if you want to pronounce a /k/, why not spell it with a k?

In the joke, however, the implicit assumption is that people process oral production by going through the conventional written representation. This in itself is patently absurd, as we know that in most cases, for the native speaker, writing is parasitic on speech, and not *vice versa*. In normal development, we first learn to speak, then to read. In this case, the suggestion reverses our conventional understanding of the process. Bounder helpfully suggests that Tourist simply changes the spelling in his head, so that he can pronounce [k] sounds in the relevant places.

Tourist seriously considers the suggestion, tries it out, and when it works, reports, with surprise, that he had never thought of using this strategy. As strategies go, it works, but it's patently absurd. As any speech-language therapist will tell you, the point of strategies is to make conscious for patients certain processing strategies that can help them to get around problems that occur in their automatic processing. Whether this strategy is likely to make Tourist's life easier or more difficult remains in question. In normal, on-line speech production, it is unusual for a speaker to first think of a written form and consider the spelling before pronouncing the word. As a matter of fact, we know from a continuation of this sketch (not produced here) that the moment Tourist is not paying conscious attention to using the strategy he lapses, with hilarious effects.

My own take on this sketch is that it is a swipe at the kind of speech-language therapists who don't bear in mind the deep systematicity and unconscious nature of language comprehension and production and suggest, instead, a surface and superficial solution that is actually immensely convoluted and doesn't address the problem at all. The notion that a speech disorder as bizarre as the one exhibited here could be cured by a little substitution exercise for each and every example, which should first be selected on the basis of its spelling properties is nearly as far-fetched as the sketch itself.

It is most interesting that the 'c' in *can't* remains [k] *i.e.*, unchanged. One would expect Tourist to pronounce it as '*ban't*, in the utterance, *I'm sorry I can't say the letter 'B'*. Perhaps the writers of the skit themselves missed it because it is a function word. If so, this is a very telling example of the claim that there is a processing distinction between lexical and function words.[20]

3.4 Phonological Processes

3.4.1 Assimilation

In the phonological process known as assimilation, the phone of a speech segment becomes more like the phone in another segment of the word or at a word boundary. We may say that a segment triggers an assimilatory change in another segment. The better knock-knock jokes make use of this process.

Example 25

Knock, knock.
Who's there?
Sam
Sam who?
Sam Pitt.[21]

The final response, *Sam Pitt* is intended to sound like *sand pit*. The way this works is as follows. The [d] in *sand* is deleted, (as word final consonants often are in fast speech in English).[22] The pronunciation of [sæm] is influenced by the anticipation of the [p] in [pIt]—the word final alveolar nasal [n] changes to a bilabial nasal [m] to become more like the bilabial stop [p] in [pIt] This yields [sæmpIt]. The knock knock joke relies on the observation that *Sam* is a common first name in English, and that *Pitt* is a recognizable last name, and (especially if you are a child) it is interesting that this sounds surprisingly like *sandpit*.

It's unlikely that the average child or adult knows the technical details of this process, yet catching the humor requires some calculation and reflection on the fact that *sandpit* sounds like *Sam Pitt*.

3.4.2 Substitution

There is frequently humor to be found in switching phonemes within words (metathesis), between words (spoonerism), and, most simply, substituting one phoneme for another.

Dorothy Parker, observing a party game, in which contestants were each required to duck their heads in to their allocated water buckets to retrieve apples that had been placed in the water for that specific purpose, is said to have remarked,

Example 26

Ducking for apples — change one letter and it's the story of my life.

(Dorothy Parker, 1893–1967)

All that is required to get this joke is a quick realization that the letter, or sound, in question is the first one in *ducking*. The joke activates our knowledge that it takes but a single phoneme to change the meaning of a word utterly. It is, of course, this insight that allows us to become conscious of the duality of patterning in language. Phonemes are meaningless units: in combination they may form the meaningful units of a language.

3.4.3 Parapraxis

The phenomenon often referred to as slip of the tongue, or *parapraxis*, was first identified by Freud in *The Psychopathology of Everyday Life* (Freud 1901/1914). He claimed that occasionally people produced utterances that were not what they consciously intended to say, but which slipped out, as a result of unconscious desires, fears or conflicts. In his honour, these are sometimes known as Freudian slips. The term *parapraxis* (meaning "another action") was co-opted by his first translator; Freud referred to the phenomenon as *Fehlleistung* in German (literally, "faulty action", or "misperformance"). Nowadays, any unintended production (in speech or writing) is loosely called a Freudian slip. This is somewhat misleading, because there are a number of implicit assumptions that go along with Freud's identification and discussion of the phenomenon.

There are a couple of jokes that wittily capture Freud's essential idea, although they certainly do not belong here, in this section on phonology. Nevertheless, they stand as a contrast to the specific linguistic phenomena—metathesis within and across words—with which I deal below.

Example 27

A Freudian slip is when you mean one thing, but you say your mother.

Example 28

A man is reporting to his analyst an interaction he has had with his mother. "While sitting with my parents at the breakfast table," he said, "I meant to say, 'Pass the butter' but instead I said, 'You ruined my life, you bitch.'"

Example 29

A patient goes to see his shrink. "Oh, I had the most awful dream last night," he said. "I dreamt that I killed my father and then had sex with my mother. Then I walked in here naked, and had sex with you! It was such a terrible, disturbing dream. I woke up feeling quite awful, had a cup of tea and a slice of toast, and came to see you right away."
"A cup of tea and a slice of toast!" exclaimed the analyst, "Do you call that breakfast?"

These jokes all play on the idea that we have unconscious thoughts, desires and conflicts, and that these often affect the language we use, and emerge in our speech production. However, for our purposes, in a discussion of the formal properties of language, with the exception of Example 27, which is a play on *another/my mother*, they are not of phonological interest, other than to highlight the distinction between what we say and what we consciously intended to say. [23]

3.4.2 Metathesis

The sort of parapraxes that occur in linguistic jokes are (deliberate) misperformances in terms of the ordering of phonemes (and occasionally morphemes) within words or across words, and the exchange or substitution of one phoneme for another, within a word. Additionally, one word in an utterance may change places with another. Technically, these may all be thought of as examples of metathesis.

For linguistic purposes, we often refer to these non-deliberate performance phenomena as slips of the tongue, and slips of the pen. In these cases, psycholinguists analyze particular misperformances as evidence of the independent psychological reality of phonemes and morphemes.

The sorts of slips that occur often produce humorous effects, whether deliberately intended or produced as speech errors that happen accidentally to be amusing. In order to discern the humor in such utterances, we need to have reference to a tacit knowledge of what the targeted phoneme or morpheme should have been, and what features, if any, the exchanged forms have in common.

Phonological exchanges are called spoonerisms, named after the Reverend William Archibald Spooner (1844–1930), Warden of New College, Oxford, known for his tendency to produce hilarious utterances of this kind. Many of the examples attributed to Spooner are apocryphal, but the phenomenon has spawned a cottage industry. One of the most well known spoonerisms (attributed spuriously to Spooner) switches the places of the initial consonants of two words in each sentence.

Example 30

"*You have **h**issed all my **m**ystery lectures. You have **t**asted a whole **w**orm. Please leave Oxford on the next **t**own **d**rain.*"

It is worth pointing out several interesting features of this utterance. First of all, in the first and second sentence, the switching of the first consonants *hissed* and *mystery* (the target words should be *missed* and *history*) and *tasted* and *worm* (the target words should be *wasted* and *term*) occurs in the environment where in fact, the nucleus and coda in the first syllable of each of the word pairs are identical. This is probably an additional spur to the misperformance. Psycholinguists (*e.g.*, Fromkin, 1980) regard this switching phenomenon as evidence for the claim that on-line planning occurs in the production of sentences, *i.e.*, that had the speaker not planned to say the [h] in *history* later in the utterance, he would not have produced it when he did, as *hissed*, three words earlier than he should have. It is also important that he produced *mystery*, instead of *history*, showing that unconsciously he knew that he had a [mɪs] syllable to produce, as well as the [hɪs] syllable he had already produced.

The same process applies to the second sentence, *tasted the whole worm* as opposed to *wasted the whole term*. The marvelous consequence of these switches is that they make their own sense, and in the case of the second one, it is syntactically, as well as semantically, perfect.

The third sentence, *Please leave Oxford on the next town drain*, exhibits a slightly different manifestation of the phenomenon. Firstly, the initial consonants that are switched are in adjacent words. Secondly, the consonants that are switched do not precede identical nuclei and codas. Nevertheless, the switch creates new words and the resulting utterance conjures up a sufficiently ridiculous picture.

There are, additionally, examples of *kniferism* and *forkerism* (terms coined by Douglas Hofstadter using a spurious backformation to claim that these are complements to spoonerism) to refer, respectively to the switching of the nucleus between two words, and the switching of coda between two words, as seen below.

Example 31

All the world was thrilled by the marriage of the Duck and Doochess of Windsor.

Example 32

John Cameron Swayze (a radio commentator) is said to have referred to a fellow journalist as a "*noted woolen communist*", when he intended to say "*a noted woman columnist*".

As can be seen, the process in Example 31 is to exchange the nucleus of the first syllable of *Duke* with the nucleus of the first syllable of *Duchess*. This is known as a kniferism, or loosely, vowel metathesis. Note as well, that the first consonant of these syllables is the same, often the case in undeliberate kniferisms. In Example 32, we see a forkerism, by some account: the exchange of coda between two words.[24]

The following example is typical of a very common class of switches, in which two words in a sentence change places, often without either hearers or speakers noticing. This too tells us something about the way in which we process utterances, particularly when the information we are getting is very familiar to us, so our processing is very fast and automatic. The example below is a very clever one, because it works on both readings, *i.e.*, "quack like a duck" and "duck like a quack", where in the form in the joke *duck* is a verb and *quack* is a noun, used to refer to an untrustworthy doctor.

Example 33

If it ducks like a quack it probably is one.[25]
(Christopher Henrich, Language Log, *July 31, 2009*)

Another manifestation of metathesis in English is to be found when two adjacent phones change places. Many languages make productive use of this process in their grammatical systems (*cf.* Hebrew, ASL) but in English it is regarded simply as one of the consequences of fast speech, or dialectal variation, yielding results such as *prehaps* for *perhaps, renumeration* for *remuneration, and aks* for *ask.* However, occasionally, this kind of metathesis yields humorous results, such as found in Example 34.

Example 34

Poor Old MacDonald was dyslexic and had a farm, Oh-eye-ee-eye-ee.

In this case, the sounds of *ee-eye-ee-eye-oh* can be easily reversed phonologically to create a humorous effect. In general, however, stereotype jokes about dyslexia, which rely on dyslexic orthography, are far more productive than jokes based entirely on the metathesis of phonemes, strictly found in spoken language.

In Example 35, Groucho Marx exploits both orthography and phonology in activating our implicit awareness of metathesis.

Example 35

What is the definition of an agnostic, dyslexic insomniac?
Someone who lies awake at night wondering if there's a dog.
(Groucho Marx, *1890–1977*)

The play here is on a few different levels. The important one for phonology is the metathesis involved in switching *god* to *dog*. The course of the joke is as follows:

an agnostic is someone who wonders whether there is a god, an insomniac may be said to lie awake at night, and a dyslexic, by sloppy definition, mixes up the order (and often orientation) of the letters s/he reads. In this case, it is the phonemes as well as the letters that are switched. Jokes as clever as this one demonstrating metathesis are hard to come by.

Sound sequences may also be reassigned in order to yield several new words from the utterance that primes for them. Some rather skilful wordplay is involved in reassigning sound sequences in such a way that new morphemes are formed, particularly if, as a result, new syntactic structures, as well as an entirely different sense can be created. Two of the best examples I know of this kind of metathesis in English lead to new words and new syntactic structures being formed.

Example 36

I'd rather have a bottle in front of me than a frontal lobotomy.[26]

and

Example 37

Q: How do you titillate an ocelot?
A: You oscillate its tit a lot.

In Example 36, for the joke to work maximally, the pronunciation should be *in fron' a me*, [ɪn frɒn: ə mɪ] which is the fast speech likelihood, in any event. A frontal lobotomy is a surgical procedure in which the pathways connecting the frontal lobe to the limbic system are deliberately damaged to reduce the patient's distress levels. This used to be the treatment of choice for certain kinds of mental illness. Presumably, given the side effects, most people would rather have anything than a frontal lobotomy.

However, the originator of this witticism (probably Dorothy Parker) managed to shuffle the syllables in such a way that from *frontal lobotomy* she derived *bottle in front a me.* (or, more probably, but equivalently, from [frɒnʔl ləbɒrəmɪ] she derived [bɒɾl ɪn frɒn:əmi]. *Bot* from *lobotomy* is conjoined with *al*, from *frontal*, to make *bottle*; *front* from *frontal* is conjoined with the [ə] from *lobotomy*; *me* from *lobotomy* remains. *In front of me* is a Preposition Phrase embedded in a larger Preposition Phrase. *A frontal lobotomy* is a compound Noun Phrase or a Noun Phrase incorporating an adjective and noun. The reassignment of morphological and syntactic structure is masterful, and the sense that is made is incontrovertible. Who wouldn't rather have a bottle in front of them (the allusion is to a bottle of alcohol, almost certainly) than undergo a frontal lobotomy?

Dean Martin (1917–95), the singer and entertainer, well known for his fondness for Vat 69 Scotch whisky, further extended this to *I would rather have a **free** bottle in front of me than a **pre**-frontal lobotomy*, deftly adding one more syllable switch into the mix, and name-dropping a little neuroscience to emphasize the particular importance of the pre-frontal cortex.

Example 37 follows a similar pattern to the one demonstrated above. An *ocelot* is a type of wild cat living in Central and South America. For the purposes of definition, *to oscillate* means to swing or move backward and forward. It happens to be intransitive, but this is not of much significance for the purposes of the joke. *To titillate* means to arouse by stimulation. Could any stage be better set for the joke?

So, how do you arouse an ocelot? By moving its tit a lot. The joke is in a question-answer format, and it is conventionally felicitous. The creativity is in the reassignment of the sound sequences. The way the reassignment works is as follows. The *os* of *oscillate* comes from the *os* of *ocelot*; the *illate* of *oscillate* comes from the *illate* of *titillate*, *its* is additional; *tit* comes from *titillate*, *a* comes from *ocelot*; *lot* comes from *ocelot*. The new words that are formed are *oscillate*, *tit* and *a lot*. All the sound sequences necessary for rearrangement are available in the question part.

In this chapter I have shown that play at morphological and phonological levels is extremely rich in many linguistic jokes. Since few phonological or morphological rules can be said to have been learnt consciously, in order to appreciate these jokes, listeners have to rely on their implicit knowledge of the rules of phonology and morphology of the language they know. There are, naturally, many other jokes in this book that rely on play with morphological and phonological rules, but I have used them in different chapters to demonstrate other linguistic phenomena. The reader will find them easy to identify, especially subsequent to the highlighting of rules presented in this chapter.

Notes

1 When I use *phoneme* here I refer specifically to phonemes that do not function morphemically.

2 I am grateful to Mary-Ann Kemp for inventing this one.

3 http://heideas.blogspot.com/, accessed March 8, 2010. I strongly recommend any serious student of linguistics, or indeed, of *The Simpsons*, to check out this site.

4 Benjamin Zimmer, on Language Log, January 29, 2006, comments on this process, calling it cran-morphing, and notes that it has yielded many productive suffixes in the 20th century: *-burger*, *-(o)holic*, *-(o)rama*, *-(a)thon*, *-(o)mat*, *-(o)nomics*, *-gate*, etc. See section 2.3.3 for a detailed discussion of cranberry morphemes.

5 Advertisements and other media flagrantly flout the selection restrictions in order to draw attention. Thus, there is an advertisement for *uncola* (a drink that is entirely unlike other soft drinks). The rule that is flouted is one that restricts the use of the prefix *–un*, disallowing its attachment to nouns. Another flout is the use of the slogan for NRMA (the National Roads and Motorists' Association (Australia)) that reassures customers by telling them to *unworry*. In this case, the prefix *-un* is illegally attached to a psych-verb, *worry*.

6 http://itre.cis.upenn.edu/~myl/languagelog/archives/000018.html. Originally this posting was made on September 30, 2003.

7 See http://eggcorns.lascribe.net/browse-eggcorns/ and *Language log* http://languagelog.ldc.upenn.edu/ under the category *Eggcorns*.

8 See Chapter 7 on jokes that require knowledge of more than one language, for an extensive discussion of this and other related topics.

9 I cannot help mentioning the joke about the guy who went to the Buddhist hamburger bar and said, "Make me one with everything". The ambiguity here is between, "Make me a hamburger which has everything on it," and "Make me at one with everything", a tenet of Buddhist thought.

10 In the US, however, *hamburger* is often used to describe the minced or ground meat itself. This would explain the use of the term hamburger rolls, to describe the bread-like substance that the hamburger (meat) is put in.

11 These forms are possible not because *frock* and *frost* are nouns but through their derivations as verbs (in participial form). Thus, at a push, we may find *deregister* (even here, *register* might be a verb form) but the only other examples that I can find that are clearly and unambiguously *de-* + *noun* are the likes of *de-hair, de-flea, de-tick,* meaning "take off + noun". These too are not terribly productive; we can't get *de-nail, de-spider* or *detooth*. There has been a recent debate (2009 *ff.*) about the term *defriend*, meaning to remove a person from one's social networking site; the debate, however, is about the most acceptable form of the word this process should take: *defriend v. unfriend.* Apparently *unfriend* is regarded as the preferred item. Either way, *de-* + *noun* or *un-* + *noun* are not regularly used in English derivational morphology. I would speculate that *unfriend* and *defriend* arose by analogy with *befriend,* "to make a friend of". If the formation of *befriend* follows a morphological rule, it would be *be-* + *verb.* There is an attributed earlier use of *friend* as a verb, said to be rare and archaic.

12 The joke does not function on all the levels it might, in that the surface reading *comes innuendo* is not strictly grammatical or usual in English, since *innuendo* is a noun, unless we are to read the term *innuendo* as meaning "by nodding" or "by hinting" as it would be in direct translation from Latin. My own reading is that Groucho preferred to create an innuendo by saying *innuendo,* rather than paying attention to how much sense accompanies the grammatically correct VP *comes in your window,* if it is to be parsed simultaneously as *comes innuendo.*

13 For an early discussion on phonological and grammatical words, see Lyons, 1968.

14 Strictly, the VP shell is [make go the van].

15 I am indebted to David Schalkwyk, the Shakespeare scholar, for this one.

16 The use of the term "phonology" (as the term "grammar") is systematically ambiguous—between the abstract and unconscious knowledge of the speaker, and the systematic study of such knowledge.

17 Of course this type of partial reduplication is a common phonological strategy of word formation in many languages such as Samoan, but in those instances, there is a language-specific morphological rule, whereas the generalization in this joke is based simply on noticing an accidental property of the sound sequence.

18 For a brief discussion of attempts at spelling reform in English, see Chapter 8.

19 For a detailed discussion about ethnic jokes, see particularly Davies, 1990.

20 This very astute observation was made by Mengistu Amberber, and the account is his, not mine.

21 Another *knock, knock* joke using a couple of extra phonological processes to aid the assimilation is this one:
Knock, knock
Who's there?
Banana
Banana who? (this interaction repeated three times)
Knock, knock
Who's there?
Orange
Orange who?
Orange you glad I stopped saying banana?

In this case, the joke is slightly more sophisticated, implicating deletion and elision, as well as assimilation.

22 Deletion, too, is a common phonological process that occurs in fast speech in English.

23 I suppose, however, that we might say that there is something more than a phonological slip involved in Example 28, since a phonologically entirely unrelated utterance is produced, and the reasons are unlikely to do with linguistic planning. Example 29 is yet another contribution to the discussion of naming, use and mention explored in Chapter 2.

24 This would depend of course, on how the inter-vocalic consonant (VCV) is syllabified: wom.an/wool.en (as opposed to wo.man; woo.len).

25 It has been suggested to me by Colin Mierowsky that these should be called *cutleryisms*. Strictly speaking they are not examples of phonological phenomena, but are included here for completeness.

26 In trying to acknowledge this, I discover attribution to WC Fields and Dorothy Parker. Apparently the source is, indeed, Dorothy Parker.

5

PLAYING WITH SYNTAX

Sentence structure is innate, but whining is acquired.

(Woody Allen, 1976)

1.0 Introduction

Essentially, the claim I make in this chapter is that it is the innateness of our knowledge of sentence structure that enables us to appreciate linguistic jokes, as I have defined them. However, it is not **simply** the innateness of the knowledge of our grammar that allows us to understand the humor in jokes of this sort. Knowledge of the grammar is tacit, *i.e.*, not readily available to consciousness. However, if successful, a linguistic joke opens up access to some aspects of our tacit knowledge of the grammar of our language and causes us to reflect upon the particular language phenomenon afresh. This, it seems to me, is the best account for why jokes of this sort are considered to be funny. Linguistic jokes are only funny if we perceive a contrast between what we know about language and the way in which language works in the joke. The joke pinpoints the ambiguity inherent in the linguistic structure in such a way that the discrepancy is incongruous, and surprising. Incongruity and surprise are generally regarded as the crucial features of jokes, linguistic or otherwise. I hope to show that the audience for linguistic jokes is not restricted to linguists, but made up of people who have an everyday, unarticulated knowledge of the grammar of their language.

Unlike Woody Allen, my preoccupation in this chapter is not with whining, but with syntax. Whining, as he observes slyly, may be acquired, as a result of exposure to others who whine. The crucial point to be made here is that when we whine in language, we use our unconscious, innate knowledge of syntax to do so. Whining *per se* does not thrust us into an awareness of the structure of our language, as the language of jokes does. Joke appreciation, like whining, may be acquired, but the underlying capacity to appreciate a linguistic joke is based on the innateness of our knowledge of sentence structure.

Jokes that exploit our innate knowledge of syntactic structure are legion. In this chapter, I explore how humor is created by the disruption of the usual, automatic expectations that we have of language use (particularly as they apply to syntax), resulting in the necessity for conscious awareness of knowledge that is normally tacit.

1.1 Sentence Structure

The grammatical structure of a sentence, as has been argued most clearly in Chomsky's earliest work, cannot necessarily be read off its surface structure realization. The sorts of sentences used to demonstrate this fact most dramatically are the ones used by Chomsky in *Syntactic Structures* (Chomsky, 1957). For instance, Chomsky showed that although Examples 1 and 2 appear superficially to have the same grammatical structure, in fact, even a cursory examination reveals that at anything other than the surface level, their structures are fundamentally different.

Example 1

John is easy to please.

Example 2

John is eager to please.

As Chomsky explains, in more exquisite detail and compelling precision than I can, a paraphrase of Example 1 yields Example 3.

Example 3

It is easy to please John.

However, a paraphrase of Example 2 yields Example 4.

Example 4

John is eager to please others.

Thus, despite the fact that the sentences differ only in the choice of the verb following the infinitival *to*, in the case of Example 1, *John* is, in fact, the object of the verb *please*, whereas, in Example 2, *John* is the subject of the verb complex *is eager*.

These examples serve as the fundamental illustration of the claim that not all sentences that look or sound as though they have an identical structure, actually do. Sentences with entirely different underlying structures may manifest with identical word orders. Thus sentences that look the same may not share an underlying structure.

Additionally, one sentence may have two or more underlying structures. Such sentences are called structurally ambiguous. Again, I draw the examples from Chomsky (1957).

Example 5

Visiting relatives can be boring.

Example 6

Flying planes can be dangerous.

Example 5 can be read in at least two ways, *i.e.*, it can have at least two different underlying structures. These readings might be paraphrased as in Example 7 and 8.

Example 7

Relatives who visit can be boring.

Example 8

The process of going to visit relatives can be boring.

Similarly, Example 6 can be read in at least two ways. These may be paraphrased as in Example 9 and 10.

Example 9

The activity of flying planes can be a dangerous one.

Example 10

Planes that fly can be dangerous (to those things or people that they might hit).

These facts about English syntax have been used, *inter alia*, to show that a superficial examination of utterances does not immediately reveal their unique underlying structure. The essential idea is that the sentences we produce are assembled in the mind, out of hierarchically organized phrases, according to universal rules of combination. Phrases in a sentence are liable to various transformations, depending on what the language allows. It is only once these transformations (known also in various incarnations of Chomskyan theory as movements, merges, copies and deletions) have taken place that a sentence is actually produced.[1]

For our purposes, here, the fundamental issue is structural ambiguity, *i.e.*, one utterance (sentence) may have more than one underlying structure. This kind of structural ambiguity at the sentence level (*a.k.a.* syntactic ambiguity) is an abundant source of jokes in English. Syntactic ambiguity may be created by exploiting any overt syntactic manifestation in order to cast doubt on its underlying structure. The kinds of jokes discussed in this chapter are, in the main, contrived to take advantage of syntactic ambiguity and to exploit the resultant, usually witty, incongruity in the different senses that are yielded. The more absurd, ridiculous and witty the relation between the different senses, the better the joke.[2]

2.0 Syntactic Ambiguity

2.1 Ambiguity in PP placement

This classic Vaudeville/burlesque joke is due originally, most probably, to the noted misanthrope, W.C. Fields (1880–1946).

Example 11

Would you hit a woman with a baby?
No, I'd hit her with a brick.

This joke template exploits a particular sort of syntactic ambiguity in the question part of the utterance. The easiest way to see the ambiguity is to examine the answer part first.

I'd hit her with a brick has one preferred reading, which is "I'd use a brick to hit her". The structure of this sentence, thus, is one in which the Prepositional Phrase (PP) *with a brick* functions as an adjunct to the verb *hit*, in other words, the Verb Phrase (VP) consists of *hit her with a brick* (see Figure 5.2). *With a brick*, in this instance, plays the thematic role of instrument. (The Noun Phrase (NP) *her* is the direct object, taking the semantic role of theme).[3]

It is in processing the preferred reading of the response according to the proposed structure that we are impelled to go back to the question part of the exchange. If we were to hear the question part in isolation from the response, we would no doubt assign it the following structure, that of the preferred reading. We would decide that *woman with a baby* is a complex noun phrase (NP), made up of a noun *woman* and a prepositional phrase (PP) *with a baby*. We know *woman with a baby* is a NP because we can substitute *her* for the entire string, in this sentence, yielding a new formulation of the question by substitution: *Would you hit her?*

However, as a consequence of seeing or hearing the response part, we may decide to revise our analysis.

Now, looking at the structure of the question part, we may legitimately ask: (a) is *with a baby* a Prepositional Phrase (PP) that is part of the Noun Phrase (NP) *woman with a baby?*; or (b) is *with a baby* a PP adjoined to the verb *hit*, as it would

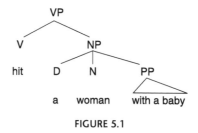

FIGURE 5.1

be by analogy to the structure of the response part, *hit her with a brick,* which is unambiguous?

The ambiguity in the question part is genuine: both readings are allowable in English. In (b), the structure would reflect that the PP *with a baby* is adjoined to the verb *hit, i.e.,* it functions analogously to *with a brick* (see Figure 5.2). In this case, *a baby* may be considered to be playing the semantic role of instrument.

There is probably very little doubt that the question has a preferred reading, something along the lines of *Would you hit a woman who was holding a baby?* The expected answer, if the interlocutor wants to be considered a civilized person, is *No, I would not hit a woman who was holding a baby,* or *No, I would not hit her.* However, the response, *No I'd hit her with a brick* alerts us to the alternative and (dispreferred reading) which is that he would not use a baby to hit her with, but would rather use a brick. In this case, he is answering the question *Would you hit her **with a baby**? (v. would you hit **a woman with a baby**?)* Bricks are probably better used as instruments for hitting people than babies are. Fields exploits the idea that whereas hitting a woman holding a baby is socially unacceptable, using a brick to hit the same woman is much more effective than using a baby for the purpose of hitting her. His intention is to offend utterly rather than simply to be accused of socially unacceptable behavior.

The syntax of the question part allows both readings. The humor is created by the answer part that highlights the ambiguity of certain kinds of sentences containing PPs. The linguistic question raised here is whether PPs function as modifiers of nouns, or as adjuncts to verbs. It is in the process of reflecting on why the joke is funny that we are made conscious of the potential ambiguity caused by the multi-fit nature of PPs in English—the fact that they can adjoin sentence initially, sentence finally, before the verb phrase, after the verb phrase, to noun

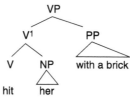

FIGURE 5.2

FIGURE 5.3

phrases, to nouns, essentially almost everywhere except between a verb and its sister NP, as shown in Figure 5.3 and below.

★VP→V PP NP

Groucho Marx is the source of scores of these sorts of jokes that exploit the promiscuity of PPs. This one from the movie *Animal Crackers* (1930) parallels the Vaudevillian one above.

Example 12

This morning I shot an elephant in my pajamas. How he got in my pajamas I don't know.
(Groucho Marx, 1890–1977)

In the first sentence, the ambiguity turns on the structural position of the PP *in my pajamas*. It could be adjoined elliptically to the NP *I*, yielding *I, in my pajamas, shot an elephant* or it could be part of a complex NP *an elephant in my pajamas*. On the first reading, it is the speaker who is wearing his pajamas when he shoots the elephant. This is the preferred reading, ridiculous as it may be (see Figure 5.4). The second reading is that the elephant is in the speaker's pajamas, a considerably more hilarious image, given the relative differences in their size, among other things (see Figure 5.5). When we process the next sentence, it is clear, however, that it is the second reading that has been exploited. The speaker shot the elephant that was wearing the speaker's pajamas.[4]

In the case below, the American stand-up comedian, Jackie Mason, exploits the potential ambiguity opened up by PP placement, homing in on the syntactic

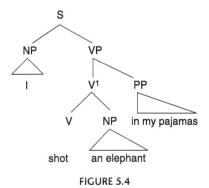

FIGURE 5.4

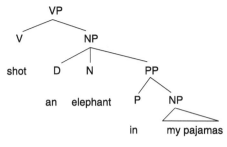

FIGURE 5.5

ambiguity to make a succinct, yet unexpected generalization. He takes particular advantage of the topic/comment discourse structure that is set up by the first sentence.

Example 13

Eighty percent of married men cheat in America. The rest cheat in Europe.

As in the previous couple of jokes, the syntactic ambiguity here relies on the place of attachment of the PP, in this case, *in America*. The first sentence contains the ambiguity and sets up the joke. The sentence could be interpreted either as: (a) *eighty percent of married men in America cheat* (implied, *on their wives*) (see Figure 5.6) or, equivalently, on the same reading, *In America, eighty percent of married men cheat* (implied, *on their wives*) (see Figure 5.7). The other reading that the ambiguity allows is: (b) *Eighty percent of married men cheat* (implied *on their wives*) *when they are in America* (see Figure 5.8).

The preferred reading is probably (a) *In America, eighty percent of married men cheat.* However, readings (a) and (b) are both legitimate, since in English, PPs are allowed to attach, as adjuncts, to the left of the subject NP, to the right of the VP, or to the right of the V^1. The joke relies on the interpretation in which the PP attaches to the right of the V^1 itself, yielding the VP *cheat in America*.[5]

Mason sets up the joke in the first sentence by relying on the expected reading, (even though this is a somewhat more colloquial, oral style than *e.g., In America,*

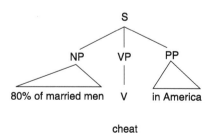

cheat

FIGURE 5.6

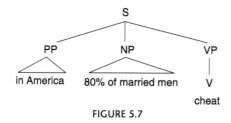

FIGURE 5.7

80% of men cheat on their wives). Then, because of the discourse expectations he has set up that the topic is **married men in America** in contrast to **married men elsewhere**, he is able to turn it around, so that he is, in fact, focusing on **where** married men do their cheating, rather than on **the number of married men** in America who cheat on their wives.

Thus, as a result of processing the second part of the utterance, we are forced back to the (b) reading, on account of the unexpected parallelism created by *The rest cheat in Europe*. The structure of *The rest cheat in Europe* is unambiguous; the PP is a sister to the V[1] under VP as in Figure 5.8. The contrast is therefore based on where they cheat, the implication being that all married men cheat—it's simply a matter of where they go to do the cheating.[6]

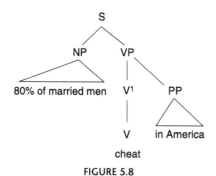

FIGURE 5.8

In some of the scripts and jokes written for the radio program *The Goon Show*, by Spike Milligan and his collaborator Larry Stephens, there is, in addition to other language play, a level of craziness in which blind logic applied to syntactic structure triumphs over referential meaning. This craziness is not unlike some of Groucho Marx's one-liners, which also send us spinning before we know where we are. (See, for instance, Example 16 below). As Groucho once remarked, "Humor is reason gone mad". The following exchange from the Goon Show exemplifies the claim. This exchange contains a number of tricks.

Example 14

Grytpype-Thynne: Moriarty—go and slam the door in his face.
Moriarty: He hasn't got a door in his face.

Grytpype-Thynne: Then he's trapped, and he can't get out!

(The Goon Show, *1957. Series 8; episode 2)*

The phrase, *Slam the door in his face* in almost all contexts, has the preferential reading of (a) "Slam the door while he is standing on the other side of it, trying to get in".

The structure of the sentence with the reading in (a) is (b) or (c):

(b) S→ NP VP PP
     VP → *slam [the door]*
     PP→ *[in his face]*

     or

(c) S→ NP VP
     VP→ V NP PP

where the PP is *in his face* and is a sister to NP *the door.*

(b)

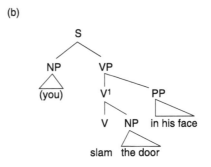

OR

(c)

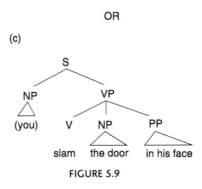

FIGURE 5.9

Moriarty, however, takes the reading

(d) "Slam the door (which) is in his face"

shown in (e).

(e) VP → slam [the door [in his face]]

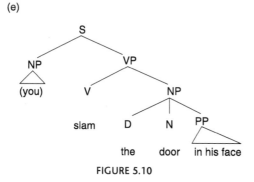

FIGURE 5.10

The structure yielding the reading in (d) is shown in (f).

(f) S→ NP VP
     VP→V NP
     NP→ D N PP.

The relevant rule relied on here is NP→ D N PP.

FIGURE 5.11

Although it is not clear why a normal person would take the reading in (d), Moriarty takes it, and in response to the patent absurdity, makes a valid observation, one that is generally true of faces, *i.e.*, *He hasn't got a door in his face.*

It is at this point that the regular, run-of-the mill joke involving syntactic ambiguity would end. However, Grytpype-Thynne's comeback spins us into a different dimension. By his logic, if something doesn't have a door, then what is inside is trapped in that doorless thing. He somehow manages to equate a face with a room (one that doesn't have a door) and sets up the scenario so that the person in whose face he had recently wanted a door slammed, is in fact, trapped inside. If the person is trapped, then he can't get out, even though at first Grytpype had not wanted to let him get in. In setting up this mind-shredding scenario, Milligan and Stephens also evoke the putative split between a person and his physical body that has perplexed Western philosophers for centuries. Such a notion allows us to make remarks like, "He is trapped in his body". *Trapped in his face* is a new take on this. Within the space of three short utterances, the listener has been spun dizzily and it is not immediately clear how the ambush happened. Quite formally, however, it is certainly the case that English allows us to process readings in which a PP is part of a complex NP (*the door in his face*) no matter how silly the result. Once again, a joke enables us to see the workings of our language, which we control, but don't really think about.

2.2 Lexical Semantics and Syntactic Ambiguity

Lexical ambiguity is discussed in greater detail in Chapter 3 and Chapter 4. Here I consider lexical ambiguity to refer to words that have more than one sense, thus words that participate in either homophonous or polysemous relationships, as well as words that are multicategorial depending on their context of use. In this section, we see how these lexical ambiguities enter into conspiracies with syntactic ambiguities.

The following exchange, from Groucho Marx again, exploits both syntactic and semantic ambiguity.[7]

Example 15

Call me a cab!
Ok, you're a cab.

The joke in this exchange hinges on an ambiguity in the lexical semantics of *call*, but also on a subtle syntactic ambiguity in the first utterance.

To highlight the syntactic ambiguities in the joke, I briefly discuss what linguists call dative alternation here. For example's sake, contrast the two sentences below.

(a) Sam gave a box to Pat.
(b) Sam gave Pat a box.

The alternation is in the VP. In (a) the VP is constituted of V NP PP. In (b) the VP is constituted of V NP NP. Both sentences are acceptable in English. It appears that certain English verbs allow this alternation, for example, *give*, *show*, *write*, *cook* and others.

Turning to the lexical ambiguity of *call*, we see that there are at least two separate meanings that the joke taps.

Inter alia, *call* (verb) may be used to mean

(a) *call* = "hail" (verb) or indeed "telephone" (verb)
     but also

(b) *call* ="name" (verb) or "say" (say + proposition).[8]

In the first part of this exchange, presumably the intended meaning is

(c) "Call a cab for me"
   The response, however, picks up on the meaning in (d).
(d) "Say that I am a cab".

Thus, one ambiguity that is exploited is the lexical ambiguity of *call*: the first speaker wants a cab to be called for her. The second speaker, Groucho, obliges by saying that she is a cab. The next ambiguity, the syntactic ambiguity in the first utterance, can be found if we understand that the intended meaning has the structure of a double object construction, best paraphrased by the nearest dative alternation, *i.e.*, as shown in (c).[9]

If we examine the paraphrase expressed in (d), it turns out that we do not have a double object construction at all, but a true small clause, rendered as (e).[10]

(e) "Call me 'a cab'"

The sentence in (e) is parallel structurally in a fundamental way to an utterance like "Call me John," or to less obvious utterances like "Make me an honest woman."

I use the utterance, "Call John for me" as an example equivalent to the reading in (c), to make the distinctions clearer.

Thus, to disambiguate the structures in (c) and (d), we might test the nature of the double object constructions we find in each. First, the structure of the reading in the alternation in (c) is as shown in (f) (see Figure 5.12).

(c)   (i)   "Call a cab for me"
      (ii)   "Call John for me"

(f)   S→ NP VP; VP→ V NP PP

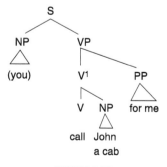

FIGURE 5.12

The structure in (g), however, is not valid as an alternation on the reading in (c) (see Figure 5.13).

(g) S→NP VP; VP →V NP NP.
    ★ "Call me a cab"   ★on the reading in (c).
    ★ "Call me John"

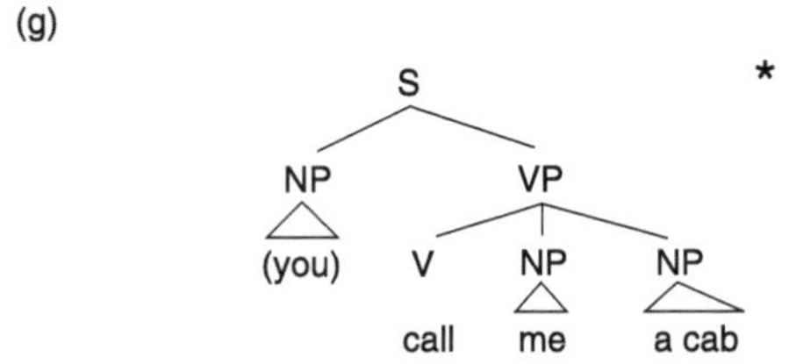

(g)

*On the reading in (c) above

FIGURE 5.13

Thus, (g) is not the correct structure for the sentence paraphrased as "Call John for me".

Recall that the correct structures in (f) and incorrect structures in (g) are related to the reading of the paraphrase in (c).

The correct structure of the paraphrase in (e), however, is shown in (h) (see Figure 5.14). The alternation shown above in (f) may be seen to be ungrammatical on the reading in (e) as shown in (i) (see Figure 5.15).

(e) "Call me 'a cab'"
    "Call me 'John'"
    "Make me an honest woman"

(h) S→NP VP; VP →V NP NP.

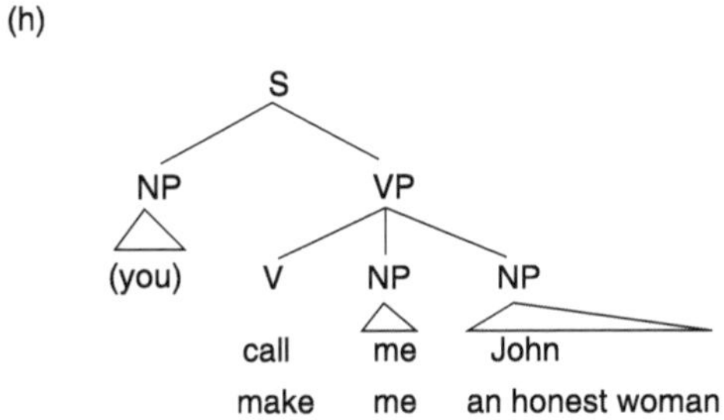

(h)

FIGURE 5.14

(i) S→ NP VP; VP→ V NP PP
    ★ "Make an honest woman for me" on the reading in (e)

(i)

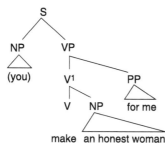

*On the reading, "make me an honest woman"

FIGURE 5.15

We see that (d) then, in its reading shown in (e), with a structure as in (h) refuses the alternation, in the way that "Make me an honest woman" could not faithfully be paraphrased as "Make an honest woman for me" if the meaning intended was "Make an honest woman out of me," as it is in (e).

Thus, the rejoinder, *Ok, you're a cab,* is perfectly legitimate in terms of the structure proposed for (d), shown in (h) and is completely bizarre in terms of the structure proposed for (c), shown in (f). Of course, the preferred reading is surely the one in which the speaker asks for a cab to be summoned. The syntax of the utterance *Call me a cab,* however, is ambiguous and the hearer is entitled to pick up on the ambiguity.

I think it extremely unlikely that any listener to the two-liner in Example 15 would go through the convolutions I set out above in order to understand the joke. Nevertheless, that the joke is funny, and accessibly so, should be evidence for the claim that jokes are powerful instruments in evoking tacit knowledge of language.

Groucho Marx is perhaps foremost among humorists in exploiting semantic and syntactic ambiguity to create witty, sidesplitting cracks. The joke that follows is a two-liner, with the joke in the second line. The first line sets it up.

Example 16

Outside of a dog, a book is man's best friend. Inside of a dog, it's too dark to read.

(Groucho Marx, 1890–1977)

The first sentence plays on the well-known adage that a dog is man's best friend. The priming template is as follows: with the exception of a dog, a book is man's best friend. Grammatically, *outside of a dog* is a rather complex prepositional phrase. Both *outside* and *of* are prepositions in at least one reading of this. ($PP_1 \rightarrow P_1\ PP_2$; $PP_2 \rightarrow P_2\ NP$).[11]

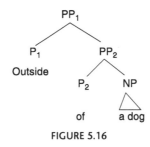

FIGURE 5.16

We are thus primed for the reading "with the exception of". In the second sentence, he sets up the parallelism: *outside of a dog/inside of a dog*. However, the priming by the first sentence has led us up the wrong path: we are expecting to continue with the "with the exception of" reading, instead we get the "outside/inside" reading. This is because Groucho has associated *outside* with *inside*—this is an association with another sense of *outside*, the more literal one, whereas, on the reading "with the exception of", *outside* is used to derive a complex idiom.

So, now we are faced with processing the sentence, and more strenuously, processing the idea of someone trying to read inside a dog. Groucho's joke demonstrates that following the rules of language can get us into very strange situations, helplessly and quickly. We don't even see the slide coming here. One moment we are thinking about man's best friend; within a couple of words we are contemplating the idea of sitting inside a dog, trying to read a book, but unable to do so because it's too dark.

The linguistic aspect on which the joke turns is, in fact, the ambiguity in the meaning of *outside of*. However, the genius lies in the way Groucho recognizes this and spins it away into pure absurdity, using a well-worn adage as a vehicle for doing so. To recognize how the joke works, we need to see that the phrase *outside of a dog* is a PP, which attaches at the left edge, above the level of the sentence *a book is man's best friend*. Similarly, to achieve the same reading, the PP could attach to the right edge of the sentence, also above the level of the sentence, yielding, *A book is man's best friend, outside of a dog*. In both cases, the reading is "with the exception of a dog, a book is man's best friend".

Inside of a dog is also a PP, apparently analogous in structure to *outside of a dog*. However, using *inside* forces the reading away from "with the exception of", and instead towards "on the inside". This then drives us to analyze the structure of *Inside of a dog, it's too dark to read* as, underlyingly, "It is too dark to read inside a dog". On this reading, the PP *inside of a dog* must be adjoined to the verb *read*. Even if expressed as *Inside a dog, it's too dark to read*, the PP may be seen to be pre-posed, moved from its underlying position as adjoined to the verb, rather than simply attached above the level of the sentence. We can see this by testing its constituency. We may say, "*It is inside of a dog that it is too dark to read*", or "*Inside a dog is where it is too hard to read*", or even "*Where is it too dark to read?*"

A structure that might disambiguate this reading even more clearly is one that might be paraphrased thus: "It's too dark, inside a dog, to read". In this case, the PP *inside a dog*, is placed parenthetically, between the main and subordinate clauses. It is clear, on that reading that it is inside a dog that it is too dark.

Thus, this joke is a subtle case of ambiguity with regard to PP placement that works as well as it does because it turns, in addition, on a little explored lexical ambiguity.

Example 17 is another well-worn joke that plays on the complications arising out of both semantic and syntactic ambiguity. More specifically, Example 17 turns on lexical ambiguity in addition to a very subtle variation in alternation arising out of the English double object construction.

The lexical item, *make*, however, although it allows alternations does not allow these alternations in quite the same form as in (a) and (b) below. One of the reasons is that the lexical item *make* has a few different (often quite closely related) readings in English. Note too that it is also the case that *make* can subcategorize either for a clause or NP.

The joke in Example 17 relies on semantic and syntactic ambiguities created by *make*.

Example 17

A: My mother made me a homosexual.
B: If I give her the wool, will she make me one too?

The ambiguity arises, first of all, out of the semantic ambiguities of the verb *make*. In this case, one reading of *make me* could be as in (a).

(a) "cause me to be", or "turn me into".

So A's utterance on this reading would be something like, "My mother caused me to be a homosexual" or "My mother turned me into a homosexual".

The other relevant reading of *make* is more or less synonymous with (b).

(b) "create" or "construct".

The easiest way to think of the utterance on the (b) reading, would be to consider A's utterance as parallel to *My mother made me a scarf*. This use of *made* could refer to the activity of knitting or sewing, so we could further paraphrase the utterance as "My mother knitted me a scarf."

The only reason to think of knitting scarves or such-like is B's response which is what triggers the association that making a homosexual is equivalent to making a scarf, *i.e.*, creating it using wool.

The preferred reading of *My mother made me a homosexual* is the first one: there was something my mother did that caused me to become a homosexual. However,

B's utterance causes a new possibility to be opened up: that my mother knitted me a homosexual. This is obviously bizarre, as homosexuals are not objects to be created using wool, but people who are attracted to members of their own sex.

How can we resolve the puzzle of why it's unremarkable to say *My mother made me a homosexual*, but odd to say *If I give her the wool will she make one too?* In order to solve this problem, we need to note that not only is *make* polysemous, but also, that in this joke there are actually various syntactic constructions that are being played off against one another.

My mother made me a scarf is a double object construction that has as its alternation *My mother made a scarf for me.*[12] In the first instance, the VP may be analyzed as V NP NP (see Figure 5.17). In the alternation, the VP may be analyzed as V NP PP (see Figure 5.18).

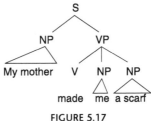

FIGURE 5.17

On the other hand, *My mother made me a homosexual*, although also a double object construction, does not undergo the same alternation. The VP may be analyzed as V NP NP. However, if we activate the parallel V NP PP alternation, we get *My mother made a homosexual for me*, which is not the preferred or intended reading. The correct alternation would be something like *My mother made a homosexual out of me*, but this does not parallel *My mother made a scarf for me*. However, the joke turns on precisely the parallelism evoked between the readings of *My mother made a scarf for me*, and *My mother made a homosexual for me*, both superficially identical V NP PP structures, with the only observable difference being the lexical items *homosexual* and *scarf* (see Figures 5.18 and 5.19).

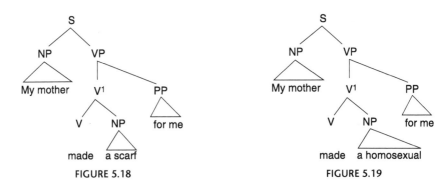

FIGURE 5.18   **FIGURE 5.19**

Thus, in effect, we can see that the utterance *My mother made me a homosexual* cannot be analyzed in the same way as *My mother made me a scarf.* B's utterance picks up on the idea that it could be, if one did not have a deep knowledge of the argument structure of verbs and the syntactic rules of English. It is when B says, *If I give her the wool, will she make me one too?* that we realize that there are two different syntactic constructions at work here. The idea that someone might knit a homosexual is absurd, but when we become aware that the language affords us the possibility to entertain the absurdity, we may experience a sudden reflective consciousness of certain rules that are generally tacit, and are, in fact, rather difficult to articulate.

In August 2008, Pope Benedict XVI visited Sydney, Australia, as a culmination of the *World Youth Day* festivities. Catholic pilgrims from all over the world swarmed to Sydney, to be blessed by the Pope himself, identifying themselves by means of various WYD paraphernalia: backpacks, T-shirts, banners, caps and so on. The local population was less than charmed by the invasion, and soon a T-shirt came into circulation, bearing the slogan shown below in Example 18.[13]

Example 18

I was touched by the Pope down under.

This slogan works because of both syntactic and semantic ambiguity. For Australians and non-Australians alike, *down under* is often used synonymously with "Australia". So, the slogan, on the surface is read as in (a)

(a) "I was touched by the Pope in Australia".

However, there is a widely known euphemism *down under* which is used to refer to a person's genitals. So, the slogan might also be read as in (b).

(b) "I was touched by the Pope on my genitals".

Given the history of scandal within the Catholic Church regarding sexual abuse by some of its clergy, this is an implication that is well understood, and considered by some to be a timeous jibe.

We would not get both readings if the syntactic ambiguity were not present. This ambiguity hinges on the attachment of the PP *down under.* Had the slogan been phrased as in (c), the simple reading would have been as in (d) without any ambiguity at all.[14]

(c) "I was touched down under by the Pope"
(d) "I was touched on the genitals by the Pope".

There is no obvious way in which (c) might be interpreted as being identical with (a). The reason for this is twofold. Firstly, the prepositions *down* and *in* function differently in this case. *Down under* is interchangeable with "Australia", in some senses, and with "in Australia" or "to Australia" in others.

Crucially, as in Figure 5.20, the PP *down under* cannot be a part of the VP, *touched by the Pope* and mean either that the wearer was touched by the Pope in Australia, or that the wearer was touched by the Pope on the genitals. Depending on who you are, there is a preferred reading. However, if we analyze the PP *down under* as being attached to the V^1, *touched*, as in (c), there would be almost no ambiguity (see Figure 5.21). The reading would be as in (d). The fact is that, although strictly, the reading in (d) would most closely be expressed as (c), it is nevertheless possible to get the reading in (d) from the original *I was touched by the Pope down under.* This is of course, precisely the reading that the T-shirt was designed to highlight. It is also the case that if the T-shirt were to have read *I was touched down under by the Pope* that the reading in (a) would be possible, although massively dispreferred.[15]

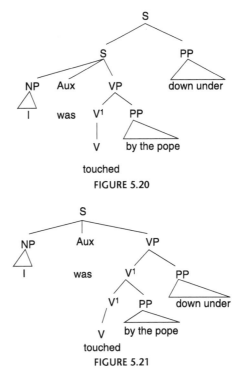

FIGURE 5.20

FIGURE 5.21

Another reason that this particular joke works so well hinges on the general distributional fact that in English, at least, locational PPs attach freely at the level of the clause, and, indeed, at any level of the VP. PP *by*-phrases, in contrast, attach more regularly to the V in its passive form, as one would expect, since they are underlying agents that have been demoted to *by*-phrases. The statement in the slogan may be an answer to one of two questions: *Where were you when you were touched by the Pope?* or *Where on your body did the Pope touch you?* The fundamental ambiguity created by both the semantics and the syntax of this slogan was a source of great merriment for the Sydneysiders who felt that their city was taking the papal visit too seriously.

In the riddle-joke in Example 19, we see yet another demonstration that the structural equivalence of two sentences at surface level is not necessarily identical at the level of their underlying structure. There are several different sources of ambiguity contributing to this joke, including semantic ambiguity, and the syntactic ambiguity of null subject constructions.

Example 19

Q: *What's worse than raining cats and dogs?*
A: *Hailing taxis.*[16]

The semantic ambiguity of *hailing* is the most obvious source of the joke. *Hailing* can mean (1) the falling of icy pellets from the sky, or it can mean (2) the process of flagging down, or calling, *e.g.*, a taxi. The argument valencies of (1) and (2) are different.[17]

Hailing (1) is identical in its valency to *raining*. *Rain* takes no arguments, but requires a dummy subject, because of the thus far unexplained stipulation that all sentences in English must have subjects.

Thus,

(a)   It is raining
(b)   * Is raining
(c)   * Raining.

Hailing (1) follows the identical pattern.

(d)   It is hailing
(e)   * Is hailing
(f)   * Hailing.

The utterance, *What's worse than raining cats and dogs?* is actually an elliptical form of *What's worse than when it is raining cats and dogs?*

We should bear in mind that *it* in *it is* is merely a pleonastic pronoun, a dummy. It is there because English requires lexically filled subjects. It has no deictic function.

Raining cats and dogs is an idiomatic expression in English that means the rain is pelting down. *Cats and dogs* (although a compound NP in form) does not have the status of an argument, since rain does not take any arguments. Thus *cats and dogs* functions adverbially, providing information about how heavily it is raining. There is no equivalent expression for heavy falls of hail (*e.g.*, ✶ *it's hailing elephants and hippos*). The first part of the joke primes us both semantically and syntactically for what is to follow. We wait to hear what is worse than this terrible rain. Hail is worse than rain. Taxis are heavier than cats and dogs. But *hailing taxis* is not a viable expression in English with the reading "very heavy hail". So, on this basis, there is nothing terribly funny about the joke. We are forced then to consider an alternative reading, since we know we are listening to a riddle/joke.

Hail (2), the process of calling or flagging down some person or vehicle, requires one internal argument, and one external, or subject argument. This is to be contrasted with *rain* which takes no arguments at all.

So, the answer to the question, may be expanded, on the reading of *hail* (2), to be

g.   When you are hailing taxis *or* When one is hailing taxis.

The meaning to be understood, presumably is this: it is a worse experience to be hailing taxis which don't stop, than for it to be raining heavily. Or, my understanding of this joke, which may be the product of an overanxious imagination, is that the really awful experience is to be standing in the pelting rain **and** trying to flag down a taxi.

In the case of *hailing taxis*, in the joke, the subject of *hailing* (2) is an empty pronoun, licensed by the gerund-participle form, *hailing*.[18] It is important to recognize that *hailing (2)* as in *hailing taxis* is a gerund-participle, whereas *raining* has no such status, as it is simply a participle, an elided form of *it's raining*.

The difference between the two senses of *hailing* can be seen in the construction *John's hailing (2) of taxis...*, which cannot work with the sense of *hailing* (1) or *raining*.

On the surface, in the two parts of the joke, both *raining* and *hailing* have null subjects, but on further examination we discover that they are different kinds of null subjects. Any appreciation of the joke has to tap the knowledge, tacit or otherwise, that these are different sorts of null subjects. The gerund-participle in English does not require an overt lexical subject. Thus, *hailing* (2) here, because it is a gerund-participle does not take a lexically filled subject. In contrast, *hailing* (1) as in *raining* (although it has been omitted here in the particular token [*it's*] *raining cats and dogs*) in its canonical sentential form requires the expletive *it* in subject position.[19]

Thus, the fact that English verbal gerund-participles do not require overt subjects allows both utterances to look similar superficially. However, the twist comes when we realize that in the first part of the riddle the participle *raining* has as an **elliptical subject** and auxiliary. Its elliptical subject is the pleonastic *it* and the elliptical auxiliary is *is*, (together, *it's*) whereas *hailing* in the second part has an **empty subject**. The ambiguity in interpretation of what the subject is in *raining cats and dogs* and *hailing taxis* depends on two independent facts about English:

(i)   the peculiar requirement that in the absence of real subjects, a pleonastic *it* or *there* should occur in subject position in **tensed** clauses (for example *it rained*) and

(ii) the licensing of empty pronoun subjects before **gerund-participle** forms of verbs that do take real arguments in subject position when they are not in the gerund form (for example, John *hailed a taxi*)

The joke is an elegant demonstration of the subtle fact that there are different kinds of null subjects in English.

In Example 20, we find an astute remark, reportedly made by the Mahatma Gandhi, in this, apparently genuine, piece of repartee. Gandhi's remark exploits a very fine point regarding the relationship between English syntax and semantics.

Example 20

Reporter: *Mr. Gandhi, what do you think of Western Civilization?*
Gandhi: *I think that it would be a very good idea.*

The joke is easy to understand, but it is not immediately obvious to see how it works.[20] In his response, Gandhi has skillfully manipulated some of the more complex features of English event structure.

Western Civilization is a nominal, a NP. It is odd, in general, for a referent to be said to be a good idea, or for the phrase *is a good idea* to be attributed to a common or garden nominal.

The second part of each example reveals the unnaturalness.

a.   Mr. Gandhi, what do you think of John?
     I think he would be a good idea.
b.   Mr. Gandhi, what do you think of China?
     I think it would be a good idea.
c.   Mr. Gandhi, what do you think of the music?
     I think it would be a good idea.
d.   Mr. Gandhi, what do you think of the pyramids?
     I think they would be a good idea.
e.   Mr. Gandhi, what do you think of old ladies?
     I think they would be a good idea.

Clearly, outside of a very restricted context, none of these sounds quite right. We would, instead, expect the answers to be along the lines of:

f.   Mr. Gandhi, what do you think of John?
     I think he talks too much.

g.   Mr. Gandhi, what do you think of China?
     I think it's an interesting country.

h.   Mr. Gandhi, what do you think of the music?
     I think it was played too loudly.

i.   Mr. Gandhi, what do you think of the pyramids?
     I think they're a tribute to the ingenuity of the Ancient Egyptians.

j.   Mr. Gandhi, what do you think of old ladies?
     I think they're crusty but sweet.

Clearly, then, these sorts of nominals can occur as part of a subordinate phrase in which the nominal is the subject NP and the tense of the verb is either past or present. None of them appears to be able to take the construction *would be a good idea.*

If we examine the problem further, we find that *Western Civilization* is part of a class of NPs known as event nominals. An event nominal is a NP that refers to an event as a single thing even though it might be made up of many actions that occurred over a period of time. Examples of event nominals are *Roman Civilization, The Paleolithic Age,* and *The Destruction of the Temple.*

We might test to see if Gandhi's retort would work with other event nominals we can list.

a.   */? *Mr. Gandhi, what do you think of Roman Civilization?*
     I think it would be a good idea.

b.   */? *Mr. Gandhi, what do you think of the moon landing?*
     I think it would be a good idea.

c.   */? *Mr. Gandhi, what do you think of the First World War?*
     I think it would be a good idea.

d.   *Mr. Gandhi, what do you think of water purification?*
     I think it would be a good idea.

e.   *Mr. Gandhi, what do you think of the banning of the bomb?*
     I think it would be a good idea.

f.   *Mr. Gandhi, what do you think of world peace?*
     I think it would be a good idea.

g.   *Mr. Gandhi, what do you think of dinner?*
     I think it would be a good idea.

Notice that (a)—(c) above do not work, but (d)—(g) do. The NPs in question are all event nominals, but only a subclass of these is able to work in conjunction with the response *I think it would be a good idea.* The only obvious difference between the two sets is that in the first one, (a)—(c), the events referred to have already taken place, *i.e.*, they have been completed. It is not particularly natural or logical to say that something that has already been completed would be a good idea, *i.e.*, that it would be a good idea if it were to take place in some unspecified future. The last four events, (d)—(g), on the other hand, could all take place at some unspecified future time. So, we can propose that it is only uncompleted, or uninitiated, events that might be appropriate in the slot *X would be a good idea*.

The joke is to be found in Gandhi's unpredicted response to the interviewer. When asked what he thought of Western civilization, he was probably expected to answer, *It's very impressive* or provide some such positive evaluation. Instead, he uses the event nominal in such a way that the very clear implication is created that Western civilization hasn't yet come into being, and, moreover, that he thinks it would be a good idea if it did. This is a masterful put-down, particularly since the interviewer was clearly fishing for a complimentary evaluation from Gandhi. The suggestion is also present that the West is not civilized at all, and Gandhi considers this lack of civilization to be a very undesirable situation.

Appreciation of the humor in this joke does not require sophisticated linguistic training. In that sense it stands as a marvelous example of a linguistic joke. All native speakers are able to get it, however, explaining why it strikes us as funny is not part of the package. A linguistically unsophisticated listener might be driven by the extraordinariness and unexpectedness of Gandhi's response to consider why this exchange is funny. The listener is not likely to engage in an analysis of event nominals, however; simply recognizing that the utterance is odd and wondering why is evidence for the claim that jokes evoke tacit linguistic knowledge. On the other hand, understanding how the joke works linguistically, as has been demonstrated in the analyses of many of the sorts of jokes considered here, is a technical matter. When fully explicated, of course, linguistic jokes are rarely funny anymore, but spoiling the fun is a widespread occupational hazard of dissection.

2.3 Lexical Ambiguity, Multicategoriality and Syntactic Ambiguity

The message shown in Example 21 is often found on the office doors of syntacticians, or used in introductory linguistics classes.

Example 21

Time flies like an arrow. Fruit flies like a banana.

(Groucho Marx, 1890–1977)

Apparently this message has the effect of making passersby think that syntacticians have no life, or that the passersby themselves are stupid. In general, this does not contribute much to the recruitment of hordes of first year linguistics students. The remark is one of those jokes that you can't sort of get. You do or you don't, and it is set up so you don't until you do.

There is an expanding set of jokes that are dependent on the sort of garden path effect used in this joke.[21] The first sentence primes the listener to parse the second sentence in the same way as the first, *i.e.*, by analogy with *time flies like an arrow: fruit* (NP) *flies like a banana* (VP); the VP is made up of *flies* (V) and *like a banana* (PP); *the PP is made up of like* (P) and *a banana* (NP) (see Figure 5.22). There's nothing particularly funny if we parse the second sentence in parallel with the first. *Time flies like an arrow:* we know this old chestnut, comparing the passage of time to the swiftness of an arrow shot from a bow. On the other hand, *fruit flies like a banana?* Why should fruit fly in the same way as a banana does? It makes no sense.

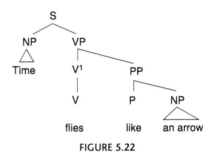

FIGURE 5.22

The joke hinges on the ambiguities inherent in the relevant words used in different syntactic categories. *Fruit* could be a noun phrase or the modifier of *flies; flies* could be a singular present tense verb or a plural noun and *like* could function as a comparative preposition or a plural verb.

Thus, once we realize that the second sentence should be understood as *Fruit flies* (NP subject) *like a banana* (VP) we understand that this is a simple descriptive fact about fruit flies, insects, who, acting in accord with their name, like to swarm around bananas (see Figure 5.23).

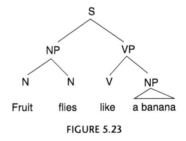

FIGURE 5.23

Along the same lines, Example 22, cast as a Question-Answer pair, plays with *flies*.

Example 22

Q: *What has four wheels and flies?*
A: *A garbage truck.*

Or, for even more grim clarity, consider Example 23, a more appealing one, right out of my childhood.

Example 23

Q: *What has four legs and flies?*
A: *A dead horse.*

In both these cases, the ambiguity turns on the multicategoriality and lexical ambiguity of *flies*. Since children, for whom these jokes are intended, are used to Question/Answer riddle jokes with a similar syntactic format (although a different humor mechanism) such as found in Example 24, they are probably primed to think that *flies* in Examples 22 and 23 is a verb.

Example 24

Q: *What was purple and <u>conquered</u> the world?*
A: *Alexander the Grape*

Following this sort of template, listeners would process *flies* in Examples 22 and 23 as a verb. Getting the joke consists in realizing that trucks don't fly, and therefore, to make any sense at all, *flies* must be a noun. It's not necessary that this knowledge be articulated for the joke to be appreciated, simply that the listener notices that there's something odd about the way that *flies* is used. And, of course, in natural discourse, trucks do fly.

2.4 Homophony and Syntactic Ambiguity

As we have already seen, syntactic ambiguity stemming from lexical ambiguity and lexical multicategoriality is a source of linguistic humor in English. The fact that English is replete with homophones, as well as multicategorial lexical items, allows jokers to exploit syntactic ambiguity based on homophony. In Example 25 we see how syntactic ambiguity based on certain homophonous items produces this cynical take on George W. Bush (president of the USA at the time of the joke, 2005). *Roe v. Wade* was a landmark case that was decided by the US Supreme Court in 1973, as a result of which abortion (up until the time a fetus became viable) was declared to be legally available on demand by a pregnant woman.

Example 25

Q: *What is Bush's position on Roe v. Wade?*
A: *He really doesn't care how people get out of New Orleans.*

The riddle/joke manages, at the same time, to criticize Bush's well known objection to the rulings emerging from the case of *Roe v. Wade* as well as to suggest that Bush doesn't care much for the poor people of New Orleans stranded by the floods that occurred in the wake of Hurricane Katrina in 2005. The homophonous *row* and *wade* are verbs in English. *Row* is phonologically identical to *Roe*. The joke works better orally, as do many jokes that depend on sound. Given that this joke was circulating around the time of the aftermath of Hurricane Katrina, and the Bush administration was generally regarded as not doing enough in the way of disaster relief, the context is the factor that vitalizes the joke. As always, the context (in this case of time and place, particularly) legitimizes the interpretation of the question that is posed. The question in the first part, which concerns Bush's position on a court ruling, is answered, quite legitimately, as a comment on his callousness regarding the indigent people of New Orleans who had been struck by the disaster. The question in the first part is, therefore, understood as asking whether it would be better for people if they were to row, as opposed to wading through the floodwaters. The sound of the question allows the implicature to be drawn that Bush doesn't care if people row or wade to get out of the flooded city of New Orleans.

This response is a clever use of phonological identity, as well as a swift reassignment of syntactic category in the case of the two names, *Roe* and *Wade*. *Roe* and *Wade* are nominals, whereas *row* and *wade* are verbs. Moreover, the joke manages to comment on Bush's stance on the landmark court ruling at the same time as on his indifference to the victims of the disaster.

A very simple demonstration of how phonological identification and multicategoriality are exploited can be seen in the following quasi-riddle in Example 26. It's not a real riddle because its only *raison d'être* is to be a vehicle for some shrewd and witty wordplay.

Example 26

Q: *What's the difference between roast beef and pea soup?*
A: *Anyone can roast beef.*

Roast beef is a certain kind of beef, and *pea soup* is soup consisting primarily of peas. Of course, in English, *roast* can be used as a verb as well as a noun and an adjective. In the question part here, *roast* functions as part of a noun–noun compound (or as an adjective modifying *beef*), and in the answer part as a verb.

The syntactic structure of *roast beef* in the first sentence is probably a noun–noun compound, behaving like a simple Noun Phrase.[22]

The syntactic structure of *roast beef* in the second part of the utterance is Verb Phrase, analyzed as V NP. The joke rests in the fact that *pea soup* may be regarded as a Noun Phrase and analyzed roughly and superficially in the same way as *roast beef* in the first utterance (on the reading that *roast beef* is a kind of beef, and *pea soup* is a kind of soup). *Pea soup* may be analyzed, like *roast beef*, as a composite nominal NP. The expectation set up on the basis of the surface similarity between *roast beef* and *pea soup* is that if one can roast beef, one can pea soup. Of course, *roast beef* is beef that is roasted and *pea soup* is not soup that is *pea*-ed, whatever that might mean. The similarity of structure goes only as far as the proposal that they are both Noun Phrases, although different in kind. However, the pivot of the joke is that there's a homophonous pair implied here: *pea* (the legume) and *pee* (to urinate). Of course, *pea* and *pee* do not mean the same thing and are in no way related words—they simply sound the same. The joke rests in the fact that although soup is a liquid, the only liquid that can be urinated is urine. The joke does not actually say that nobody can pee (*pea*) soup, it simply creates the inescapable implicature by setting up the scenario, using a particular syntactic structure, inviting the parallel structure (having set up *roast beef* and *pea soup* earlier) and then activating the contrast by using *Anyone can* to introduce the VP structure.

Example 27 also plays with homophony in interaction with multicategoriality, leading to syntactic ambiguity of the whole. The relevant items here are *ark/Arc*, and *made/Maid*.

Example 27

If Noah's Ark was made of wood then Joan of Arc was Maid of Orleans.

As we all know from the Bible story in Genesis, Noah was a righteous man who built an ark (something like a big covered ship) out of wood to save some of the living from a huge flood sent as a punishment by the god of Genesis. Joan of Arc, or more precisely, Saint Joan of Arc, Jeanne d'Arc, (ca. 1412–1431), a French heroine and a Catholic saint, born in Orleans, was said to be a maid who led the French forces to victory before being burned at the stake. "Joan of Arc" is the referent of *Maid of Orleans*, since it is claimed that she was a virgin girl who led the troops to victory. The first play we get, then, is that of the homophonous *ark/Arc*. In English these sound the same. *D'Arc*, was, in fact, Joan's identifier (equivalent in use to a surname). In translation this is "of Arc". So she is Joan of *Arc*, in English; and Noah's *Ark* was a wooden vessel, according to legend.

The two statements comprising Example 27 sound as though they each convey information that is in some way parallel. The utterance takes the form of an *if p then q* proposition, which further reinforces the structural parallel between the two sentences. However, of course, one *ark* is a common noun, the other *Arc* is a place name; *made* is a verb, whereas *maid* is a noun. The first part tells us the materials of which a vessel was constructed; the second part tells us that a certain person was also known by another name.

Thus, the first part proposition tells us that Noah's Ark was made of wood, or made out of wood. The PP *of wood* is attached to the V *made*. The second proposition tells us that Joan of Arc was Maid of Orleans. *Maid of Orleans* is a NP, consisting of a noun *maid* and a PP, *of Orleans*. The NP *Maid of Orleans* is sister to the V *was*. There is almost no parallel between the two propositions in meaning, nor in any structure other than the totally superficial surface one, and the utterance itself is totally nonsensical. However, the utterance sounds like a philosophical proposition from which some deep insight is to be gleaned. We hear something like "if aX was made of Y; then bX was made of Z", and because of the structural similarity of the propositions, we assume there is some kind of connection.

Essentially, the effect of this incongruous and gratuitous parallel is gained by exploiting sound parallelism and also the similarity of overt syntactic structure. The cleverness consists in the fact that these two entities have nothing whatever to do with each other (despite a well-known fallacious piece of nonsense that perpetuates the idea that Joan of Arc was Noah's wife). The joke is thus an exploitation of homophony, multicategoriality (*maid* is a noun, whereas *made of* is a complex adjectival construction) and syntactic ambiguity.

Interestingly, if the propositions were to be reversed, the resulting utterance would not be nearly as amusing. Thus,

If Joan of Arc was Maid of Orleans, then Noah's Ark was made of wood.

The reason is probably because in the joke, the trigger word is *made*, just as the trigger phrase is *made of wood*. This phrase is necessary for the following proposition to have even a semblance of sense. Thus, it is *made* that triggers the use of *Maid*, and not vice versa.

In Example 28 we see homophony, multicategoriality and syntactic ambiguity used as logical ju-jitsu. Just when you think you are going one way, you find yourself and your expectations overturned. In the example, the speaker exploits the distinction between *over* (with the reading "above") and *over* (with the reading "again") by using them in superficially similar syntactic positions, although the two sentences are quite clearly syntactically very different.

Example 28

If I had to live over again, I'd live over a delicatessen.[23]

The first part begins with a counterfactual, *If I had to live over again*. It's reasonable to expect that the speaker will now tell us what he would do if he had the opportunity, or was compelled, to live over again, *i.e.*, to have his life again. We expect that he will tell us about different choices he would make, and indeed he does. He says he would choose to live over a delicatessen. Punning on *over*, he has entirely rearranged the phrase structure of the first utterance. *Live over*, as a phrase, means "have my life to live again". *Live over a delicatessen* means to "live above a delicatessen". *Over* in the second sentence is a simple preposition, in no way part of the verb as it is in the phrasal verb complex, **live over** again. The analysis of *live over* as a phrasal verb is ensured by the use of the adverb *again*. If we examine the surface parallelism between (a) and (b), we can see that they have entirely different underlying structures.

(a) I would live over again
(b) I would live over a delicatessen.

    In the first case, the VP consists of phrasal V+adverb (see Figure 5.24); in the second, the VP consists of V¹+PP (see Figure 5.25)

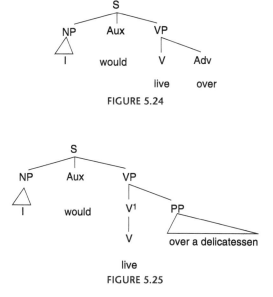

FIGURE 5.24

FIGURE 5.25

    The humor is to be found in the contrast between the rather profound first part of the conditional, in which the speaker considers revising his major life choices, and the second part, which, for most of us, is somewhat more trivial, the decision to live over a delicatessen rather than in some other location. The joke suggests that for some, perhaps, the decisions are equivalent.

    Example 29 is a clever example of a children's riddle, in which we see some sophisticated word play involving superficially similar syntactic structures and exploiting distinctions between phrasal and non-phrasal verbs, specifically playing on the ambiguous sense and syntactic class of the word *down*.

Example 29

Q: *What do ducks do before they grow up?*
A: *They grow down.*[24]

This riddle recruits a play between two meanings of a particular word, *down*, and the ambiguity in sense between the phrasal verb *grow up*, and the verb *grow* in its sense as a middle verb, such as in *grow hair*.[25] In both cases, *grow* is used as a verb. *Grow up* is a phrasal verb meaning "to advance in age". *Grow down* is something that ducks do, *i.e.*, acquire a sort of feathering. In this case, *up* is part of the phrasal verb *grow up*, but by logical analogy (and no reference to semantics), ducks that grow up should also grow down. And indeed, the answer is that ducks do grow down. If we read *down* as the directional opposite of *up*, the answer makes very little sense. However, *down* is also a noun, with the sense of "feathers". The joke-evoking contrast is between *up* and *down,* the polar opposites of directionality. The structure of *grow up* is VP →V+particle (see Figure 5.26), whereas the structure of *grow down* is VP→V+NP (see Figure 5.27). The lexical ambiguity and multicategoriality of *down* is responsible for the possibility of syntactic ambiguity.

FIGURE 5.26   FIGURE 5.27

The contrast is as follows:
$[_{vp} [_v \text{grow up}]]$
$[_{vp} [_v \text{grow}] [_{NP} \text{down}]]$

The beauty of the joke is that it is true.

Sometimes, even when no syntax is overtly present, it is evoked as a result of homophony, or a bad pun. Example 30 comes from the movie, *Young Frankenstein* (1974), which is a spoof on the genre of Frankenstein movies. We encounter a character called Igor, who is Dr. Frankenstein's factotum. Igor, being foreign for the purpose of the movie, (in which everyone is actually foreign, since it is set in Transylvania) lapses into his idea of foreigner talk, when dealing with new foreigners. We hear an animal howling sound in the background. Inga is the young lab assistant.

Example 30

Inga:	*Werewolf!*
Dr. Frederick Frankenstein:	***Werewolf?***
Igor:	*There.*
Dr. Frederick Frankenstein:	***What?***
Igor:	*There, wolf. There, castle.*

In this exchange, the surprised and anxious question, *Werewolf?* uttered by Frankenstein, wondering if the sound they had heard was made by a werewolf (actually hoping that what Inga was saying was not what he thought she was saying) is interpreted by Igor as a question as to the whereabouts of a wolf. Igor does not bother with the niceties of the missing copula *is*, but simply provides the answer to the question he thinks he hears, *Where wolf?* and helpfully answers, *There.* When Frankenstein doesn't seem to understand the answer, Igor elaborates, *There wolf,* again omitting the copula by way of responding to the form of the question. And in case Frankenstein still doesn't get it, pointing in another direction, *There castle.*

As we have seen, the jokes in this chapter are extremely (English) language specific, because they turn on language particular structural ambiguities in conjunction with words that are multicategorial. Jokes like these, or parallel to these, tend to be produced in spoken language, or in some cases (with varying degrees of success) in writing as well. In terms of faithful translatability,[26] these linguistic jokes are well nigh impossible, unless the translation is into a language that is historically related to the extent that there are structural as well as lexical similarities, *e.g.*, with luck, English into German, or German into Dutch.

Example 31 exhibits semantic and syntactic ambiguities, but although it can be told orally, it relies additionally on our knowledge (or recollection) of a punctuation ambiguity. In the famous panda joke, as retold by Lynne Truss, a panda goes into a bar, asks for a ham sandwich, eats it and then takes out a revolver and fires it into the air. When the barman asks him what on earth he is doing, he throws a book on to the bar and growls: "This is a badly punctuated wildlife manual. Look me up." The barman looks through the book and, under the relevant entry, reads: "PANDA. Large, black-and-white bear-like mammal native to China. Eats, shoots and leaves." (Truss, 2003).

Example 31

Eats, shoots and leaves

The joke centers on the absence or presence of a particular comma, or in speech, on the pause structure *i.e.*, whether the relevant fragment should read, or be heard as, "*Eats, shoots and leaves*" or "*Eats shoots, and leaves.*" Truss uses this joke to illustrate a point about punctuation. In fact, the joke turns on the semantic and syntactic ambiguity involved in whether *shoots* is to be understood as a noun, the plural of *shoot*, "a new plant growth" or as a verb, meaning "to fire a projectile from a weapon", as well as the semantic and syntactic ambiguity of *leaves*. *Leaves* may be understood as a noun, the plural of *leaf*, or as a verb, present tense, meaning "to depart", to be co-ordinated with the verb form *shoots*.

There's a slightly raunchier Australian equivalent in which it is the Wombat, rather than the Panda, that is the animal to be defined. The details and the set up of the joke need to be changed to fit the context more appropriately. However, in this case it is the Wombat that *eats(,) roots(,) and leaves*. The verb *root* in Australian

English is a slang term meaning "to copulate". There are also jokes about the Australian surfer who is like a wombat, because he eats (,) roots (,) shoots (surfs a wave, or ejaculates) and leaves. There's even an Australian joke about a Wombat and a prostitute (whom the Wombat shoots when she demands payment), in which the punch line is *Look me up. WOMBAT: Eats(,) roots(,) shoots and leaves.*[27]

In the Panda/Wombat examples, I would argue that actually the semantic and syntactic ambiguities are the conditions of possibility for the joke. Punctuation, or pause structure, would alert the listener/reader to the preferred phrasal categories, but it is essentially the semantic and hence syntactic ambiguities that create the possibility for the joke to be made. The badly placed (or omitted) commas simply accentuate the possibility of ambiguities. The real issues here are homophony, grammatical category and syntactic structure, rather than simply punctuation. Truss uses this joke as an illuminating example for her argument that punctuation is underestimated in terms of its functional importance for communicative clarity (and, as in this case, as serious a matter as life-or-death). In my view, the joke works even if it is not in written form. Comprehension of oral language precedes that of the written word, although, indeed, as Truss claims, in written languages, clear punctuation may sometimes give us a way out of ambiguity.

The sorts of jokes discussed in this chapter do not require any great technical knowledge about language in order to be enjoyed. Although they are linguistic jokes, they can be appreciated not only by language boffins, linguists and language teachers. So, why is it that people think these jokes are funny? Is it because of the ambiguity of meaning? We can explain that ambiguity in linguistic textbooks. Humor needs more than ambiguity. The trick seems to be in turning the linguistic ambiguity or problem into the pivot for a situation that spirals out of control because of the absurdity inherent in the ambiguity.[28] Why we consider a joke to be funny is a matter for humor theorists. Recognizing the joke requires access to tacit knowledge of language, and this is a matter for linguists concerned with grammatical knowledge and ways in which it might be accessed.

Notes

1 For reasons of simplicity, I have taken for granted that phrases are made up of morphological units (words) and that these, in turn, are composed of phonemes.
2 A discussion as to what causes a joke to be a joke is, strictly, beyond the scope of this book. However, I take a broadly Incongruity Theory based approach to why people find jokes funny. My concern is to show systematically how the humor in a linguistic joke is created, rather than to distinguish between jokes and non-jokes.
3 I use the standard abbreviations for phrases, thus Noun Phrase is NP; Verb Phrase is VP; Adjective Phrase is AdjP; Preposition Phrase is PP; AdvP for Adverb Phrase. Similarly I use N for noun; V for verb; Adj for adjective; P for preposition; Adv for adverb; D for determiner; Aux for auxiliary and Part for particle.
4 This remarkable discourse continues in order for Groucho to manage to get in a spectacularly egregious pun.

It's hard to get ivory in Africa, but in Alabama the Tuscaloosa
This pun is noteworthy also because it condenses almost an entire sentence into a phonological word. *The* remains *in situ* for the reading "Tuscaloosa" and "tusks are looser".

5 In these examples I am ignoring X bar levels unless absolutely necessary, because although technically more precise, they obscure the central point I am trying to demonstrate.

6 Presumably the ambiguity would disappear if there were a phonological pause before the post-verbal PP as in: *Eighty percent of married men cheat, | | in America.*

7 The original of this joke apparently dates back to the 1800s. There are a number of variations. See for instance, *Flywheel, Shyster and Flywheel,* a radio program featuring Groucho and Chico Marx.

8 Technically, *say* subcategorizes for what linguists nowadays call a Complementizer Phrase (CP). Traditionally, this is known as an embedded subordinate clause.

9 A double object construction is one in which both the direct object and indirect object occur as NPs, thus VP→VNP NP.

10 Small clauses are minimal predicate structures. They consist of arguments and predicates, but no tense. They usually occur within the context of a main clause, and may serve as the internal argument of the verb. Thus, in the examples below, the italicized words are small clauses.
We painted *the house white*
I saw *John eat the apple*
I consider *him a fool*
I believe *him guilty*
Eggs make *me sick.*

11 More accurately NP should be DP, but this is simplified for the purpose of not obscuring my central point, which is about the embedded PPs.

12 See the discussion of small clauses following Example 15 above.

13 The wearing of this T-shirt during World Youth Day celebrations was prohibited, under threat of an AUD$5, 000 fine.

14 Obviously, the ambiguity can be avoided if *down under* is kept *in situ* and another PP of place is added: *In Rome, I was touched by the Pope down under.*
Clearly the slogan was meant to be ambiguous, however, because it was just too good to be true.

15 In these trees I have represented Aux as a separate category and oversimplified the passive construction. Nothing in my analysis hinges on this, since I am concerned here only with the placement of the PP.

16 I am grateful to David Schalkwyk for giving me this joke.

17 I use the term "valency" here to refer to the number of arguments (role players) a verb requires for the sentence to be grammatical.

18 Huddleston & Pullum remark that English has no gerund form *per se*; it has a single form of the paradigm that approximates the work of the Latin present participle and the Latin gerund. They call that form the **gerund-participle** (Huddleston & Pullum, 2002).

19 It's possible that one account for the omission of *it's* in *it's raining* is phonological. *It*, being pleonastic, cannot bear stress, and in fast speech *it is* may be pronounced *ts*, leading to a form like *tsraining,* which very easily allows the deletion of *ts.*

20 I'm grateful to Mengistu Amberber for helping me with this, among many other analyses.

21 The garden path effect is so known because it describes constructions that (often deliberately) lead hearers/readers up the garden path, *i.e.,* astray. Garden path sentences are used in processing experiments in order to show that the syntactic parser can occasionally be tricked.

22 To test this idea, we might try modification with an adjective. If a compound NP is modified by an adjective, the adjective cannot come between the two lexical items: *i.e.*, we can say *The French roast beef* but not *✶The roast French beef*.

23 I am unable to find the source of this remark. I've seen it attributed to different people, including Woody Allen and some Country 'n Western composers.

24 I am grateful to James Schalkwyk for giving me this wonderful joke.

25 Verbs that allow the middle alternation express the bringing about of a change of state. However, unlike in the causative alternation, in the middle alternation, there is no agent, simply a theme in subject position. For a more detailed discussion of this topic, see Riemer 2010, p. 251ff. and the references therein.

26 This diagnostic for linguistic jokes goes back to Cicero. Issues regarding humor and translation are given a full treatment by Chiaro 2008. See also Chapter 1.

27 I bracket the commas, for the purpose of presenting both readings.

28 For a fuller treatment of ambiguity theories, see Attardo (1994), Raskin (2008) and Ritchie (2004).

6

A CASE STUDY: *WORD ASSOCIATION FOOTBALL*

In order to demonstrate the kind of humor that can be created using ambiguity at phonological, morphological, semantic, syntactic and pragmatic levels of linguistic knowledge, I dissect a remarkable and extended joke, first appearing on the album, *Monty Python's Matching Tie and Handkerchief* (Chapman, Cleese, Gilliam, Idle, Jones, & Palin, 1989/90).

The comedy team, *Monty Python's Flying Circus* is the source of many extended jokes that exploit different aspects of the structure of English to humorous effect. One such skit, *Word Association Football*, uses a well-established technique of psychoanalysis, often played as a verbal game, "word association". The idea of the technique, and now of the game, is for a person to free associate and supply any word that a previous word evokes. The Pythons take this basic format to new heights, specifically because of their crafty use of pseudo-morphemes, homophony, morphemic reanalysis, lexical-semantic and syntactic ambiguity.

Of course, much of the humor also lies in the presentation—the speaker barely pauses for breath, interspersing word and sound associations with fragments of embedded speech acts, appropriately enunciated. However, the genius of the wit is to be found in the recognition that syllables are essentially meaningless, morphemes are very often sound-meaning combinations only in context, and words can be multicategorial.

Word Association Football

Tonight's the night I shall be talking about of flu the subject of word association football. This is a technique out a living much used in the practice makes perfect of psychoanalysister and brother and one that has occupied piper the majority rule of my attention squad by the right number one two three four the last five years to the memory. It is quite remarkable bakercharlie how much the miller's son this so-called

while you were out word association immigrants' problems influences the manner from
heaven in which we sleekit cowering timrous beasties all-American Speke, the famous
explorer. And the really well that is surprising partner in crime is that a lot and his
wife of the lions' feeding time we may be c d e effectively quite unaware of the fact or
fiction section of the Watford Public Library that we are even doing it is a far, far better
thing that I do now then, now then, what's going onward Christian Barnard the
famous hearty part of the lettuce now praise famous mental homes for loonies like me.
So on the button, my contention causing all the headaches, is that unless we take into
account of Monte Cristo in our thinking George the Fifth this phenomenon the other
hand we shall not be able satisFact or Fiction section of the Watford Public Library
againily to understand to attention when I'm talking to you and stop laughing, about
human nature, man's psychological make-up some story the wife'll believe and hence
the very meaning of life itselfish bastard, I'll kick him in the balls pond road.

(Cleese, John 2000 in A Pocketful of Python, *vol. 2)*

At risk of destroying this forever, I attempt to explicate as many of the jokes in
this piece as I can, firstly, find, and secondly, understand. It should be remembered
that this speech is delivered orally, ostensibly as a presentation, so the listener does
not have much hope of catching all of it on the first listening. Luckily, I have a
copy of the scripts, so was able to piece together most of what I think was said
on the recording.

Strangely enough, there is an underlying template of sensible and logical
discourse in this piece, although it is in no way necessary for our understanding
of the linguistic humor. We cannot speculate on John Cleese's creative process
here, but if I were to dare to do so, I would say that he probably started out with
a piece of coherent text and then dealt with it in his virtuoso way, following the
principles of word association to the maximum.[1] Below is what I consider to be
his original text, which is perfectly coherent and logical, and even makes sense. I
have reconstructed it from a time-consuming, but not unrewarding unpicking of
each and every joke.[2]

Word Association
**Tonight I shall be talking about the subject of word association.
This is a technique much used in the practice of psychoanalysis
and one that has occupied the majority of my attention for the
last five years. It is quite remarkable how much this so-called
word association influences the manner in which we speak. And
the really surprising part is that a lot of the time we may be
effectively quite unaware of the fact that we are even doing it. So,
my contention is that unless we take into account in our thinking
this phenomenon we shall not be able satisfactorily to understand
human nature, man's psychological make-up and hence the very
meaning of life itself.**

The speaker starts out by creating a particular speech event: he is delivering a speech and as is customary with this formal sort of speech event, he begins with an introductory speech act, *i.e.*, telling his audience that he is going to talk and what he is going to talk about. However, taking Austin's (1962) notion of performativity to a new height, he is not only going to say what he is doing, he is going to do it. Since he is giving a talk on the topic of word association, while giving the talk, he is practicing word association. Word association is a technique first developed by Carl Gustav Jung (1875–1961). Its purpose was to unearth the unconscious connections in the psyche, by asking people to talk aloud about any topic and allow themselves to free associate on each word or phrase they come up with. The connections are neither expected nor required to be logical. For the linguist, as opposed to the (psycho)analyst, this sort of technique may tell us about how lexical items are arranged in the mind, either by sound relationships, meaning relationships, form relationships or other, non-linguistic associations in the world or the mind of the speaker. Cleese undertakes this task thoroughly, demonstrating, among other things, that these associations do not have to be restricted to whole words, but to any part of words or to more than one word as a chunk. The presentation is a demonstration to the letter (or sound) of the technique as intended by its originator. At the same time it explodes conventional psychoanalytical expectations and ravages what we know about linguistic categorization.

The title itself is a joke: *word association* is the name of the technique; the first word the speaker associates is with *association*, i.e., *football*. *Association Football* is the official name of soccer. This word game the speaker is playing, previously regarded as a kind of verbal ping pong if played by more than one person, is now recast as a kind of football game. Then he starts the talk itself, by announcing, *Tonight*. Immediately he associates that with the well-known phrase *tonight's the night*, the rest of which he inserts. Then he moves back to the template *I shall be speaking about*. Immediately, the two syllables in *about* trigger a reanalysis, into *a bout*, and are then associated with flu, rendering *a bout of flu*. So what started out as a preposition (*about*) becomes a noun phrase. Then he returns to the sentence he began and says he will be talking about the subject of word association football (repeating the association first made in the title). He continues, *This is a technique*, and then misanalyzes the sound of the last syllable of *technique* as the verb *eke*, which then triggers the verb phrase *eke out a living*. He returns again to the sentence from which he had strayed, and explains that the technique is much used in the *practice*, (which he then associates with *perfect*, producing the phrase *practice makes perfect*, then continues as though the interruption did not happen) *of psychoanalysis*.

The last syllable of *psychoanalysis* is similar in sound to the first syllable of *sister*, so he continues with the word *sister*, which in turn is associated with *and brother*. The sentence interrupted at *psychoanalysis* is then continued, along the track I mapped above, *This is a technique much used in the practice of psychoanalysis and one that has occupied....* The last syllable of *occupied, pied* then triggers an association with *piper*, so is now to be understood as forming the adjective *pied* and a new noun phrase, *pied piper.* Then, without pausing, as though uninterrupted by *piper*, he continues from *occupied* to *the majority*, completing the verb phrase, *occupied the majority. Majority* then triggers an association with *rule*, so yielding the noun phrase, *majority rule.* Again, as though uninterrupted, he returns *to the majority*, in order to complete the complex noun phrase with its prepositional phrase, *of my attention. Attention* then triggers the military order, a barked *Attention squad by the right number.* Whilst in the midst of this order, he associates *number* with *one two three four*, returning to his proposed message where he had left off at *attention*, seamlessly transforming *four* into *for* and completing a prepositional phrase, *for the last five years.* From *years* he finds a sound association with *here's* and produces an association with *Here's: Here's to the memory.* So the sentence he began is completed, and without associations, reads perfectly grammatically and logically as follows:

> *This is a technique much used in the practice of psychoanalysis and one that has occupied the majority of my attention for the last five years.*

He then resumes his talk, beginning the next sentence *It is quite remarkable*, when he is ambushed by *able* in *remarkable* which he then associates with *baker charlie*, to produce *able baker charlie*, the first three words in the NATO alphabet, corresponding to a, b, c. Returning to *remarkable*, he continues, [*It is remarkable*] *how much*, and interrupts himself to add *the miller's son*, alluding to a character in English folklore, Much the Miller's Son. Recalling *how much*, he continues *this so-called*, and once again interrupts his flow by finding an association with *called*, to produce the phrase *called while you were out.* Returning to *so-called* he adds the noun phrase *word association.* Thus far, according to my mapping of his intentional text, he has reached *It is quite remarkable how much this so-called word association.* The last two syllables of *Association* sound enough like *Asian* to trigger the remainder of the phrase, *immigrants*, and to yield the noun phrase, *Asian immigrants. Immigrants* in turn triggers *problems*, forming *immigrants' problems*, a well-worked phrase in Britain at this time (the early 1970s). The sentence he is busy trying to produce is re-joined thus, according to my map [*It is quite remarkable how much this so-called word association*] *influences the manner. Manner* sounds the same as *manna* and thus triggers the noun phrase incorporating the prepositional phrase, *manna from heaven*, so he inserts *from heaven* before he returns to modify *manner*, by adding *in which we.* Instead of supplying the verb or auxiliary one would expect to follow *we*, he notices the sound of *we* is identical to that of *wee*, and inserts the opening line of Robert Burns' poem, *The Mouse: "Wee, sleekit, cowrin, tim'rous beastie"*, (translated as "small, sleek, cowering little beast"). Next he adds *−al* to the end of *beastie*, making *bestial*, and then using *−al* as similar enough to *all*, he creates *all-American. Speke* follows the *can* of *Americans (I think)*, forming *all-Americans speak.* Speke was indeed a famous explorer as the speaker points out. He completes the phrase that had begun with *we*, adding the verb phrase to produce *we speak.* Thus, we can extract another fully formed sentence, *sans* interruptions and associations: *It is quite remarkable how much this so-called word association influences the manner in which we speak.*

The speaker begins the next sentence, *And the really*, then associates *really* with *well*, so producing *really well*, followed by another association with *well, well well,* which leads him to add, *that is surprising*, a common expression*,* that returns him to his target, which he seems to intend, *the really surprising part.* However, *part* immediately triggers *partner*, which is then associated with *crime* to yield *partner in crime.* Recalling the noun phrase headed by *part*, he adds what starts out as a verb phrase, *is that a lot. Lot* triggers the biblical association *and his wife.* Returning to *lot*, he continues, *of the.* Instead of completing the phrase, *lot of the time*, he links *of* with *the lion's feeding time. Time* brings him back to what he was going to say anyway and he begins the new clause with *we may be.*

Be triggers *c, d e* and *f*, neatly bringing him to the first syllable of *effectively quite unaware of the fact. Fact* is then associated with *fiction. Fiction* triggers the association with *the fiction section of the Watford Public Library*, before he resumes the clause embedded into *fact: that we are even doing it. It* unleashes a string of associations: *It is a far far better thing that I do now than*, the beginning of the famous last line from *A Tale of Two Cities*, by Charles Dickens. *Now than* triggers an association with the rather predictable British Plod catch phrase, famous from other parodies, *Now then, now then, what's going on?* He integrates this into the preceding string, creating, *It is a far far better thing I do now then now then what's going on. On* triggers the association with the hymn *Onward Christian Soldiers*, but before completing the full phrase, he associates *Christian* with *Barnard*. Christian Barnard was a famous heart surgeon who successfully performed the first heart transplant in the late 1960s. So he continues *Christian Barnard the famous heart*, then transforms *heart* into *hearty* which triggers the association *lettuce.* The hearty part of the lettuce is where the heart of the lettuce is. *Lettuce* is reanalyzed because it sounds the same as *let us*, so we now have what was a noun transformed into a hortative construction (*lettuce* into *let us*). Once again, a catch phrase is triggered, *let us now praise famous men.* The sound of the noun *men* is identical with the first syllable of *mental* so this causes *mental homes* to be produced, and with not much of an associated jump at all, triggers *for loonies like me.* Thus, all of this was generated in the attempt to produce the sentence: *And the really surprising part is that a lot of the time we may be effectively quite unaware of the fact that we are even doing it.*

As he no doubt is.

He begins the next sentence, *So*, immediately recognizing its identical pronunciation this with the sound of the word *sew*, then adding the association *on the button.* The logical connector *so* is transformed first into a verb (sew) and then a phrasal verb (sew on) followed by its object. He continues his rhetoric, using *my contention* as his introductory noun phrase. The last two syllables of *contention* sound the same as *tension*, and with this he associates *causing all the headaches.* Ignoring his own interruption, he continues the sentence he began that started

So, my contention and adds to it *is that unless we take into account.* The last syllable of *account* is homophonous with the word *count*, which is, of course, associated with *of Monte Cristo*, a character out of a book by Alexander Dumas. Resuming the sentence in his conscious planning, [*So my contention is that unless we take into account*] *in our thinking*, he is triggered by the last syllable of *thinking* the sound identity with the word *king*, and immediately associates with that *George the Fifth*. Undeterred, he pushes on, remembering to add *this phenomenon* after ignoring his own interruption after *take into account in our thinking.* The last syllable of *phenomenon* is reanalyzed as the preposition *on,* and this triggers the phrase, *on the other hand.*

Having now managed to sustain the entire clause, *unless we take into account in our thinking this phenomenon*, he begins uttering the new clause, *we shall not be able satisfactor-.* We would predict he would be aiming to produce *satisfactorily*, but his associations are triggered by the last two syllables he produces, *fact-or.* These are reanalyzed into *fact or,* and he is driven to add *fiction,* and then to this attach the previous association *of the Watford Public Library* and then add *again* to this, to remind us that he remembers that he has mentioned this section of the library before. However, not forgetting that he began the word *satisfactor-,* he adds the missing morpheme, *-ily* to the end of the infixed association, producing *againily.* So, the clause beginning *we shall not be able satisfactorily* continues with the infinitive *to understand.* The last syllable of *understand* is identical in sound to the verb *stand,* and this is associated with the military (or school) rebuke, *stand to attention when I'm talking to you and stop laughing. Laughing* triggers *about* and then he neatly adds the noun phrase he was aiming for, to the preposition *about,* forming *about human nature.* In apposition to *human nature,* he adds *man's psychological make-up.* So the clause thus far, without the associations, is probably *, we shall not be able to understand human nature, man's psychological make-up. Make-up,* a noun in this case, is then reanalyzed into a phrasal verb, and triggers another catch–phrase, *make up some story the wife'll believe.* Ignoring the interruption completely, the speaker returns to his argument, having completed the clause and now launching the final proposition, *and hence the very meaning of life itself.*

This is where the sentence ends, grammatically, and is a suitable note on which the argument could end, but *self* triggers the association *selfish* and *selfish* triggers *bastard. Selfish bastard* triggers a phrase often used in talking about selfish bastards, *I'll kick him in the balls. Balls,* a noun, triggers *Ball's Pond Road,* the name of a road in Islington, London; the pond presumably named after someone called Ball, and the road the one that runs to the pond.

The planned sentence, which triggered all these associations, is most likely the following: *So, my contention is that unless we take into account in our thinking this phenomenon we shall not be able satisfactorily to understand human nature, man's psychological make-up and hence the very meaning of life itself.*

In the exposition above, I have attempted to show how in this inspired piece of brilliance, Cleese exploits the phonetic, syllabic, morphological, semantic and syntactic characteristics of English, showing that linguistic association does not have to respect constituent boundaries, and that widespread application of linguistic rules can lead to chaos and nonsense. The fact that English draws on a small number of phonemes and phoneme combinations and that these are combined productively, either to form morphemes or meaningless sound sequences, is a cause of some of the chaos. The fact that we speak in a sound stream, and need to know a language to parse what we hear into component phrases, words and morphemes is not the same as a person randomly parsing a sound sequence when he notices it or feels like it. A crudely programmed machine, set to associate sound sequences with particular phrases could come up with an equivalent piece of nonsense (except that Cleese's is spectacular nonsense).

It is also a most interesting fact about English (actually about language in general) that associations may be either sound or meaning based, or even simply based on their clustering in a phrase. When we make associations, they can be based on any or all of these facts. Psycholinguists tend to represent the connections in lexical storage as consisting of any/all of these. The fact is that in order to understand an utterance in a language we need to know the phonology, morphology, lexis, syntax and semantics of that language, and most often, its context of use, too. If any of these is missing, our understanding is in trouble. If any of these are rattled around enough, randomly punctuated with other bits, and delivered with due attention to the overt form of production, as Cleese has done, it's either garbage or very funny.

The reason the piece is so successful, in my view, is that at some level, because he abides by the rules, although misapplying and overgeneralizing them, it is possible to reconstruct his "intended" meanings. That means that we too need to think about what the rules are that he has broken, misused, misapplied or over-applied. Obviously, the whole performance is a virtuoso joke, which most people other than those conducting this painful analysis would have uppermost in their mind, but it is worth showing how the humor works, if only to reconfirm for ourselves the reality of linguistic rules and the tacit or semi-tacit use we make of them most of the time.

Naturally, it would be impossible to translate something of this sort. However, there is no reason, in principle, that just such an exercise could not be conducted on any other natural language, with the same sort of humorous effects being created. The humor resides in the knowledge we all have of the combinatorial properties of the elements of language. Knowledge of the language we use enables us to distinguish between meaningful and meaningless elements. Unconscious knowledge of the combinatorial rules allows us to see the humor in alternative possibilities. The Cleese example is more skillful and more creative than most of us are capable of producing, but the fact is, we can process and understand it. To understand the humor of this particular joke and its complex combination of smaller jokes is to know our language, and indeed, to have no idea of the extent to which we actually know it.

TABLE 6.1 Key to the associations

Word/sound association	Lexical association
association	football
tonight	's the night
about	a bout
technique/eke	out a living
practice	makes perfect
psychoanalysis/sister	and brother
occupied/pied	piper
majority	rule
attention	squad
number	one, two, three
four/for	the last few years
years/here's	to the memory
able	baker charlie
much	the miller's son
called	while you were out
association/Asian	immigrants
immigrants	problems
manner/manna	from heaven
we/wee	sleekit cow'ring, tim'rous beastie
beastie	bestial
bestial/all	All American
speak/Speke	the famous explorer
really	well
well	well
well, well	that is surprising
part/partner	in crime
lot	and his wife
be	c, d, e, and f
f	effectively
fact	or fiction section of the Watford Public Library
it	it is a far far better thing I do now
now than	now then now then what's going on?
on	onward
onward	Christian
Christian	Barnard
heart/hearty	lettuce
lettuce	let us now praise famous men
men	mental hospital
mental hospital	for loonies like me
so/sew	on the button
contention/tension	causing all the headaches
account/count	Count of Monte Cristo
thinking/king	George the Fifth

TABLE 6.1 *(continued)*

Word/sound association	Lexical association
phenomenon/on	the other hand
satisfactor-/fact or	fiction section of the Watford Public Library
understand/stand	stand to attention
laughing	about
make-up	some story the wife'll believe
itself/selfish	bastard
selfish bastard	I'll kick him in the balls
Balls	Pond
Balls Pond	Balls Pond Road

Notes

1 John Cleese is a member of the Monty Python's Flying Circus comedy troupe. He is the performer, and apparently, the originator, of this sketch.
2 Fortunately, I need never say truthfully that this is what I do for a living.

7

JOKES IN MORE THAN ONE LANGUAGE

1.0 Introduction

1.1 Bilingual Humor

The ability to make or understand jokes that involve knowledge of more than one language does not always require that a person is fully bilingual. Many jokes involving more than one language require competence in one language and often, simple acquaintance with another. Usually, the crucial components are knowledge of the pronunciation system of both languages, and of the basic lexicon of the lesser-known language. Naturally, the more linguistically sophisticated a bilingual joke is, the greater the knowledge of both languages that is required. Interlingual, or multilingual, jokes exploit the fundamental fact that a string of phonemes, outside a context of use, may mean nothing in one language, but may have one or many meanings depending on the languages available to joke tellers and joke listeners in the context of use.

Bilingualism is a fruitful source of linguistic jokes. The notion of bilingualism is itself the topic of some jokes, some of them rather tired, but all of them catching the intrinsic oddness in the fact that there are many different linguistic ways to express a thought. The essential arbitrariness of the sign is underlined by the existence of multilingualism. Before settling down to a discussion of the mechanisms involved in the creation and recognition of humor in bilingual jokes, in the interests of egalitarianism, I proffer my version of one of the most popular bilingualism jokes to be found on the Internet.

Example 1

A police dog responds to a classified advertisement for a job with the FBI. The Human Resources manager is very officious.

"You'll have to meet the selection criteria. Can you type 60 words a minute?"

The dog, balancing on his hind legs, applies his paws to the computer keyboard, and types 80 words in a minute.

"Now," says the Human Resources manager, "It is part of the essential criteria that you pass a physical examination and run the obstacle course without knocking over any hurdles."

The candidate completes the obstacle course flawlessly, breaking all records.

"The final requirement," says the HR manager, smugly, "is that you have to be bilingual."

The dog looks up at him, batting his eyelashes, and says, "Meow!"

I don't think that any part of this joke needs exposition, other than to say that the idea of a dog using language is contrary to the notion of language as a uniquely human characteristic. Other species may make sounds, but everything we know about animal communication systems points to the fact that they are limited, unproductive, and not made up combinatorially of discrete elements.[1] The noise that dogs make, or the noise that cats make, cannot be assumed to be language in the way it has been defined by linguists, since, at least, Hockett's formalization of Design Features (Hockett, 1960). Mapping equivalence between two animal sound systems could be considered bilingualism only if we believed that animals actually use language and that language could be understood across species. In the world of the joke, in which a police dog wants to work for the FBI, can type, jump hurdles and already talk English, it is quite likely that he should have very little difficulty with the language Cat.

One of the most clichéd of all jokes about bilingualism is the one in Example 2. As usual, there is probably some truth in the stereotype, at least recognizably for the purposes of the joke.

Example 2

If someone who speaks three languages is trilingual, and someone who speaks two languages is bilingual, what do you call someone who speaks one language?
An American

This joke mocks the tendency of many Americans to underestimate the value of knowing more than one language, and in some cases, to actively discourage bilingualism (*i.e.*, knowledge of a language other than English) in the children of immigrants. Of course, there are many Americans who are bilingual, trilingual or multilingual, but the perception in many parts of the world where bilingualism is a way of life is that Americans disdain the languages of other people, believing that others should communicate with them in English (thereby demonstrating, that in any event, they think that bilingualism is fine for others, as long as one of the languages is always English).

The joke in Example 3 demonstrates a European perception about Americans and their attitudes toward learning a language other than English.

Example 3

A Swiss motorist, looking for directions, pulls up at a bus stop where two Americans are waiting. "Entschuldigung, koennen Sie Deutsch sprechen?" he asks.

The two Americans stare at him.

"Excusez-moi, parlez vous Francais?" he ventures.

The Americans continue to stare.

"Parlare Italiano?" Nothing. "Hablan ustedes Espanol?"

Still no response. The Swiss motorist drives off, irritated and frustrated.

The one American turns to the other and says, "Maybe we should learn a foreign language."

"Why?" says his companion. "That guy knew four languages, and it didn't do him any good."

The point of this joke is the same as the one in Example 2, mockery of American monolingualism and attitudes to the languages of others. However, the twist is that one of the Americans recognizes that the Swiss motorist has used four different languages. That's an advance. But it's in the world of the joke; in the same world, the Swiss motorist does not think to try asking for directions in English.

Now that I have engaged in the mandatory jibes, I will give up on the easy target of American monolingualism.[2]

1.2 Sound Similarities in Different Languages

Those who are lucky enough to know more than one language are able to exploit their linguistic resources fruitfully in the area of making and appreciating jokes that involve more than one language. Interlingual jokes, as a rule, involve using strings of sounds that might make up individual words in one language and reassigning them a new analysis in another language. Such strings might be reanalyzed as syllables, morphemes, words or phrases, in many cases not retaining a shred of their original meaning or grammatical function, and in some cases maintaining vestiges of original meaning and function whilst being reconstrued as part of the reanalyzed utterance in the other language.

The joke in Example 4 is from Ted Cohen's book, *Jokes*, although he attributes it to Cathleen Cavell. It works better spoken than read, although if first encountered in print, there's a chance to think about it without the pressure of having to get the joke immediately.

Example 4

According to Freud, what comes between fear and sex?
Answer: Fünf

(Cohen, 1999)

When I first read this joke I couldn't get it. I couldn't even imagine what *fünf* was, nor did I have any particular idea of how to pronounce it except according to my English grapheme-phoneme mapping rules. The clue is to think of the German counting system, *ein, zwei, drei, vier, fünf, sechs* (1, 2, 3 etc.). *Fear* and *sex* sound something like the way the numbers 4 and 6 are pronounced in some dialect of German, or, for the purposes of the joke, as a novice English-speaking learner of German might say them.

So, at the most basic level, the question as asked in the joke is, what did Freud, a native speaker of German, say came between 4 and 6? Well the answer is surely obvious, 5, or *fünf* in German. This is the sort of joke in which the punch line focuses the listener's attention on the code. In this case, although we don't know it from the outset, there are two codes involved, English and German.

The way the joke is set up is masterly. The Austrian, Sigmund Freud, father of psychoanalysis, had something original, and often shocking, to say about the human psyche. A large part of his theoretical apparatus concerns the most primitive human drives and emotions, among them fear and sex. Additionally, Freud believed that the human psyche develops in the infant in stages, starting with the oral, then the anal, and finally the genital. If we know this much about Freud, and are primed by the question to think of 'fear', 'sex' and the notion of 'between', we might ponder Freud's theory of drives and of emotional development, and wonder which developmental stage could come between fear and sex. However, once we hear the answer, we realize that the phonological sequences of *fear* and *sex* are similar to the phonological sequences of *vier* and *sechs*. We remember, too, that Freud was German-speaking. This joke works well if told in a German accented English, because, stereotypically, German speakers tend to use /z/ in alternation with /s/ word initially.[3]

In any event, to understand this joke, we need to play at the same time with the sound of the German counting system, and with Freud's obsessions. We need to know, at least, the counting numbers to ten in German to understand the joke. After racking our brains to answer the general knowledge question, we are reminded that the meaning of sound sequences differ from language to language. This is strong evidence for two different claims that may or may not be related. One is that there is nothing inherent in the sound stream that means one thing or another. The claim that the relationship between signifier and signified is arbitrary was made by Saussure, although he was not the first to make it, as he acknowledges (Saussure, 1910/1993). Saussure later prevaricated on whether the relationship was entirely arbitrary, pointing out that it was contingent within the system of any particular language, *i.e.*, the current state of the language, and the way it is used. Jakobson provides a very sensitive discussion of Saussure's major claim that every signifier must have a signified, and similarly that every signified must have a signifier, and, importantly, that a comparison of similar signifiers across languages does not reveal absolute equivalences in the signified (Jakobson, 1937). The arbitrariness of the sign is a cornerstone of 20th and 21st century linguistics, although this claim in its most absolute form has been challenged increasingly by philosophers and linguists, in a charge first led by Benveniste (Benveniste, 1966–74) and continuing today in the work of cognitive linguists.

The second claim is based on the idea that there is nothing inherent in the sound stream that means one thing or the other. This claim is that it is the individual mind that makes meaning of the sounds that it hears, constantly assigning structure on the basis of what it expects, and reassigning structure on the basis of surprising input. The notion is that the mind assigns structure to sound sequences, and derives meaning on that basis.[4]

Thus, on the basis of these claims, it is all in the mind of the perceiver (because of membership in a language community whose language is in a state of dynamic systematicity and because of the way in which the mind/brain perceives language input). When the perceiver knows more than one language, and is reminded, by a joke like Example 4, that we can assign more than one structure to a sound stream, using knowledge of different languages at the same time or in quick succession, surprise at the freshness of the perception is likely to result in delight and laughter. This double take is a more complex variant of the way in which ambiguity of sound sequences within only one language is processed.

Children who know, or are learning, more than one language delight in this feature of the sound stream. Growing up in South Africa, where we were obliged to learn English and Afrikaans (a Germanic language creolized from Dutch and contact with Malay, Portuguese, Bantu, and English), there were certain words, which thrilled us English speakers at school. Specifically, we loved to fill in the front covers of our exercise books in the slot called *Subject/Vak*. *Vak* is the Afrikaans word for subject and is homophonous with *fuck*. The joke never got stale. "*Vak* – *Off*" was the standard way of filling in the front cover, and the variations were endless. *Vakansie* [fɑkɑnsi] is the Afrikaans word for vacation, and we never tired of this joke either.

The philosopher, Sydney Morgenbesser (1921–2004), is reputed to have found himself in trouble over his correct pronunciation of the name of the German philosopher, Immanuel Kant, and his application of the categorical imperative. The anecdote is reproduced in Example 5.

Example 5

*Morgenbesser was leaving a subway station in New York City and on the stairs on his way out, preparatory to leaving the station, put his pipe in his mouth. A police officer stopped him and reminded him, officiously, that it was forbidden to smoke in the subway. Morgenbesser replied that he was actually on his way out of the subway and that he hadn't, in any event, lit his pipe yet. The officer responded, "If I let you do it, I'd have to let everyone do it." Morgenbesser, never one to miss an opportunity to apply a philosophical point to an everyday situation, said, "Who do you think you are, Kant?" The policeman heard '***Kant***' as an English obscenity, thought Morgenbesser was swearing at him, and hauled him off to the police station to explain his offensive behavior.*

The police officer heard a sound sequence that he interpreted as an English obscenity. The structure of the utterance was such that he heard Morgenbesser's answer to his own rhetorical question, *Kant*, as name-calling, and was duly insulted.

Example 6 goes back to the early days of the Johnny Carson show in the USA. In order to understand this joke, phrased as a riddle, we need to know that the German word *nein*, pronounced like the English *nine*, means "no".

Example 6

A: If 9 W is the answer, what is the question?
B: Herr Wagner, does your name begin with a "V"?

The joke is a very simple and silly one. Wagner is a German name, pronounced something like "Vahgner". The questioner wants to know if Herr Wagner spells his name with a V. His response, in German, is quite to the point: *Nein, W* ("No, W"). The joke rests in a simple reassignment of the German *nein* (no) to the English *nine* and the appropriate answer to the question: it is spelt with a W not a V.

It's likely that this joke in its original incarnation incorporated the idea that *9W* referred to Route 9W, a highway in New York City. In this case, the opening line, *If 9W is the answer, what is the question?* was intended to lead the listener astray in priming for the answer about the highway.

Example 7 is a joke based on knowledge of Yiddish pronunciation. Yiddish, too, is a Germanic language, with a counting system ripe for interlingual jokes with English.

Example 7

Some years ago, a nouveau-riche Yiddish-speaking couple who had recently moved to the leafy suburbs joined an exclusive country club. They were keen to lose their immigrant customs and tastes, as they were aware that these would mark them out as Jewish. One evening, before dinner at the club, the husband gave his wife some advice.

"When we get there, please, don't ask for a soft drink or some sweet kosher wine. Order a martini, or a gin and tonic."

The wife agreed to this, although she was not much of a drinker, since she wanted to appear smart and sophisticated, and to please her husband.

The waiter approached to take their order, "Ma'am, may I bring you a cocktail?"

"Yes, indeed," she replied, "We'll have martini."

"Dry?" inquired the waiter.

*"No, no!" she said, in horror, "**tzvay iz genug**."*

Once again, the joke is based on the fact that there is a sound sequence in the counting system of one language that means something entirely different in another language.[5] In Yiddish, *drei*, pronounced like the English word *dry*, means three. *Tzvay iz genug* means "two is enough".

Since this couple is clearly not accustomed to martinis, dry or otherwise, part of the joke is her horror at the idea that she and her husband might have to drink three of them. When the waiter says *Dry?*, she thinks he is speaking Yiddish and intends to ask if she wants "three". Triggered back into the language with which she is more comfortable, she immediately assures him, in Yiddish, that two will be enough. The humor in the joke emanates from the idea that this couple is terribly eager to disguise their Yiddish roots by pretending to do what others at the country club do, but it is a matter of a single word that shows them, and us, that they are still the people they started out as. Stereotypically, Jews don't belong to WASPy country clubs, nor do they drink martinis at the country club or anywhere else. Not only is this stereotype reinforced by the fact that her knowledge of martinis is so minimal that she has no idea what *dry* refers to, but also that the mere suggestion of three alcoholic drinks horrifies her. This is a joke that is made by Jews in America against themselves. The woman in the joke tries to be what she is not, and is caught out by being what she is, a speaker of Yiddish, and not much of a drinker.

There are a number of Russian jokes that are puns based on the fact that a common Chinese syllable (spelled *hui* in pinyin) is homophonous with the vulgar Russian word for penis (хуй), to be understood as equivalent in connotation to the vulgar *dick* in English.

In Example 8, we see a joke popular in Russia during the Gromyko period, although it's easy to see how it could be adapted to other historical contexts.

Example 8

A new Chinese ambassador has an appointment to meet Gromyko. The Chinese ambassador introduces himself: "Zhǔi Hui!" Gromyko does not bat an eyelid. "Zhui sam!" he replies. The unsuspecting Chinese ambassador asks, "And where is Gromyko?"

Zhui hui is a mock Chinese name of the order of *Hoo Flung Poo* or *Wee Chew Fat*. It is rendered as "Chew a dick!" in Russian. By way of reply, Gromyko responds, *Zhui sam*, which, in Russian means "chew [it] yourself".

Andrei Gromyko was the Soviet Foreign Minister from 1957 for about eighteen years. The joke has very little chance of being a true record, but that's irrelevant to the point at hand. The joke is in the fact that the Chinese ambassador genuinely thought he was introducing himself (saying something like, "I am Zhǔi Hui") and the Soviet minister thought he was being insulted in Russian. So the sound sequence *Zhǔi hui* is analyzed by Gromyko as Russian, and therefore, he misunderstands the speech act, which he interprets as an insult and returns it in kind. However, his comeback is in Russian, *Zhui sam* ("chew it yourself"). The Chinese ambassador does not understand Russian, and believing that the other man, too, had introduced himself, wonders next about the whereabouts of Gromyko, the man he had come to meet. *Zhui (Sam)* sounds, to those of us who don't know, sufficiently like the kind of Chinese sounds we hear in *Zhǔi (huî)*. The same principle at work in the previous jokes using two languages is to be found here too. In the case of the joke in Example 8, interestingly, the sound sequence in both languages is longer than a single syllable, and may be heard as two words in both Chinese and Russian.

Canada, a country in which both French and English are widely spoken, with some friction as to bilingual language policies, also boasts some jokes that require knowledge of two languages. Various versions of the joke in Example 9 can serve as an example of bilingual French/English jokes. This is, in fact, an English joke, with some French words in it.

Example 9

A young Canadian boy, desperate for a pet, nags his parents to get him a cat. However, they tell him that they are poor and have no money to feed a pet. They offer him a deal, though, that if he contributes to the household income by ferrying people across the river, he can bring a pet into the house. As it turns out, he is lucky enough to acquire three kittens from a cat owner across the river. Proudly he names them Un, Deux and Trois before heading back home across the river. Alas, his boat capsizes; he survives, but is emotionally shattered. Arriving home hysterically, he tries to explain to his parents what has happened. All they can get out of him, panting and incoherent, is "Maman! Maman! Un, Deux, Trois cats sank!"

This is one of the more contrived bilingual jokes I have come across. In order to understand the punch line, we need to know that the utterance *Un, Deux, Trois cats sank* sounds like the first five numbers in the French counting system, *un, deux, trois, quatre, cinq*.

Example 10 contains another, slightly less clunky version of Example 9.

Example 10

There's 2 cats, One Two Three Cat, and Un Deux Trois Cat. They're swimming across the English Channel in a race. Only One Two Three Cat got to the other side. Why? Because Un Deux Trois Cat sank.

The joke in Example 11 is an ingenious use of the sound sequence of a whole sentence in one language, which is heard in another language as spelling out the sound of the letters that make up a word in that language. This joke appears on many websites where it is discussed for its educational purposes, but I cannot track its origin.

Example 11

A speaker of Spanish who knows no English goes into a department store in the USA and wants to buy an item of clothing but doesn't have the English to ask for it. The helpful assistant shows him almost every kind of clothing item in the store. Finally, when she shows him a pair of socks, the Spanish speaker says: "¡Eso sí que es!" (That's what it is!) The assistant, whose patience has been somewhat taxed, explodes. "If you could spell it all the time, why didn't you say so?"

The sound sequence, "¡Eso sí que es!" is homophonous with the sound of the English letter sequence S-O-C-K-S. The joke, of course, is that if the Spanish speaker could have spelled the word *socks*, the whole exercise would have been entirely short-circuited. On the other hand, if he could have spelled it, no doubt he would have done, unless he was of a sadistic mindset.

Jokes, alas, seldom respect the criterion of political correctness. Example 12 requires some knowledge of Yiddish as well as English, and is extremely offensive. Nevertheless, it demonstrates an interesting and very neat way of using two languages to tell a joke that is intended to be funny in both languages.[6]

Example 12

What's the definition of a dead homosexual?
Geh in drerd.

In order to understand this joke, we need to know the meaning of some Yiddish words and expressions. *Geh in drerd* is a Yiddish curse, which might be translated as "Go to hell". *Geh* (pronounced like the English word *gay*) is a verb that means "go", in this instance *in* means "into" and *drerd* means "the ground", and metaphorically, "hell". However, as we know, *gay* is a noun in English, sometimes an adjective, colloquially used as a descriptor for homosexual people. The punch line, thus, if we code-mix, can be rendered as, "a gay person in the ground", which is, I suppose, one answer to the question posed in the first part of the joke. The offensive undertones probably emanate from the fact that *Geh in drerd* is a curse, and, thus, the implication by Speaker 2 might be that gay people are on their way to hell. An alternative effect of the force of this Yiddish curse is that Speaker 2 might be telling the questioner to go to hell for asking questions of that nature.

The joke in Example 13 uses sound sequences in Portuguese to play on an English idiom. Because it is possible to compare the two NPs, *snow* and *milk*, on the basis that they have a certain feature in common (whiteness) and the possibility that they might have certain common uses, it's not completely far-fetched to ask which of the two substances is better.

Example 13

*Which is better, snow or milk? Better **leite** than **neve**.*

In Portuguese, *leite* means "milk" and *neve* means "snow". There's a double pun here, because each sound sequence has an English equivalent with an entirely different meaning. *Leite* in Portuguese is pronounced the same as *late* in English, and *neve* in Portuguese is pronounced the same as *never* in English.

The English idiom, *better late than never*, means that if something happens later than expected, this is nevertheless better than if it never happens at all. In the Portuguese context of the joke, however, the answer is that milk is better. There is even a context in English in which this construction could be grammatical. "Better milk than snow, if those are the only options for diluting my coffee". Of course, *late* and *never* function adverbially in this English utterance, as opposed *leite* and *neve*, which are Portuguese NPs. Nevertheless, the puns work on both the English structural readings. It's not really a Portuguese joke; it's an English joke that exploits the fact that two sound sequences in Portuguese are found that by happy accident are related semantically if heard as English, and are semantically related by at least one feature in Portuguese.

Example 14 is an English joke on a French sound sequence that is used semantically appropriately as a French word appearing in an English sentence, but that also functions as a bilingual pun. As is often the case in this sort of joke, the reanalysis of the sound sequence leads to a change in its syntactic category.

Example 14

Q: *Why do French people only have one egg for breakfast?*
A: *Because one egg's **un oeuf***

This is a rather obvious made-up joke, the purpose of which is to demonstrate the point that the sequence *un oeuf*, which means "one egg" in French can be reanalyzed as the English word, *enough*. The joke is rather clever, however, because the sentence works equally well in English on both its readings, *i.e.*, "one egg's *un oeuf*" (one egg is *un oeuf*, in French) and "one egg's enough" (for a person to eat for breakfast).

Example 14 highlights the commonness of a certain kind of ambiguity to be found in a language like English. The forms of the verb *to be* in English span a variety of grammatical functions. For instance, *is* can be used to state that two terms have the same referent or the same denotation. An egg is *un oeuf*, in French. This construction allows us two ways of referring to the signified, an egg, using two languages. And additionally, then, the claim is made that *an* (or one) *egg is enough*. That certainly doesn't imply that *one egg* is identical to *enough*. It is a predication (one that is, also, elliptical) about an egg. This joke exploits the use/mention distinction, and, moreover, employs two languages to do it. On one reading, thus, we could say "the denotation of 'an egg' is identical to the denotation of '*un oeuf*'".

But, of course, in English we can also say *An egg is an oval, cream- or light-brown embryo enclosed in a protective covering, produced by a hen, used for food.* In this case, we use *is* to introduce a definition of a hen's egg. We can also, however, use *is* to predicate something of the egg: *An egg is brown* or *delicious* or *very healthy* or *the perfect breakfast. Is* may also function as a main verb, as in *An egg is on the table. Is* can also be found as an auxiliary in a verb complex: *An egg is boiling in the pot,* or *an egg is hatching in the box.* So, to say that "one egg is enough" is simply to make a predication about "one egg", *i.e.,* that it is sufficient for the purposes required.

These are just some of the main uses of the verb/auxiliary *be* in English. It is no wonder, then, that the possibilities of exploiting these multiple ambiguities are rife in English. Famously, Bill Clinton, in his impeachment hearing, uttered the immortal line: *It depends what you mean by 'is'.* Leaving aside Clinton's problems, we see that the joke in Example 14 exploits a very complex issue in English. Once we get involved in using *is* to make claims about terminological equivalence between languages, we add a new dimension to what we mean by *is*.

An egg is an *oeuf*; but an egg is a *beitzah* too (*beitzah* is the Hebrew word for *egg*) and an egg is an *eier* (the Afrikaans word for *egg*) and so on. Referential equivalence is sometimes possible when we are translating between different languages and sometimes it is not, hence the long-time problem known as *Indeterminacy of Translation* in the philosophy of language (Quine, 1960). Returning to Saussure's point about the inequivalences of signifiers in different languages, we may see, for instance, that *un oeuf* may signify an egg to be eaten but not a human ovum.

As an exercise in bilingual homophony, spanning more than the word as the unit for play, it is illuminating to look at some creative uses of macaronic language.

1.3 Macaronic Language

Macaronic language is a form of humor that relies on knowledge of the orthographic-sound system of at least two languages and of the form-meaning system of at least one of those languages. There have been some ingenious products that play on the arbitrariness of the sign's form: the following examples show that the homophony existing between a string of sounds in two different languages can be exploited for humorous effect.[7]

A famous collection of macaronic verses, in the form of nursery rhymes, named *Mots d'heures: Gousses, Rames—the d'Antin Manuscripts*, written by Luis d'Antin van Rooten, was published in 1967. The basic idea here was to pronounce the text as though it were written French. Thus, the title if read aloud, using French grapheme-phoneme rules, ends up sounding like *Mother Goose Rhymes* said in French-accented English. The basic joke is that what looks and sounds like French, when processed by the English speaking/hearing brain, turns out to be familiar English, albeit a French-accented English. The book itself is a collection of English nursery rhymes, some of which are shown below. Additionally, the author creates an overall spoof, claiming that the book is a collection of medieval French verse, which he has carefully annotated. The annotations themselves are complete nonsense, since the verses themselves are meaningless. However, he makes much of parodying a particular form of over-interpreted, pretentious pseudo-intellectual analyses of obscure French literature, with earnest and nonsensical footnotes.

In order to get the joke in these, one needs to read aloud, as though reading French.[8]

Example 15

Un petit d'un petit
S'étonne aux Halles
Un petit d'un petit
Ah! degrés te fallent
Indolent qui ne sort cesse
Indolent qui ne se mène
Qu'importe un petit d'un petit
Tout Gai de Reguennes.

This majestic piece of French verse is, in fact, equivalent to a phonetic transcription of the stereotypical French-accented English in which the English nursery rhyme, *Humpty Dumpty sat on a wall* might be rendered.

Another version of this great poem (not d'Antin's) has also appeared.

Example 16

Un petite d'un petite s'attendre vol.
Un petite d'un petite a d'egrait vol.
Al de kien souer c'est, et al de kiens mien,
Que dont peut un petite deux g'edeur a'gien.

It's noteworthy that both of these French nonsense verses yield the same sound sequences, and to the English ear, mean the same. The assignment of orthography and meaning to the string of sounds are separate issues. Once again we see that it is the mind that processes language, and the bilingual mind is fertile for even more fun and ambiguity than the monolingual one is.[9]

In d'Antin's collection, we may also find this old classic of the English nursery.

Example 17

Et qui rit des curés d'Oc?
De Meuse raines, houp! de cloques.
De quelles loques ce turque coin.
Et ne d'anes ni rennes,
Ecuries des curés d'Oc.

If your knowledge of French is as limited as mine, I'll give you a clue: think *Hickory Dickory Dock.*

Some other favorite characters also make an appearance in the collection: "*Chacun Gille*" and "*Pis-terre, Pis-terre, Pomme qui n'y terre*" (*Jack and Jill*, and *Peter Peter Pumpkin Eater*).

I'll leave this one for the reader to figure out.

Example 18

Lit-elle messe, moffette,
Satan ne te fête,
Et digne somme coeurs et nouez.
À longue qu'aime est-ce pailles d'Eure.
Et ne Satan bise ailleurs
Et ne fredonne messe. Moffette, ah, ouais!

Essentially, all uses of macaronic language make a very simple point. To get the joke we need to understand that it is the mind that processes sounds and structures, and the mind that assigns one structure rather than another to a sequence of sounds. Sounds (phones) by themselves are not language; the mere combinations of sounds are not language. Sounds have to be processed as pieces of language by the human mind.[10] We hear what we can make sense of; the more languages we know, the greater our recognition. Reflection about the reasons we can make sense of one language that sounds like the words of another, or about the possibilities of processing the same string of sounds in one language in different ways, should remind us of how we process visually confusing stimuli, such as the Necker cube. In a related fact, in musical experiments conducted to investigate how listeners, exposed to hearing four identical beats in a bar played at the same tempo and at the same rhythmic intervals over and over again, perceive these beats, it has been revealed that they eventually start to assign unequal stress to one of the beats.[11] This is further evidence for the claim that it is the mind that assigns structure to the incoming stimulus.

1.4 Cross-Modal Similarities

For those who know a signed and a spoken language, the possibilities for joking using both languages are very tempting. There are a number of different kinds of jokes that exploit knowledge of both a signed and a spoken language. The joke in Example 19 requires a short description of the formation of a single sign, but is worth trying to follow. The sign is found in ASL (American Sign Language) and it means MARRY (as in a man marrying a woman). The sign is made with the left palm turned upwards at waist height. The right hand, palm facing outwards, starts with the right tip of the index finger on the right temple and moves downwards to clasp the upturned palm of the left hand.

The story is generally told in ASL, but I will paraphrase it loosely till I get to the relevant part.

Example 19

A giant falls in love with a very tiny princess and decides that he wants to marry her. Her father, the king, will have nothing of it, but the giant hangs around, and begs and pleads. He promises he will nurture and nourish his princess, swears undying love and offers to perform any tasks that the king will set him, so that he may show how much he loves the princess and what he is prepared to do to win her. The king grudgingly sets the giant three tasks. He is to empty the Aegean Sea and bring the water to the Sahara desert; he is to carry enough bricks to build a castle to the top of Kilimanjaro; he is to squeeze coal into diamonds. Willingly, the giant goes to work and after three years completes the tasks as set. He arrives, exhausted, at the palace of the king, and finds his princess. Gently setting her in the palm of his hand he looks lovingly down at her and signs, "My darling, I have done the tasks that were set for me. I have now returned to claim my reward. I love you and I want to marry you."

Remember the sign for MARRY? Imagine the giant right hand crushing the princess as it descends to meet the upturned left hand.

The story has a moral: don't talk with your hands full!

As the joke is told, it sometimes has a more sardonic moral, one that is limited to insider knowledge of the conflict among signing Deaf people and mainstream educators. Many Deaf people see it as their right to use signed language, the more obviously natural face-to-face language of Deaf people, and mainstream educators of the deaf for many years insisted upon a teaching philosophy of Oralism, *i.e.*, teaching deaf people to read lips and try to produce the sounds of oral language.

So, the alternative moral, produced tongue in cheek (if I may further muddy the metaphors) is: *You see, Oralism is better!*

The joke uses the genre of the fairy story—there's nothing besotted giants can't do, after all. Entering into the world of the story, we can imagine a tiny princess standing in the palm of a giant's hand. It is only when the form of the language interrupts the content, and the princess is crushed by her betrothed, that we are aware that language has a life of its own: iconicity collides with arbitrariness. If the joke were to end here, it would be a funny piece of slapstick, relying on the similarity between a particular sign and a mimed action. The fact that the joke has a moral, though, allows a sophisticated interlinguistic joke. We are all told as children that we shouldn't talk with our mouths full (although we are not always given a reason, other than table manners). Now, if hearing people shouldn't talk with their mouths full, by analogy, deaf people shouldn't sign with their hands full. And indeed, the consequences can be devastating. Fairy tales have morals, and this one is drawn for us. And, as far as the Oralists are concerned, maybe we shouldn't sign at all. Because this is a joke told in signed language, the ironic perspective of the teller should be clear.

2.0 Mark Twain and the Awful German Language

Mark Twain (Samuel Leghorn Clemens, 1835–1910) had much to say about the learning of German, and his experiences of this language.

Example 20

Whenever the literary German dives into a sentence, that is the last you are going to see of him till he emerges on the other side of the Atlantic with his verb in his mouth.

(Mark Twain, 1889)

This remark refers to the grammatical tendency of Germanic languages to place the verb at the end of the sentence, *i.e.*, that they seem essentially to be SOV languages. Since German sentences of the literary variety are known to be particularly long, the activity of producing one of those sentences requires even more stamina than required for producing a basic German sentence.

In order to demonstrate his horror at the particular differences between German and English, and how difficult these were for him to learn, he included in his book, *A Tramp Abroad* (1880), an appendix he called *The Awful German Language*. I quote liberally from this source. His most egregious remarks concerned the propensity of German to form multimorphemic words, a tendency he calls the compounding disease, and the terrifying syntactic rule in Germanic that requires verbs to occur in word-final position in a number of clausal types.

Example 21

Some German words are so long that they have a perspective. Observe these examples:

- *Freundschaftsbezeigungen.*
- *Dilettantenaufdringlichkeiten.*
- *Stadtverordnetenversammlungen.*

These things are not words, they are alphabetical processions. And they are not rare; one can open a German newspaper at any time and see them marching majestically across the page—and if he has any imagination he can see the banners and hear the music, too. They impart a martial thrill to the meekest subject. I take a great interest in these curiosities. Whenever I come across a good one, I stuff it and put it in my museum...

Of course when one of these grand mountain ranges goes stretching across the printed page, it adorns and ennobles that literary landscape—but at the same time it is a great distress to the new student, for it blocks up his way; he cannot crawl under it, or climb over it, or tunnel through it. So he resorts to the dictionary for help, but there is no help there. The dictionary must draw the line somewhere—so it leaves this sort of words out. And it is right, because these long things are hardly legitimate words, but are rather combinations of words, and the inventor of them ought to have been killed. They are compound words with the hyphens left out. The various words used in building them are in the dictionary, but in a very scattered condition; so you can hunt the materials out, one by one, and get at the meaning at last, but it is a tedious and harassing business...We used to have a good deal of this sort of crime in our literature, but it has gone out now.

Twain here is satirizing the rule of compounding that anyone learning certain Germanic languages as second languages must have come across. As he points out, these are compound words with the hyphens left out. This kind of compounding process is extremely productive in German. Because the compounds can just as soon be decomposed, *i.e.*, their morphemic elements are, in the main, separable words, such multimorphemic "crimes" cannot be easily located in a dictionary. This is a problem for dictionary makers and users of most polysynthetic languages. The separate morphemes are listed as independent words; finding out the meaning of a word is not as simple as looking up a word in a dictionary. One has to understand not only the individual words in the compound, but also the rules forming these compounds. As is the case with compounds in many languages, not only German, the sum of meanings of the independent words does not always yield the meaning of the compound as a whole. Twain's overall point, apart from mockery, of himself, and of any hardily monolingual speaker of English encountering German, is to highlight the enormous differences in the ways of expressing the same idea in different languages. German is the case in point, as its compounds are notorious to speakers of English, but it is no worse or better than any other language. Twain is also playing with idea of naturalization. He pretends that any deviation from the rules of English is a crime against language and literature, a matter for moral indignation. This is the tendency that many of us have to believe that any way of constructing language other than the one we know is weird.

Of course, orthographic convention aside, compounding in English also has similar properties. For instance, Heidi Harley (2006) provides this example.

Example 22

Scandal investigation committee chairperson appointment meeting ruckus investigation...

Twain also recoils in terror before the phenomenon of verb separability, a well-known phenomenon of Germanic languages in general. He slightly overstates the case.

Example 23

The Germans have another kind of parenthesis, which they make by splitting a verb in two and putting half of it at the beginning of an exciting chapter and the other half at the end of it. Can any one conceive of anything more confusing than that? These things are called "separable verbs." The German grammar is blistered all over with separable verbs; and the wider the two portions of one of them are spread apart, the better the author of the crime is pleased with his performance.

Twain is here referring to the construction in Germanic languages that makes use of separable prefixes or of separable verb compounds. In Germanic, a large class of verbs uses one of a number of separable prefixes that when prefixed can change the meaning of the root verb. However, the prefix does not always need to remain attached to the root verb for the entire verbal complex to retain the changed meaning. As Twain is at pains to point out, many sentences in German appear to have a verb in second position, even though the same verb may occur sentence finally in other sentences. There are some peculiar syntactic consequences, in the case of sentences containing separable prefix verbs. The prefix might occur in sentence final position either on its own (i) or prefixed to the main verb root (ii). In the case (i) in which the prefix occurs on its own, sentence finally, the main verb root is to be found in second position in the sentence. It's also possible for the infix *–ge* (past particle marker) to be infixed between the prefix and the main verb root, as in (iii).

i. Morgen **kaufe** ich **ein**.
   Tomorrow buy I in
   "Tomorrow I'll shop"
ii. Wo wirst du morgen **einkaufen**?
    Where FUT you tomorrow in-buy
    "Where will you shop tomorrow?"
iii. Gestern *habe* ich **eingekauft**.
     Yesterday PERF I in-*ge*-buy (perfect)
     "Yesterday I bought" (ungrammatical in English as *Yesterday I have bought*)[12]

The examples in (i), (ii) and (iii) show the separable verb phenomenon (or crime) that Twain alludes to.

Starting from the perspective of English, which, in general assigns gender biologically for humans and mammals, and uses a gender-neutral pronoun for all other nouns, Twain professes to be baffled by the illogicality of gender assignment in German.

Example 24

In German, a young lady has no sex, while a turnip has. Think what overwrought reverence that shows for the turnip, and what callous disrespect for the girl. See how it looks in print—I translate this from a conversation in one of the best of the German Sunday-school books:

"Gretchen: Wilhelm, where is the turnip?
Wilhelm: She has gone to the kitchen.
Gretchen: Where is the accomplished and beautiful English maiden?
Wilhelm: It has gone to the opera."

....a person's mouth, neck, bosom, elbows, fingers, nails, feet, and body are of the male
sex, and his head is male or neuter according to the word selected to signify it, and not
according to the sex of the individual who wears it—for in Germany all the women wear
either male heads or sexless ones; a person's nose, lips, shoulders, breast, hands, and toes are
of the female sex; and his hair, ears, eyes, chin, legs, knees, heart, and conscience haven't any
sex at all. The inventor of the language probably got what he knew about a conscience from
hearsay.

Now, by the above dissection, the reader will see that in Germany a man may think he is
a man, but when he comes to look into the matter closely, he is bound to have his doubts; he
finds that in sober truth he is a most ridiculous mixture; and if he ends by trying to comfort
himself with the thought that he can at least depend on a third of this mess as being manly
and masculine, the humiliating second thought will quickly remind him that in this respect
he is no better off than any woman or cow in the land.

German is hardly unusual in its assignation of grammatical gender. French
is no more logical, neither is Hebrew. In English, for all its supposed logical
perfection in this regard, ships are female, as are automobiles, dogs tend to be
regarded as masculine and cats as feminine. The point is that English does not have
grammatical gender other than for human pronouns. German has three genders
and gender agreement. Interestingly, many languages of the world have rather
complex systems of grammatical gender, often described as noun classes. These
have been famously dealt with by Dixon (1972) in his discussion of Dyirbal, an
Aboriginal Australian language, well known among linguists for its system of four
noun classes, which are assigned according to the following semantic criteria:

I — animate objects, men
II — women, water, fire, violence
III — edible fruit and vegetables
IV — miscellaneous (includes things not classifiable in the first three)

(Dixon, 1972)

This classification led the semanticist George Lakoff to entitle his volume on
categories of the mind, *Women, Fire and Dangerous Things* (Lakoff, 1987).

Other languages, *e.g.*, Luganda, a Bantu language spoken in parts of East Africa,
have been found to have up to ten noun classes (or grammatical genders). The way
in which these are assigned might be regarded as arbitrary, but in all the systems of
noun class assignment, there is some semantic motivation. In Luganda, these are,

more or less, people, long objects, animals, miscellaneous objects, large objects and liquids, small objects, languages, pejoratives, infinitives, and mass nouns.

Twain, who was dealing with only three genders in German, mocked the lack of logic this assignment displayed. What we know of gender in German, however, does have a certain grammatical pattern. The word *madchen*, (maiden) derived as a diminutive of *magd* using the suffix *–chen*, is neuter because, historically, in German, all diminutives (as a semantic class) were at one stage classified as grammatically neuter. The overall point, of course, is that depending on your initial language perspective, all other languages are weird. The more different they are from where you start, the weirder they are.

In regard to linguistic classification taxonomies, Jorge-Luis Borges (1942) writes about a taxonomic system, which he says was attributed by Dr. Franz Kuhn to a certain Chinese encyclopedia (Borges, 1999).[13]

Example 25

These ambiguities, redundancies, and deficiencies recall those attributed by Dr. Franz Kuhn to a certain Chinese encyclopedia called the **Heavenly Emporium of Benevolent Knowledge**. *In its distant pages it is written that animals are divided into (a) those that belong to the emperor; (b) embalmed ones; (c) those that are trained; (d) suckling pigs; (e) mermaids; (f) fabulous ones; (g) stray dogs; (h) those that are included in this classification; (i) those that tremble as if they were mad; (j) innumerable ones; (k) those drawn with a very fine camel's-hair brush; (l) etcetera; (m) those that have just broken the flower vase; (n) those that at a distance resemble flies.*

This is a very famous, and much-used, quotation from Borges. Although Dr. Franz Kuhn was a real person, and although all the dialects of Chinese make use of a noun classifier system, there is no reason to believe that such an encyclopedia exists. Strangely enough, there are a number of scholars who take this classification seriously, and some who have gone so far as to suggest that this arrangement of the universe is no more random than serious taxonomies that exist in languages of the world. This interpretation seems to me to be relativism gone mad: *those that have just broken the flower vase?*

The central point that is made by Borges here, however, is that for an outsider to observe the linguistic categories that a particular language allows, is to feel that the other linguistic world is illogical, irrational and insane. The grammatical world of one language can be so far from another as to cause profound confusion and madness. Borges' taxonomy (in my view) is simply an extension of Twain's pain.

Twain, who was clearly fascinated with German and its differences from English seems to have made a fairly serious effort to get to the bottom of the differences between German and English. In 1897 he delivered a speech in German *Die Schrecken der deutschen Sprache* (The Horrors of the German Language) to the Vienna Press Club to show off his mastery of these differences. The humor of it, however, lies in his own literal translation of the speech, which demonstrates the more terrifying aspects of German.[14]

In his speech, he plays particularly with use of the verb final constructions, verb fronting, object fronting, temporal and locative adverbial fronting, negative placement, and separable verb constructions. Additionally, he deftly demonstrates his ability to construct long, subject heavy sentences, filled with parentheses. His register, too, is exquisitely appropriate for the delivery of formal speeches in German-speaking contexts.

As a sample of various linguistic jokes in this speech, I'll provide an example (taken from the speech) of some of the phenomena he is satirizing.

The terrifying German language has the astonishing property of piling up modal auxiliaries sentence-finally. It is unclear if there is a limit to the number that can be stacked. In Example 26, the final four words (written, indeed, with dashes in between) are all used grammatically in their German equivalents, with no dashes.

Example 26

How so had one to me this say could—might—dared—should?

The use of more than one modal auxiliary in a simple sentence is extremely unusual in English, although it does occur in certain varieties. English, in any event, does not pile up its verbal forms sentence-finally. (*cf.* English: *How should it be that one might have dared to possibly say this to me?*) This property is well known in some Germanic languages, however.[15]

Next, in Example 27, we see an example of object fronting.

Example 27

The German language speak I not good.

Here, the object is in sentence-initial position, followed by the main verb in second position, then the subject followed by the negation marker and finally the adverb (uninflected for superlative, as opposed to the way it would be in English) (*cf.* English: *I do not speak the German language well*).

In Example 28, the auxiliary *has* is in second position, whilst the verb is in final position with the prefix *in-* preceding it, so that the phrasal verb becomes one word form (*cf.* English: *has **pushed in** the whole history of the Thirty Years' War between the two members of a separable verb* or *has **pushed** the whole history of the Thirty Years' War **in** between the two members of a separable verb*). Note that this is precisely what Twain has not done in this example, by keeping the elements of the phrasal verb together.

Example 28

he has the whole history of the Thirty Years' War between the two members of a separable verb in-pushed.

He does however, do it, egregiously, in Example 29.

Example 29

On the one end of the railing pasted I the first member of a separable verb and the final member cleave I to the other end—then **spread** *the body of the sentence between it* **out**!

In this case he takes the verb *spread out*, places one part *spread* in second position and the other part *out* absolutely sentence-finally (cf. English: *On the one end of the railing I pasted the first member of a separable verb and the final member I cleaved to the other end—then* **spread out** *the body of the sentence between it*).

Interestingly, Twain has used two different sentence structures to demonstrate that, sometimes in German, the entire prefixed phrasal verb appears sentence-finally, and sometimes it is only the prefix that must appear in the final position. Either way, these sentence structures are different from English, because even though English has the phenomenon of pied-piping, this occurs within the limits of the smallest VP, not across a whole sentence. Thus, in English, in a pied-piping construction, we would have

i.   **spread** *the body of the sentence* **out** *between it*
      v. the (literal rendering of the) German,
ii.   **spread** *the body of the sentence between it* **out**.

Twain has at some length demonstrated what he finds strange about German, by simultaneously showing it as well as commenting on it. Of course, anyone who knows two languages can translate literally from one language to the other on a word-for-word basis and come up with ridiculous results in the target language. However, Twain's particularly skilful way of writing about what he is satirizing whilst using the very forms he is satirizing is what provides the humorous dimension to the product. Additionally, Twain is also belly-achingly funny, to me at least, in the examples he chooses, and the particular vocabulary, metaphors and tone he adopts, as well as in his clear analysis of linguistic differences, demonstrating dextrous proficiency and knowledge of both English and German.

Interestingly, Twain's bilingual humor is not paranomic, or homophonous, the way most of the jokes in this chapter are. In contrast, in these long pieces, Twain uses the structures of one language and the words of another. The effect is to sound like he is speaking German in English. The accent, however, is not in the phonology, but in the morphology and the syntax.

In this chapter I have shown that certain kinds of jokes easily evoke knowledge of more than one language in bilinguals, even in people who are not truly bilingual. Appreciating these sorts of jokes requires listeners to consult their tacit knowledge of both languages and to notice the strangeness of the similarities as well as the differences.

Notes

1 For an extensive discussion on animals and communication, see Stephen Anderson's *Doctor Doolittle's Delusion: Animals and the Uniqueness of Human Language* (Anderson, 2004).

2 Nevertheless, I need to point out that the famous, and probably apocryphal, remark about the modernization of the English text of the King James Bible, "It (the King James version's English) was good enough for Jesus Christ, it's good enough for me", is unattributed, but almost certainly American.

3 It's easier to get away with this joke if the relevant bits are said in a stereotypical German accented English, since *sechs* (/zeks/) and *sex* are not really pronounced identically.

4 The notion that it is the mind that assigns structure and therefore meaning to language has not gone unchallenged. However, the claim I am making here is actually about perception; the idea that it is the mind that assigns structure to incoming visual or auditory stimuli. The relationship between structure and meaning is one that I am happy to say does not belong in this footnote, but see Chapters 2, 3, 4, and 5.

5 It's interesting to note that the counting system of a language is so often the source of wordplay.

6 When I first heard this joke, after hearing the opening utterance, I said, "I don't want to know." The person telling it absolutely insisted, promising me I would think it extremely clever. I do, but I still find it totally offensive.

7 On the fascinating topic of translingual homographs, *i.e.*, words that are spelt the same, but have different meanings in each of the two languages, see http://languagelog.ldc.upenn.edu/nll/?p=1074. Fortuitous examples include *autiste*—in French "autistic"; in Italian "drivers".

8 Since I barely speak French, but more or less know the rules of French pronunciation, it is reasonably easy for me to do this. However, people who do know French often find this a very difficult task, as their processing is interrupted by actually knowing the language, and finding that they are reading total nonsense.

9 The fact that these items are written in what appear to be French words, does, of course, deliberately lead the reader astray into thinking that it is French that will be spoken and heard.

10 For helpful discussions of this point, see most recently, Isac and Reiss 2008; Boeckx, 2010.

11 A full and interesting discussion of this and other cognitive phenomena related to music cognition can be found in Iain Giblin's *Music and the Generative Enterprise* (2008).

12 I have borrowed these data from http://www.vistawide.com/german/grammar/german_verbs03.htm, accessed October 28, 2010.

13 The essay was originally published as *El idioma analítico de John Wilkins*, La Nación, 8 February 1942, and republished in *Otras inquisiciones*.

14 The full text of the translation, appearing in the *New York Times*, translated by Twain himself, may be found at http://www.twainquotes.com/18971127.html.

15 There are dialects of English in which it is perfectly acceptable to say *he should'na oughtta done that*, for example.

8

JOKES ABOUT LANGUAGE

1.0 Introduction

There is a particular category of jokes that are primarily about language. Most of these point directly to a perceived absurdity in what we think we know about language. Some of these are funnier than others: there are vast collections of jokes on the Internet about what a strange language English is. However, many of these are not jokes as much as they are simply pithy little remarks pointing out the absurdities of English. The best of these are found in the writings of Richard Lederer (1989, and too many to reference).

Such remarks are of general interest to most people who speak English, probably because they speak English, and no doubt, because at some time or another, everyone has reflected on the language they use and how weird it is. Thus, as Lederer points out, in English, *we drive on a parkway and park on a driveway.* In what other language, he asks, *can your nose run and your feet smell?* Or indeed, in what other language do you *play in a recital* but *recite in a play?* These sorts of observations are pointers to the places at which the relationship between language and logic is most strained, and are very good illustrations of Wittgenstein's argument that meaning is use.

As a rule, people do not examine the language they use for logical inconsistencies, nor do we look for explanations of why we say what we say. This is probably because our normal use of language is automatic. We tend to assume that there is a transparent relationship between what we say and what we mean or what we say and what we think it means. Jokes about language are reflexive, however. They allow us to think about language as an object, and our use of language as a phenomenon.

Most of the jokes in this book alert us to aspects of our language without directly indicating that it is language that we should examine. In this chapter, however, I discuss some jokes that are overtly about language—*i.e.*, the topic of the joke is an aspect of language or language use.

2.0 Jokes and Linguistic Form

2.1 Jokes About English Orthography

Much fuss is made of English spelling rules, and the logical absurdities yielded by maintenance of orthography that provides us with the equivalent of fossil evidence for the archaeological record of some part of our linguistic past. These strange, apparently illogical, inconsistent orthographical forms remind us what an arbitrary object the language we use is, and how particularly arbitrary are the conventions we use to write it. Learning to read English is learning that the relationship between phoneme and grapheme is only sometimes reliable. As has been pointed out, there is sufficient evidence in the spelling rules of English to insist that the word *fish* is to be spelt *ghoti*. The way this works is to use *gh* pronounced as in *laugh*, *o* as in *women*, and *ti* as in *nation*.[1] This proposal highlights the absurdity and inconsistency that is rife in the English spelling system, which is, in many ways, only remotely a system. It takes but one good demonstration of the absurdities to point this out. The arguments against spelling reform are about connections other than those between phoneme and grapheme. They invoke connections with our past, our traditions, and with speakers of English worldwide who speak with different accents. The idea here is that all speakers of English are united by a common written language. To believe, however, that the written form of our language will never change, is to miss the essentially dynamic nature of language, even in its print form. The rapid spread of Internet communication has shown that even the written system can change and grow dramatically in a fertile context.[2]

Many books, learned, commercial, amusing and pedantic, have been produced that dwell on the particular spelling absurdities of English. They are of use to language teachers, pedants and comedians. However, for my purposes here, spelling absurdities in and of themselves are not actually jokes, so I do not include many of them here, except when they make an additional humorous point.

Dorothy Parker, a humorist always intensely conscious of the structure of language, is said to have made the following remark *extempore*, when invited to play a party game involving ducking for apples in a bucket of water.

Example 1

Ducking for apples—change one letter and it's the story of my life.

$$(Dorothy\ Parker,\ 1893–1967)$$

This is, *inter alia*, a joke about language, because it directs the listener to pay attention to orthography and phonology. The listener is not told which letter to change, but it takes a small step to figure it out. The joke itself of course, has nothing to do with ducking for apples, other than that the phrase is set up as a minimal pair for the phrase *fucking for apples*, which probably means having sex for no real reward (*cf.* working for peanuts).

2.2 In Two Words

Dorothy Parker was known not only for her witty comments on her unsuccessful love affairs, but also on her constant need for more money. She captures her ongoing desperation for money with the following plaintive linguistic observation.

Example 2

The two most beautiful words in the English language are "check enclosed".
(Dorothy Parker, 1893–1967)

Words, as we know, cannot in and of themselves be beautiful although this phrase is a cliché, usually employed for sentimental purposes.[3] Parker satirizes this sentimentality, by listing what for her are the two most beautiful words, especially when issued in the correct order, under the most conventional of contexts, *i.e.*, that her cheque is enclosed with the note bearing these words.

Samuel Goldwyn (1879–1974), famous for his many malapropisms, logical contradictions and mixed metaphors, additionally had a fine understanding of the rules of English morphology. He is reported to have offered the following response when asked to do something.

Example 3

In two words, im possible

Impossible is one word, not two. However, it may be analyzed as two phonological words, particularly if said slowly and with emphasis. Impossible has two morphemes, or meaning units. *Im-* contains the idea of 'not' and *possible* the idea of 'do-able'. Essentially, *impossible* contains two basic concepts, so indeed, *impossible* may be represented as two words in the morphological systems of some languages, including in English, where it might be rendered as *not possible*.

There is quite an industry now in the utterances that follow the introductory trope *in two words....* They are all based on the same joke, that is, what follows is never two words. Thus, as in Goldwyn's remark, the utterance that follows *in two words* is one word, three, or many, never two.

So, for instance, in *Mystery Science Theater 3000*, Joel is complaining about something and elicits this response from Dr. Forrester, who counts each of the two words on his fingers.

Example 4

Two words, Joel: Get Overit.

Here, of course, *Overit* may indeed be a single word—but at a phonological level, not in terms of English semantics and its expression.

In the original Australian version of the TV sitcom *Kath & Kim*, the one word trope is employed as a running gag. The excerpt below is a more than usually over-the-top example of the way this joke works.

Example 5

Kath: Now Kimmy, look at me. I've got one word to say to you: Move out tout-de-suite, go back to Brett. Get real, you'll never get any better!

3.0 The Medium is the Message but is the Message the Message?

A particular feature of many jokes about language is that they have the effect of making the joke more than once: one might say that in these cases, the medium is the message and the message is the message. These are a specially complex case of jokes within jokes.

The joke in Example 6 is one much beloved of linguists, and when told by a linguist usually contains elaborate exemplification. I've tried to track down the attribution, and I believe it originates with Sydney Morgenbesser. Apparently, the philosopher J. L. Austin was visiting Columbia University in the 1950s and delivering a series of lectures, including one on close linguistic analysis. Austin commented that it was curious that no languages had been found in which the use of two positive logical operators yielded a negative polarity reading. Morgenbesser, in the audience, is said to have muttered, "Yeah, yeah."

Here's a short version of Morgenbesser's witticism in joke form.

Example 6

A linguistics lecturer is giving a class on negation. He proceeds to describe how negation works in different languages of the world. In some languages, he explains, such as Italian, you need only one negative item for the sentence to have negative polarity. In some languages, such as Afrikaans, you require two negative items for the sentence to have negative polarity, whereas in some languages two negatives will give you a positive polarity, as in English. However, in no language do two positive items yield a negative polarity. From the back of the hall comes a student response, "YEAH! RIGHT!"

This is a perfect example of the kind of linguistic joke I have been describing. The technique in these jokes is either to demonstrate or undermine the point the joke is making. The punch line in Example 6 contains a linguistic demonstration of what apparently cannot be done, *i.e.*, using two positive items to give the sentence a negative polarity, and does it appropriately and efficiently, putting paid to the strong claim the lecturer is making. Of course, philosophers, logicians and semanticists will tell you that these are not real polarity items, that the lecturer is right and the student is making a category mistake, but none of these holds any water for the purposes of the joke. The pragmatics, as always in jokes, (and in life) holds the day. The lecturer says two positives cannot make a negative, and the student uses two positives to negate what the lecturer is saying. The fact that the force of the student's utterance is at once a challenge to and a denial of the correctness of the lecturer's claim, as well as an elegant demonstration of the impossible, is what makes this joke clever, as well as funny. It is, of course, the perfect put-down. Who could continue after that? As every linguist knows, data can be very inconvenient facts, especially when produced spontaneously by others at inappropriate moments.

There's another story that exploits the same principle as the joke in Example 7, but uses a different level of the grammar by which to do it.

Example 7

A linguistics lecturer is expounding on inflectional morphology. "The English language has examples of suffixes and prefixes, but we find no examples of infixes, even though these are not uncommon in other languages." A voice from the back of the room drawls, "Un-fucking-believable!"

In this case, the last speaker does exactly what the lecturer says cannot be done: he infixes *fucking* between *un-* and *-believable*. It's true of course, that English does not use grammatical infixation as productively as, *e.g.*, Tagalog, but expletives such as *fucking*, *bloody* and *blooming* often do occur intersyllabically, usually for the intensified illocutionary effects of anger, outrage, surprise, and admiration.

Another example of a joke that serves as an example of itself is the following, which, as an added twist, uses a foreign expression.

Example 8

A girl walks into a bar and orders a double entendre… so the bartender gives it to her.

A *double entendre* is an utterance that can be understood in more than one way. As a rule, this French term is reserved for those utterances that have as one of their readings a suggestion of the risqué. Thus, a remark considered to be *double entendre* is one that is sexually suggestive. It's conventional when ordering spirits in a bar that if you want a stronger drink you ask for a double, *e.g.*, *a double Scotch, a double brandy and ginger ale*, etc. It is clear that the girl doesn't know what a *double entendre* is, or if she does, she shouldn't really be ordering it in a bar. The second part of the utterance is itself a *double entendre*. It could mean, "so the bartender gives her a *double entendre*" (which doesn't make much sense, although it follows that he should give her what she asked for) or it could mean "so the bartender gives it to her", colloquial for "the bartender had sex with her".[4] In the one reading of *gives it to her, it* refers to the *double entendre*, or the putative drink she ordered. In the other reading, *it* does not refer to anything. *Give it* is a phrasal verb when part of an idiom like *give it to her*, meaning "have sex with her". The suggestion made by the joke, *i.e.*, the *double entendre*, is that the bartender gave her what she asked for, sex, generally the aim of a *double entendre*. This joke contains a *double entendre* within a *double entendre*.

Some kinds of jokes about language are produced by exploiting the ambiguity inherent in words that relate to the manner in which language is produced. This one is due to Spike Milligan.

Example 9

He walked with a pronounced limp—l-i-m-p pronounced limp.
(*Milligan, 1961,* The Sewers of the Strand)

The ambiguity here is to be found in the term *pronounced*, which on one reading means "noticeable", and on another refers to the process of pronunciation. So to paraphrase the wording of this joke, we could say, "he walked with a noticeable limp, the word spelt l-i-m-p should be spoken in the following way, *limp*." Needless to say, this is not remotely funny. The joke associates the frozen expression, "with a pronounced limp" with the frozen expression "x-y-z pronounced xyz", although the two expressions have absolutely nothing to do with each other. The repetition highlights the ambiguity in our use of *pronounced*. The humor is in the repetition of *pronounced limp*, which is simply silly, because limp has already been pronounced, in its first use, so there's no point in doubling back and saying how it's pronounced. If we were to follow the logic of this usage we would be led to an endless, insane repetition of *pronounced limp*.

In Example 10, we see another example of the loopiness of language. It's worth noting here that the property of hierarchical recursion has been postulated to be the defining property of human language (Hauser, Chomsky, & Fitch, 2002; Fitch, Hauser, & Chomsky, 2005). Jokes about recursion are very close to the soul of linguistics.

Example 10

Here's a dictionary entry for *recursion*.
Recursion *See "Recursion".*

Joseph Heller, author of the novel *Catch-22*, actually names a kind of recursive loop *Catch-22*. This is not hierarchical recursion, but an unending loop. Catch-22 is a maddening kind of paradox. Here's the explanation of Catch-22 from the novel itself.

Example 11

Yossarian looked at him soberly and tried another approach. "Is Orr crazy?"
"He sure is," Doc Daneeka said.
"Can you ground him?"
"I sure can. But first he has to ask me to. That's part of the rule."
"Then why doesn't he ask you to?"
"Because he's crazy," Doc Daneeka said. "He has to be crazy to keep flying combat missions after all the close calls he's had. Sure, I can ground Orr. But first he has to ask me to."
"That's all he has to do to be grounded?"
"That's all. Let him ask me."
"And then you can ground him?" Yossarian asked.
"No. Then I can't ground him."
"You mean there's a catch?"
"Sure there's a catch," Doc Daneeka replied. "Catch-22. Anyone who wants to get out of combat duty isn't really crazy."

(Heller, 1961, p. 45)

Another example of a Catch-22 is found a few lines later in the novel.

Example 12

He had Orr's word to take for the flies in Appleby's eyes.
"Oh, they're there all right," Orr had assured him about the flies in Appleby's eyes after Yossarian's fist fight in the officers' club, "although he probably doesn't even know it. That's why he can't see things as they really are."
"How come he doesn't know it?" inquired Yossarian.
"Because he's got flies in his eyes," Orr explained with exaggerated patience. "How can he see he's got flies in his eyes if he's got flies in his eyes?"

(Heller, 1961, p. 46)

This is Joseph Heller's definitive contribution to the problem of linguistic recursion. It demonstrates yet again that people using ordinary language need escape hatches from the analyticity of pure logic.

Using recursion in a maddening way is a trick often used by Spike Milligan. Logically and linguistically, these sorts of utterances can't be faulted. Here's a typical example.

Example 13

In the darkness we sat huddled on the fiendish Chinese river-steamer, the silence broken only by the sound of the silence being broken.

(The Goon Show, 1955. Series 5; episode 17)

The effect of this kind of language play is similar linguistically to the visual effect of mirrors reflecting each other reflecting each other. These ideas found their creative form in Lewis Carroll's *Alice Through the Looking Glass*, particularly in the major motif of the dreamer dreaming that s/he is a part of someone else's dream (Dodgson, 1871). The mathematical concept of recursion may be informing this play by Carroll. It has, in fact, been argued by Gardner that Lewis Carroll's (*a.k.a.* Charles Lutwidge Dodgson) literary work is deeply informed by his mathematics (Gardner, 1960).

These sorts of recursive embeddings are crazy-making, be they visual or linguistic. When we are made conscious of the recursive possibilities of our language, we are faced with the fact that although embedding and recursiveness are limitless, human cognitive processing, comprehension and memory are restricted. In the case of these sorts of jokes, the consciousness of the infinite possibilities of language contrasted with human cognitive limitations can be a source of bewilderment but also, of amusement.

There's little cottage industry in what have been called "Self-referential Trope Titles".[5] Examples are manifold, but a few will suffice here.

Example 14

Department Of Redundancy Department
Heävy Mëtal Ümlaut
Noun Verber

4.0 The Collision of Language and Logic

It has often been remarked that there is a particular sort of humorous play that appears in the work of (especially North American) Jewish comedians. This play seems to find its roots in the *pilpul*, or the reasoning processes engaged in by Talmudic scholars as part of the ongoing process of exegesis and interpretation of texts sacred to Jewish religion. It may be described as detailed, forensic debate over minor points of language and logic. Training in *pilpul* has always been highly regarded for the sharpening of wits, and the mode of argument is recognized (and appreciated for its sheer value in exercising the mind) although the dedication to Talmudic scholarship is no longer part of the lifestyle of many 21st century Jewish people. When displaced onto the world outside of Talmudic scholarship, the use of *pilpul* taps right into the fundamental absurdity and illogicality of language use.

The joke about the Rabbi's slippers, also discussed in Chapter 2, presents an illuminating demonstration of this.

Example 15

Rabbi Tescher, discovering that he had left his comfortable slippers back in the house, sent a student after them with a note for his wife. The note read: "Send me your slippers with this boy."

*When the student asked why the rabbi had written "**your**" slippers, Rabbi Tescher answered, "Listen, young man. **Think.** If I wrote "my" slippers, my wife would read "my slippers"—and would send me **her** slippers. What can I do with her slippers? So I wrote "your" slippers: she'll read "your" slippers and send me mine.*

(Rosten, 1985)

The linguistic issue here is deixis, or the shifting reference of certain words. As discussed in Chapter 2, deictics are inherently context bound. When a speaker pays too much attention to the use of deixis—a difficult linguistic issue as it straddles the language system and its referential uses, both endophoric and exophoric—confusion is likely to result. It is no accident that the character in the joke is a rabbi, because rabbinical scholars are trained to use this sort of reasoning. The reasoning is impeccable; the results are absurd. Using what he knows about his wife, the rabbi shows that he is sensitive to the pragmatics of the situation. On the other hand, the logic he applies to the use of deictics runs counter to their actual use. Language use is conventional, and he is flouting the conventions of deixis. It could be said, however, that he knows his wife, and how she thinks, so his communication is appropriate given the contextual factors. Of course, the story is humorous because the rabbi is in danger of getting his wife's slippers, for which, as we know, he has no use.

If he gets his slippers then he will be justified in continuing to believe that his use of language is correct, because it has worked for him. However, in order for this system to work, deictics have to cease being deictic, and simply be rigid designators. Henceforth "your slippers" will refer to the rabbi's slippers. We can only imagine what this sort of convention would do to a system of communication.[6]

Freud (1905/2002) tells the joke in Example 16, which he says is one of the most excellent in demonstrating a particular kind of Jewish reasoning.

Example 16

Two Jews meet in a railway carriage at a station in Galicia. "Where are you going?" asks one. "To Cracow" was the answer. "What a liar you are!" broke out the other. "If you say you are going to Cracow, you want me to believe you are going to Lemberg. But I know you are going to Cracow. So why are you lying to me?"

(Freud, 1905/2002)

Again, we see that logic applied to language use can lead to wild absurdity. In this case, the language that is used is disputed, since the first speaker accuses the second of lying. This goes to the heart of language use, which is intentionality. The first speaker wants to know where the second is going. He asks a simple question and gets what looks like a straightforward answer. Being of a suspicious turn of mind, he doesn't trust the second speaker's answer. He then spells out the logic underlying his accusation that his interlocutor is a liar. The paranoia is patent, but like all paranoia it has its own internal logic. He introduces the proposition *If you say you are going to Cracow, you want me to believe you are going to Lemberg.* There is no way that the first speaker can know what the second speaker wants him to believe. Nevertheless, once that proposition has been introduced into the argument, other propositions appear to follow, syllogistically. The speaker continues, *but I know you are going to Cracow.* Of course, there is no way he can know that his interlocutor is going to Cracow, other than by believing what the man has told him, but he has just accused that same man of being a liar. Having thus "deduced" that the man is indeed going to Cracow, he demands to know why the man is lying to him. But we don't know that the man has lied; he has answered his interlocutor's question. The expostulation reveals the convoluted thought processes of one who cannot trust other people's uses of language, because he cannot trust other people. He doesn't simply say to the other, "I don't believe you", for which statement, in any event, he has no evidence one way or the other, but he also subjects the second speaker to a violent verbal attack, essentially because, ultimately, the man has provided a simple answer, which the first speaker now deems to be accurate, although founded on a lie.

If logic can demonstrate to us that language is not to be trusted, where do we end up? In these cases, and the claim has been made by Oring (1984) among others, we learn that certain kinds of language use reflect the absurdity of the world and encourage us to surrender to that absurdity. This is a particularly Jewish narrative about suffering, complaint and resigned acceptance, but it is never silent, and the absurdity is highlighted by the kinds of jokes that are made and appreciated. The comedy is in the attitude—"the world is absurd so what do you expect me to do about it? I still have to eat, to live. I might as well laugh."

The influence of the jokes and the thinking behind them that emanate from the descendants of Eastern European Jewish émigrés (Examples 15 and 16) is reflected in the way Groucho Marx uses language and logic, as do many Jewish comedians of the 20th and 21st century.

Woody Allen, commenting on one of the principal debates in modern linguistics, that is, the innateness of language, made a remark that touched on the matter of constant complaining, which seems to be an identifying feature of much Jewish humor.

Example 17

Sentence structure is innate but whining is acquired.

(Woody Allen, 1976)

In fact, from the standard perspective of generative linguistics, this is a truism. Generative linguists take it as a given that sentence structure is part of our innate capacity for language; the many uses of language, including whining, are acquired as part of exposure to a culture in which such speech acts, *e.g.*, whining have a place. It is also the case that there are some cultures that appear to privilege the speech act or language activity, of whining, more than others do. (For more on speech acts, see Chapter 2). Stereotypically, one such cultural group consists of Jewish people, particularly those with whom Woody Allen seems to identify. The remark gets its humor from the rather odd choice of the speech act of whining, rather than any other speech act, and, also, from his critique of a culture in which whining is acquired as part of membership in that culture, by implied contrast with other cultures in which whining might, indeed, not be acquired.

The kind of logic applied to language use and convention is shown to lead into even deeper craziness in the joke in Example 18, which has echoes of Lewis Carroll in the way that the speaker treats null classes as though they existed. For instance, the March Hare in *Alice In Wonderland* offers Alice some non-existent wine, she is made an offer to take more tea when she has not had any, and the White King in *Alice through the Looking Glass* is impressed with Alice's eyesight which is so sharp that she can see nobody coming at a great distance down a road.

Example 18

"Why should 'eretz' be spelled with a gimmel?"
"A gimmel? It isn't."
"Why shouldn't 'eretz' be spelled with a gimmel?"
*"Why **should** 'eretz' be spelled with a gimmel?"*
"That's what I'm asking you—Why should 'eretz' be spelled with a gimmel?"
(Ted Cohen, 1999)

This exchange is another example of the power of *pilpul*. For explication's sake: *gimmel* is the third letter of the Hebrew alphabet, its pronunciation is [g]. *Eretz* is a Hebrew word which means "land" or "country". The joke is typical of the playful and infuriating reasoning which is rife in this tradition.

The trouble starts with the first question. Why should anyone reasonably ask this question? For tolerance's sake, though, it is rather typical of a certain kind of linguistic riddle, so it is as legitimate as *Why should you always refuse to lend an ape money?* (Answer: *It's dangerous to let him put the bite on you.*) The interlocutor is puzzled, since, as he points out, it is obvious that *eretz* is not in fact spelled with a *gimmel*. Then the first speaker, following some elementary rules of logical argument, phrases his second question as the flip side of his first, thus, *Why shouldn't eretz be spelled with a gimmel?* The interlocutor now gets into this game, and he too flips the question back, asking why indeed *eretz* should be spelled with a *gimmel*. The first speaker is triumphant, having got the second speaker to voluntarily express his initial question, as though it were a question worth asking. The first speaker has won the one-upmanship battle, the content being total nonsense. The skill in argument is what is at stake, and the patent ludicrousness of the outcome allows us to see where pure logic can lead.

5.0 Prescriptivism and Rebellion

In language use, as in life, people do not find stipulations easy to obey. This may have something to do with their arbitrariness, or the fact that they are imposed from without. Linguistic prescriptivism has had a terrible and complicated hold on speakers because, as we know, language is the site of struggle, and power relations always enter into language use. Most of us do not like being told how to speak, since we regard our language use as one of our personal freedoms. If our speech patterns do not match the stipulations, we may either yield to the greater force of the stipulator as in the example below, or flout the stipulation.

Example 19

The third grade teacher says, "Mary, I'd like you to give me a sentence beginning with 'I',
please."
  Mary hesitates for a few seconds then says, "I is…"
  The teacher interrupts her, "No Mary, you cannot begin a
  sentence with 'I is'—you must use 'I am'."
  Mary appears upset and tries to protest, "But Teacher…"
  The teacher insists, "I asked you to give me a sentence beginning with 'I', and use 'am',
please."
  Mary shrugs, "I am the ninth letter of the alphabet."

This is another example from the genre of teacher-pupil jokes, in which the pupil outsmarts the teacher. In this case, the teacher cannot think beyond the phenomenon of grammatical agreement that she has in mind. In her opinion, the only kind of verbal element that can follow the item *I* is marked with first person singular agreement, thus *am* rather than *is*. When the teacher hears *I is*, she cannot think beyond what to her is an unacceptable error. In her conception of the grammatical world, a child who says *I is* has got to be wrong. Although the child tries to protest, she will not allow her to finish the sentence, but insists on the correct formation, beginning *I am*. Mary, realizing she is fighting a losing battle, simply concedes, but does so either ingenuously or very cleverly, demonstrating that the teacher has caused her to make a gross grammatical error. This sort of joke has the purpose of keeping us alerted to the limited application of certain grammatical rules as they are formulated for pedagogical purposes, *e.g.*, "*I is* to be followed by a first person singular auxiliary or verbal form or a modal." These kinds of prescriptions lead immediately to the rebellious need that some of us have to show that the rule as formulated is subject to exceptions, and therefore, not much good as a rule.

It seems inevitable that any language user who is alive to the possibilities of language is impelled to regard articulated language rules, particularly prescriptive prohibitions, as a personal challenge. This is seen in both conscious and subconscious protests. It is not clear whether the line *to boldly go where no-one has gone before* from *Star Trek* is a conscious attempt to boldly split an infinitive in a television series (which no-one has had the courage to publicly do before) or whether it was preferable to recklessly split it, because that is how people speak English (and, it would appear, both Vulcans and Klingons seem to easily understand it).

The invocation against placing an adverb between *to* and the verbal form found in an infinitive in English probably derives from the 17th century purists who thought that any grammatical deviation English made from its Latin origins was ugly, reprehensible and a sign of ignorance and uncultivated sensibility. The longest lasting and most influential of the prescriptive tracts on the subject is due to Bishop Robert Lowth who published his *Short Introduction to English Grammar* in 1762. Essentially, Lowth prescribed a host of rules to ensure that English (a Germanic language in syntactic structure, at least) remained as close as possible to the structures of Latin (a Romance language). Sadly, he could not enforce word order strictures (classical Latin allowing a much freer word order, with a preference for the verb in final position) nor the elaborate morphological suffixes for case, person, number and gender (extinct from English except in personal pronouns, *who*/*whom* question words, residual verb conjugations and so forth). But he did set down the law on the splitting of infinitives and preposition-final sentences (Lowth, 1762).

Needless to say, English, a language which owes a great deal to the Romance and Germanic traditions, has developed in the many centuries since Latin passed quietly away, although its spirit continues to hover over some parts of the English speaking world. Speakers of English tend to split infinitives when they need to. Astonishingly, even today, we hear convoluted sentences uttered by speakers who tie themselves into horrendous knots and disfigure their message in their attempts not to split infinitives, or to not split infinitives.

A classic remark misattributed to Winston Churchill engages with the prescriptive, and very silly, prohibition against ending a sentence with a preposition. The speaker neatly shows the contortion that is required, and in so doing, produces a very cumbersome sentence, which is, in any event, only marginally grammatical.

Example 20

From now on, ending a sentence with a preposition is something up with which I will not put.

(misattributed to Winston Churchill, 1874–1965)[7]

And just to make the case *a fortiori*, a small industry has evolved in examples designed to demonstrate how many prepositions one can actually end a sentence with.

Example 21

What did you turn your socks from inside out to outside in for?

Example 22

Child to father: "What did you bring this book I didn't want to be read to out of up for?"

The *Guinness Book of World Records* apparently, at some stage, identified a new category called *The most prepositions at the end*. They listed the sentence in Example 23, apparently said by a boy who didn't want to be read bits out of a book about Australia.

Example 23

What did you bring that book that I don't want to be read to from out of about 'Down Under' up for?

Somewhere along the line, it became evident that this trick could be performed recursively and sentences such as the one in Example 24 started to proliferate.

Example 24

What did you use the example that the boy asked, "What did you bring that book that I don't want to be read to from out of about 'Down Under' up for?" for?

The potential for amusement palls once we see the recursive possibilities of the joke. *Guinness* abandoned the category. A pithier example says it all.

Example 25

"Excuse me, where is the library at?"
"Here at Harvard, we never end a sentence with a preposition."
"Oh, I beg your pardon, where is the library at, asshole?"

As linguists have argued for many years the prohibition is a hangover from the days of embarrassment and cultural cringe experienced by English scholars of the 17th and 18th century, when English was regarded as an inferior form of classical Latin (dead, unchanging and therefore beautiful) and, it should be said, a Romance language. The Villain of the Piece, if one is to be picked, seems to have been Lowth, although it has been suggested by Mark Liberman that it was the amateur peevologists of the 19th century who elevated this characteristic of "the solemn and elevated style" into a supposed grammatical rule.[8]

In order to understand what the fuss is about, I'll try to explain the relevant rule for case in Latin.

Essentially, in Latin, case is manifested either by suffixation on nominals and their determiners to indicate nominative, accusative, dative, ablative etc., or by an unbound preposition immediately preceding the nominal, which also carries the case marking. Thus, as I recall from my years of rote learning, *to* or *for the boy* is translated as *pueri*, where the *i* indicates dative *to* or *for*. Since *pueri* is one word, obviously the preposition is closely attached to the stem. I won't dwell on the obvious observation that the case marking follows rather than precedes the nominal stem, because I am no Latin scholar, but if we are to be consistent in our return to Latinization we should observe the niceties. In the case of unbound prepositions, we get *ad urbem*, "to the city", where *ad* translates as "to" and *urbem* is the accusative case of *urbs* meaning "city". Is this funny yet?

But many English speakers have the temerity to say, *Which city are you going to?* stranding that preposition as far away from the demonstrative interrogative *which* as possible, as opposed to *To which city are you going?* There are still those who wield the structure in question as a diagnostic of education and class, particularly when used in the written form. This shibboleth has been around for 250 odd years, but I suspect its blade has been blunted just a little. Jokes ridiculing it have done their share.

Nevertheless, we might ask why, despite the best efforts of our minders to teach us otherwise, we persist in our wrongheadedness? One reason is that English is grammatically a Germanic language, and the rule of pied-piping in prepositional phrases, or preposition-stranding, as it is also known, is deeply entrenched in Germanic syntax. Thus, in Afrikaans, for instance, also a Germanic language, prepositions are free morphemes with a tendency to appear preceding their sister noun phrases, or popping up in sentence-final position, or indeed, affixed to the beginning of verbs, in the cases of phrasal verbs (see also Chapter 7, for the discussion of German inspired by Mark Twain).

And, in fact, English is not that different in this respect. Consider the sentences, *She looked up the word* and *She looked up the hill*. We can say, *Up the hill she looked* but not *Up the word she looked*. We can say *She looked the word up* but not *She looked the hill up* (on the reading that she looked to the top of the hill). There are a number of constituency tests we can run to establish that in one instance, *up* belongs closely to *look* and in another it is more closely related to the noun phrase. So, that's the first fact to be aware of. Some prepositions are part of phrasal verbs and some relate specifically to noun phrases, and the brute application of the prescriptive rule doesn't acknowledge the difference.

The second fact is that Germanic languages allow preposition stranding in the case of non-phrasal verbs too. So in Dutch, we can say *Hij trapte de deur in*, meaning "He kicked the door in." (den Dikken, 1995). In Afrikaans, moreover, we can say *Hy loop in die kamer in* meaning, "He walks into the room", where *in* is a preposition meaning "into" and occurs both preceding the noun phrase *die kamer*, "the room," and sentence finally. In a northern dialect of German, we can say, *Da ist die Rede von*, meaning "this is the thing being talked about" (Hempelmann,

2000).[9] Like many languages, English has a mongrel heritage. And users of English are being asked to choose between their ancestors, Romance or Germanic, and they tend towards Germanic in this regard, since the morphology of case marking has all but dropped out of English, and prepositions/particles are a major category in the lexicon of Germanic.

Why has the issue of obedience to the prescription about prepositions endured this long? Surely our Germanic leanings could have been stamped out by now? Education is capable of changing so much about the way we think and behave— this preposition stranding should have been beaten out of us. But it hasn't, and thus, to understand this phenomenon, we need to consider the proposition that language use has a mind of its own and when English speakers follow their tacit rules of language, they tend to strand prepositions, particularly in complex clauses.

Further, in the case of *wh*-movement in questions in which the PP is the target, we tend to move only the *wh*-word or phrase, the NP, rather than the whole PP. So we tend to say *Who did you give it to?* when the full declarative structure is *I gave it to him.* We simply move the wh-NP *who(m)* rather than the full PP in question form *to who(m).* This is a move that English approves of (or should I say, of which English approves?). Both possibilities are grammatical in English. Since case marking on *who* is falling away, try stop it though we may, there appears now to be even less reason to move the full PP. Those who do insist on moving the full PP tend to say *To whom did you give it?* rather than *To who did you give it?,* because there is no point in being half a prescriptivist. The rest of us simply say *Who did you give it to?* and await the inevitable dislodgement from our academic pedestals.

Let's go back to the proposition about prepositions up with which we will not put. In ridiculing the unnaturalness of the PP prescription, the speaker demonstrates how pompous and ungainly it sounds. By demonstration, he does what he says he will never do, and by doing it shows it to be a rather affected and ugly construction in its execution. Another way of saying what he says (with no humorous effect) is *Ending a sentence with a preposition is something I will not put up with.* Actually, *put up with* is a multiword phrasal verb meaning something like "endure" or "tolerate". So what he has produced in the example is equivalent, structurally, to the sentence *This is the word up which she looked.* It is not grammatical in English to split a phrasal verb in this way, because the preposition belongs to the verb phrase and not the noun phrase.

The example misattributed to Churchill is made funnier by the facts that the speaker chooses a phrasal verb with not one, but two, prepositions, and that s/he embeds them in a relative clause. In so doing, s/he demonstrates that the rule is not only crudely formulated, it can yield incorrect results, and additionally, that it sounds ridiculously pompous. Of course, to understand the joke, one must have been educated in a tradition that denigrates preposition stranding. The fact too, that the remark was (mis)attributed to Winston Churchill, grand statesman, orator, and upper-class British gentleman, the paragon of English as it should be spoken, adds to the humorous effect.

Prescriptivism is itself sometimes clothed in jokes. There's an often-quoted joke that is intended to remind users of English about the necessity of abiding by the prescriptive rules governing *will* and *shall*. The story goes something like this.

Example 26

A European tourist is swimming in the ocean not far from the shore, when he gets into some kind of trouble. He shouts out to the polite English people on the beach, "I will drown and nobody shall save me!" and so, he drowns.

The humor here is predicated on a prescriptive rule of English regarding the proper grammatical use of *will* and *shall*. *Shall* is to be used as an auxiliary in the first person to indicate the simple future tense, whereas *will* is to be used in the second and third person, for the same purpose. On the other hand, *will* is to be used in the first person as an auxiliary to indicate volition, intentionality, and resolve and *shall* is to be used in the third person for the same purpose.

The joke thus relies on the English people being so secure in their use of this rule that they don't even think about it. It also relies on the perception that the English are so polite that they wouldn't dream of preventing anyone from doing what he wanted. Thus, foreign to the English language, culture and shore, the swimmer drowns, because he mixes up the uses of *will* and *shall*. What he said may have been understood by the audience as "It is my intention to drown, and it is my express desire that nobody tries to save me". He intended of course, to say, "I am going to drown and it seems that nobody is going to save me." Following the prescriptive rule is thus shown to be a matter of life and death, and also, far more important than the life of a second language speaker. The sad truth, however, is that this rule is more honored in the breach. There are, indeed, people who follow it without any conscious consideration. For the rest of us, it is long gone. *Shall* appears to be waning in its use, and both *will* and *shall* when used with the force of order or instruction are generally stressed. Even in formal writing the *shall/will* distinction appears to be on its way out. As a matter of curiosity, it will be interesting to see whether younger generations of English speakers find this joke amusing.

6.0 Use and Mention

As we have already seen in other chapters (especially Chapter 2), there is a class of jokes that play on the distinction between the formal features of language as code and language in its ideational or expressive function. These form a particular subset of a larger set of jokes that play with the distinction between use and mention. Some of these use/mention jokes are funny because they are so obvious, but they are only obvious if one is focusing on the formal aspects of language. The three jokes that follow are all jokes that can be appreciated by children, no matter whether they know the terms or names of the concepts involved in explaining why the jokes make people laugh. The genre is a very common one in children's jokes, the basic children's riddle.

Example 27

Q: *What's brown and sticky?*
A: *A stick.*

Whether we agree with Freud or not, when we think of an item that is brown and sticky, it is likely that we think of something we can eat, like toffee, or vegemite, or something messy and disgusting (like excretion, tar, or grease). For some these may coincide. *Sticky* is an adjective that could refer to something gluey, viscous, or having adhesive properties. Whatever substance we imagine should have the properties of being brown and sticky. Although *stick* is the main sound sequence in the word *sticky*, we are not driven immediately to answer *stick*. This is probably because the genre of this type of Question/Answer riddle asks us to consider a substance in terms of its properties.

When we hear the response, *a stick*, we are forced to think about why that should be the answer. It is entirely obvious from the formal properties of the word and our knowledge of English suffixal morphology that *stick-y* might mean stick-like. In fact, on this interpretation, what could be more sticky than a stick? We have to laugh, because the answer, requiring the application of a productive rule of adjective formation, add −*y*, is so obvious. Of course, the reason that *sticky* does in fact mean "gluey" or "adhesive" is because it is derived from the English verb *stick*. Some adjectives ending in −*y* **are** productively formed from verbs, such as *shiny* from *shine* (*v*), but as a rule, when adjectives are formed from nouns (rather than verbs) in English they tend to take other forms, such as −*like* in *godlike*, or −*ish* as in *boyish*.

For a deep-seated psychological reason, there is something transgressive in thinking of a substance that is brown and sticky. When we discover that, instead, we should be thinking about a stick, we laugh because we have cheated the censor (*cf.* Freud, 1905/2002) and are relieved. Additionally, we laugh because we become conscious of conflicting or ambiguous rules of word-formation in English.

Similarly, the next joke is transgressive because by exploiting phonological form whilst ostensibly posing a question about linguistic meaning, it permits the thought of excreta.

Example 28

Q: *What's brown and sounds like a bell?*
A: *Dung.*

The genre of the children's riddle is familiar. The words *sounds like* invite us to think of an item that makes the same noise as a bell does. When we hear the answer, it is obviously correct, if we are thinking about form. The answer provides us with a **word** that sounds the same as the sound a bell makes, *i.e.*, variations on *ding, dong, dung* etc. But we were not primed to think about the sound of a word, rather, the question apparently concerned the referent of a word. When we realize that the word *dung* sounds like the noise a bell is purported to make, we laugh, because we were caught, tricked into thinking of an object, rather than the sound of a word. We realize that words can sound like other words or sounds, and that the words *sounds like* as the phrase is used here refer to the phonological form of words as well as to non-linguistic sounds in the world.[10]

Additionally, dung is brown and sticky, so many people are uneasy about the word (*cf.* Freud, again), and laugh when reassured that *dung* is also a sound that a bell makes, and at the same time feel relieved that the transgressive thought is contained by a joke, as an item of play.

In contrast, the joke in Example 29 is not transgressive in making us squirm about messy words and substances that remind us of excrement, nor other substances that seem particularly to attract and repel children, simultaneously. Like the previous example, this joke exploits the polysemous use of the phrase *sounds like*.

Example 29

Q: *What's orange and sounds like a parrot?*
A: *A carrot.*[11]

The first part is right in line with the genre. In form it's identical to the previous joke. Parrots, like bells, produce sounds. We are invited, indeed primed, to think of something, probably animate, that make the same sorts of noises as a parrot. Additionally, this thing should be orange in colour. The answer is surprising. A carrot is orange and the sound string *a carrot* differs in exactly one phoneme from *a parrot*. Again, the trick is in the use of *sounds like*. Instead of searching for a vocal animal, we should have been searching for a sound string whose referent was orange in colour. Sometimes, indeed, language is just about language. Nevertheless, the noteworthy aspect of these jokes is that they set off a train of associations that may have been entirely unconscious. Explicating some of these associations reveals to us the connotative richness of the ordinary language we know and use. Jokes like the three above demonstrate that all our knowledge and uses of language are connected in mysterious ways, many of which we do not understand.

Jokes about language treat it as an object as does the practice of formal linguistics: as data to be described and then analyzed. Discovering meaning potential is not a relevant dimension, nor a goal of this formal kind of analysis.

I find the following joke among the funniest exploiting the distinction between language as code and language as a system of meanings.

Example 30

Q: *What do Alexander the Great and Winnie the Pooh have in common?*
A: *They have the same middle name.*

(Ted Cohen, 1999)

Now, certainly to some, this is no doubt a very stupid joke. Examination of the biographical and historical facts should reveal that these two characters have nothing at all in common. It is, however, certainly a joke a child could make and a riddle a child might correctly answer. As a matter of fact, I tried this one out on a couple of eight year olds, who actually came up with the answer, but didn't think the joke was all that funny. They simply responded to a question, and focused on the code to figure out the answer. So what makes those adults, who think it is hilarious, respond in this way?

I'll try to explain how and why I think it works so well. Simply, *Alexander the Great* and *Winnie the Pooh* are the names of famous figures, one historical and one fictional. These three-element names form a unit in both cases. If one were to refer to Alexander and Winnie, there are plausible referents aplenty. However, these particular three-element names pick out particular and individual referents that many people in the English-speaking world are familiar with. So, it is not just Alexander, but *Alexander the Great*, and not just Winnie, but *Winnie the Pooh*, that are the referents in this joke. The form, Question/Answer, is like one used quite conventionally in other riddle-type jokes. The expected answer would be one that picks out a feature common to both the referents; perhaps they were both short, or had long noses, enjoyed honey, or were valiant in battle. This is more or less how the listener is primed. The answer, however, picks up on a purely formal feature of the three-element names: the middle element *the* is common to both names. So, listener expectations are undercut; the search for any commonality in the lives or characters of these well-known referents is set aside; and the commonality is found to be a purely formal feature of the names. Since the answer is totally unexpected, and at the same time, perfectly correct and utterly obvious, as hearers, we are suddenly directed to attend to the form of language, and as a result, to set aside content entirely.[12] The condition of ignoring interesting content and focusing on a formal feature is further exacerbated by the fact that the formal feature is *the*, in itself a fairly contentless item. In addition, any serious consideration of the grammatical functions of *the* in English is just too difficult for anyone not considering a career in doing so. We are easily led to yield to the condition of helplessness and absurdity in the face of the complexity and mysteriousness of our knowledge of the language we use.

I imagine that another factor in the funniness of the joke is the choice of referents from within a very large set. The joker could have chosen *Kermit the Frog* and *Winnie the Pooh*, or *William the Conqueror* and *Alexander the Great*, and, in my opinion, the joke would not have been nearly as good. This is probably the case because there is such a huge incongruity between the famous Macedonian soldier and leader, Alexander the Great, and the central character of the children's story by A.A. Milne, a stuffed Teddy Bear with a penchant for honey and a fine line in narrative discourse.

7.0 Jokes about Naming

Proper names lend themselves to all sorts of jokes, not least of which are those provoked by hundreds of years of Western philosophy. The status of names in relation to sense and reference has a long and bloody history. The joke in Example 31 is not easily covered by the generalizations about naming made by philosophers and linguists.

Example 31

A grasshopper walks into a bar.
The barman says, "You know, there's a drink named after you?"
"Really? Herman?"[13]

In order to understand this joke, we need to know that there is an alcoholic cocktail called a *Grasshopper*. We also need to enter into a world where grasshoppers can speak, can go up to barmen, and barmen can speak to grasshoppers in English. This joke picks up on a very thorny problem in philosophy. What is the status of the denotation "grasshopper"? The grasshopper has a proper name, Herman. Grasshoppers are herbivorous insects of the suborder *Caelifera* in the order *Orthoptera*, but we don't need to know this to get the joke. The grasshopper is a grasshopper. He is not a Herman. But Herman, in this instance, happens to be a grasshopper. So, when the barman says *there's a drink named after you*, it is legitimate for the grasshopper to ask, curiously, *How did they/you know my name was Herman?* The confusion here is that the barman does not know that the grasshopper's name is *Herman*, but he does know that Herman is a grasshopper, and he knows that the name of the drink in question is a *Grasshopper*. However, if I were to walk in a bar and the barman were to say there's a drink named after you, I would say, *Really? Debra?* and I would not think he meant the drink was named a *Human Being*.

The issue here is whether we refer to people according to their personal names or some other kind of classification system. *Herman*, in this case, has a specific referent, a grasshopper named Herman. This is a complex philosophical point, but the joke makes it more succinctly than a lot of the philosophical literature on sense and reference.

Of course, the idea of a grasshopper hopping into a bar is absurd at the outset. That he has a name and can talk adds to the general bracketing of commonsense experience that we find in jokes. The joke is short and snappy. It makes us laugh, and leaves us wondering about how we use language to name, describe and refer. This heightened consciousness regarding naming is unusual, in contradistinction to our automatic use of names and descriptors every time we name or refer to people, places, things or ideas in our language.

Kripke (1972) and, independently, Putnam (1975) revolutionized our ideas about naming. Previous theoretical approaches were due to Frege and then Russell. The sense/reference distinction was first formalized by Frege (1892).[14] Russell (1905) on the basis of his critique of Frege's distinction, developed the *Descriptive Theory of Names*, in which he proposed that names were disguised definite descriptions. The revolution against the *Descriptive Theory of Names* took the form of Kripke's *Causal Theory of Names* (Kripke, 1972/80), among others.

Kripke's proposal to account for our use of proper names is that names are what he calls *rigid designators*. Our use of names is part of a continuing tradition beginning with the first time a person, animal or object is "baptized" or "dubbed". Thus, although the person who bears a name may not have the same properties or attributes as the original bearer of the name, the designator is rigid. We use names in the same fashion that we use deictics, or indexicals. They are driven by a particular context of use. Names do not necessarily have unique referential properties, nor do they have what is known as "sense". They point out a person, animal, place or thing **in a given context**. Names allow us to recognize their bearers. They are not necessarily accurate descriptions of their bearers, nor do they, necessarily, tell us anything about their bearers. As it turns out, some names do have additional properties, and humor can be created by exploiting these particular properties. This can be seen in the cases in which a name does have a meaning and that meaning is not arbitrarily connected with the entity in question. Kripke notwithstanding, there are jokes about names that implicate far more than the *Causal Theory of Naming* is able to provide.

Returning, for instance, to *Alexander the Great* and *Winnie the Pooh*, which pick out these entities in all possible worlds, we might like to think a bit more about the linguistic properties of these names. Although they don't have much meaning, since they are names and names (apparently) don't mean anything (*contra* Humpty Dumpty—see Example 32 on p. 215), the three-word constructions themselves each have different internal structures. Although superficially they look alike in terms of their syntax, underlyingly this is not the case.

Thus, the term *Alexander the Great* might be regarded as a rigid designator for the historical person who was first dubbed with that name—presumably not in English, originally, but in Greek, as *Mégas Aléxandros*. Syntactically and semantically, this phrase may be analyzed as follows: there is an entity named Alexander who, when considered among all other Alexanders, is the one distinguished by being great. In this case, *Great* is functioning adjectivally, picking out a particular Alexander from all other Alexanders.

As we can see, the rigid designator picks out an entity in the world; the syntax and semantics of the phrase, on the other hand, tell us something about the way this complex name is composed, restricting the particular entity from within a class of entities, all named Alexander.

Clearly here, the syntax is also crucial. If we were to say, "The Great Alexander", this would be consistent with "there is an entity named Alexander who, when considered among all other Alexanders, is the one distinguished by being great." If that is the case, it will not necessarily pick out the same entity—"Alexander the Great".

Winnie-the-Pooh, on the other hand, is the name of a particular stuffed teddy bear, who happens to be a fictional character. Winnie-the-Pooh's real name, in any event, we are told, is Edward Bear. Bear is clearly not an arbitrary name in the way that Edward is. He is after all a bear, albeit only a stuffed teddy. He is sometimes known as *Pooh Bear*. As the story goes, the bear was originally named Winnie (based on Milne's son's actual teddy bear, who had been named after a real bear in the London Zoo). In Milne's story, after a particular incident with a balloon and bees the teddy bear's arms were so stiff that the only way to chase flies off his nose was to blow them off—producing the sound *pooh*.

Like *Alexander the Great*, *Winnie-the-Pooh* is a rigid designator. The baptism of the character is described in *Winnie-the-Pooh* (Milne, 1926). The teddy bear character is there given the name Winnie-the-Pooh, and there is a long chain of causality between that character and his many Disney clones.

The complex name, *Winnie-the-Pooh*, however, may be analyzed semantically and syntactically as, "there is an entity named *Winnie* who is a member of the class of poohs" (we can read this as the class of pooh bears).[15] Thus, syntactically, *the Pooh* is an NP in apposition to the NP *Winnie*. Note the contrast in structures between *Alexander*, who was the greatest of the class of Alexanders, and *Winnie*, who was a (founder) member of the class of poohs.

To complicate the matter of naming further, however, note that the original *Pooh* was a swan, who lived in London Zoo. The teddy bear's original "baptism" was as *Winnie-the-Pooh*, although it is clear that Winnie is not a swan, but simply that the bear was given the rigid designator *Winnie-the-Pooh*. This is often reflected in the way in which the name *Winnie-the-Pooh* is yielded in other languages, when the books, and now the Disney movies, are translated. For instance, in Russian it is *Vinni Pukh*; in Spanish, *Winnie Puh*, and in German, *Pu der Bär*. However, this is not the case in French, *Winnie l'Ourson* or Polish, *Kubusia Puchatka*.

This diversity in translation practices is noteworthy: it demonstrates that translators need to make important decisions about the theories of naming they follow. Do they adopt a causal (and contingent) theory of naming, thus going with the notion of rigid designators or do they go with a sense-based theory of naming? Milne plays with a sense-based theory of Winnie's name by making the narrator offer this explanation of why Winnie-the-Pooh is often called *Pooh*:

> "But his arms were so stiff ... they stayed up straight in the air for more than a week, and whenever a fly came and settled on his nose he had to blow it off. And I think—but I am not sure—that *that* is why he is always called Pooh."
>
> *(Milne, 1926)*

Pooh, in this instance, is used to describe onomatopoeically the sound the bear makes when blowing off a fly, since his arms were so stiff. Leaving aside the fantastical nature of this entire piece, we can see that Milne thought that children, at least, expected a sense-based explanation of names.

A famous conversation about the meaning of names is to be found in Carroll's *Alice Through the Looking Glass* (Dodgson, 1871).

Example 32

"My NAME is Alice, but—"

"It's a stupid name enough!" Humpty Dumpty interrupted impatiently. "What does it mean?"

"MUST a name mean something?" Alice asked doubtfully.

"Of course it must," Humpty Dumpty said with a sort of laugh: "MY name means the shape I am—and a good handsome shape it is, too. With a name like yours, you might be any shape, almost."

(Dodgson, 1871, Chapter 6)

It was pointed out by Peter Alexander (1951) that Carroll performs an interesting inversion with proper names and ordinary words. This is part of the *Looking Glass* picture of life. As Martin Gardner reminds us, in the non-*Looking Glass* world, words have conventionalized meanings, whereas "proper names seldom have a meaning other than that they denote an individual object" (Gardner, 1960). This view of meaning can be seen in Humpty Dumpty's discourse on the meanings of words, found in *Through the Looking Glass*.

Example 33

"I don't know what you mean by 'glory,'" Alice said.

Humpty Dumpty smiled contemptuously. "Of course you don't—till I tell you. I meant 'there's a nice knock-down argument for you!'"

"But 'glory' doesn't mean 'a nice knock-down argument,'" Alice objected.

*"When **I** use a word," Humpty Dumpty said in rather a scornful tone, "it means just what I choose it to mean—neither more nor less."*

"The question is," said Alice, "whether you CAN make words mean so many different things."

"The question is," said Humpty Dumpty, "which is to be master—that's all."

*Alice was too much puzzled to say anything, so after a minute Humpty Dumpty began again. "They've a temper, some of them—particularly verbs, they're the proudest—adjectives you can do anything with, but not verbs—however, **I** can manage the whole of them! Impenetrability! That's what **I** say!"*

"Would you tell me, please," said Alice "what that means?"

"Now you talk like a reasonable child," said Humpty Dumpty, looking very much pleased. "I meant by 'impenetrability' that we've had enough of that subject, and it would be just as well if you'd mention what you mean to do next, as I suppose you don't mean to stop here all the rest of your life."

"That's a great deal to make one word mean," Alice said in a thoughtful tone.

"When I make a word do a lot of work like that," said Humpty Dumpty, "I always pay it extra."

(Dodgson, 1871, Chapter 6)

Carroll engaged in a very creative manner with the issues of Nominalism that Humpty Dumpty's view of meaning involved. When Humpty Dumpty says *When I use a word, [….] it means just what I choose it to mean—neither more nor less*, he is expressing a position that is *en route* to the solipsism of private languages. If a word means whatever its user chooses it to mean, then the possibilities of interaction with others are severely restricted, since language use is, at the very least, a system of conventionalized meanings that are negotiated in interaction.

Interesting, though, is the fact that it is the same Humpty Dumpty who wants to know what Alice's name means. The inversion is a logical one, as befits the *Looking Glass* world. The point Carroll wants to entertain is that it could all as well be otherwise. Alexander's observation goes to the heart of Carroll's position on language use. It is indeed a question of who is to be master: it appears that at present all we can have is a negotiated settlement.

It is certainly the case that some proper names have meaning, although it is not necessary. A random selection of names that share the same surface structure as *Winnie-the-Pooh* and *Alexander the Great* reveals similar ambiguities and one or two additional ones. I unearthed *Jake the Muss; Ethelred the Unready; Billy the Kid; John the Baptist; Mack the Knife; Jabba the Hutt; Robert the Bruce; Jake the Peg; Mott the Hoople;* and *Gimpel the Fool*.

Jake the Peg, Mack the Knife, and *Jake the Muss* are all names that have the structure, *First name* (arbitrary) then a description in apposition, providing the most salient feature of that character. So *Mack the Knife* was a character called Mack who was known for his prowess in dealing with his enemies by using a knife; *Jake the Peg* was a character who had a wooden leg, (*i.e.*, a peg); *Jake the Muss* was a character who was very strong (*i.e.*, had muscles).

On the other hand, *John the Baptist, Billy the Kid, Mott the Hoople* and *Gimpel the Fool* are all names that have the structure *First name* (arbitrary) followed, in apposition, by a description, much like the structure of *Alexander the Great, i.e.,*

John the Baptist is a particular John, known for introducing baptism; and this particular Gimpel was known for being a fool. *Billy the Kid*, however, was not the Billy who was known for being a kid, but had as his salient feature that he looked very young, and *Mott the Hoople* was a hobo called Mott. *Jabba the Hutt* was a Hutt, called Jabba. *Robert the Bruce* was a Scottish King, Robert I. He was probably called Robert the Bruce, because he descended from a family variously known as *a Bruius*, *de Brus*, or *de Bruys*. *The* in this case seems to be equivalent to *de* (of) as it would be in French. *Ethelred the Unready* was not unready. *Unready* is a deliberate mistranslation or a pun on the Old English *unræd* (meaning "bad counsel"); the pun is on his name *Æthelred* (meaning "noble counsel"). Some names of the form *X the Y* are simply an arbitrary *First name*, followed by *the* + *rhyme*, whether or not the rhyme has any relevant meaning, e.g., *Sam the Sham*, *June the Baboon*, or *Hector the Inspector*.

Thus, all the names I have discussed in the *X the Y* category have some meaning, but their analysis does not follow straightforwardly from their superficial structure. We cannot capture all the facts under one generalization. The structure of *Richard the First* is not the same as the structure of *Jabba the Hutt*.

In the kind of naming we do with reference to the names of well-known characters, there is certainly recourse to the connotations associated with these names. Calling someone *a little Napoleon*, or *a little Hitler* is not an arbitrary use of names. It is not because the targets of the names we assign are little—it is because they have something of the quality that is connoted by the famous names. It is interesting that these proper names take on the properties of regular nouns, prefaced by the determiner *a* and the adjective *little*.

Ted Cohen (1999, p. 34) quotes the remark found in Example 34.

Example 34

Wagner is the Puccini of music.

In order to appreciate this double-edged insult, one must despise both Wagner and Puccini, and understand what *Puccini* implies for those who don't like his music. The insult is rather complicated. Part of the insult about Puccini is that Puccini was, of course, actually a musician. If we were to say that Wagner was the Shakespeare of music, we would be paying Wagner a compliment (since Shakespeare was not a musician, but great in his field of literature). But saying someone is the Puccini of music is to say, first of all that Puccini was not a musician, and secondly that the person who is being so compared is also not a musician, despite the fact that he (Wagner, in this case) is always considered to be one. Thus, both Puccini and Wagner are damned in this insult, Puccini because he is not even considered as being in the field of music, and Wagner, because he is regarded as being like Puccini, and therefore not in the field of music, which is the field in which he is being judged.

The comedy team, Monty Python's Flying Circus, demonstrated quite vividly that naming practices are always contextually bound. In case there is any doubt that the Pythons were not aware of the linguistic and philosophical problems of naming, the fact that this is set in the Philosophy Department at an Australian University, should leave us in no doubt. Australian philosophers were well known (certainly in the 1960s and 1970s) for their Materialist-Realist views.[16]

Example 35

.... First Bruce, an Australian in full Australian outback gear. We briefly hear a record of 'Waltzing Matilda'. He is sitting in a very hot, slightly dusty room with low wicker chairs, a table in the middle, big centre fan, and old fridge.

Second Bruce: Good day, Bruce!
First Bruce: Oh, hello Bruce!
Third Bruce: How are yer Bruce?
First Bruce: Bit crook, Bruce.
Second Bruce: Where's Bruce?
First Bruce: He's not here, Bruce.
Third Bruce: Blimey, s'hot in here, Bruce.
First Bruce: S'hot enough to boil a monkey's bum!
Second Bruce: That's a strange expression, Bruce.
First Bruce: Well Bruce, I heard the Prime Minister use it. "S'hot enough to boil a monkey's bum in 'ere, your Majesty," he said and she smiled quietly to herself.
Third Bruce: She's a good Sheila, Bruce and not at all stuck up.
Second Bruce: Ah, here comes the Bossfella now!—how are you, Bruce?
Enter fourth Bruce with English person, Michael.
Fourth Bruce: Goodday, Bruce, Hello Bruce, how are you, Bruce? Gentlemen, I'd like to introduce a chap from Pommie land… who'll be joining us this year here in the Philosophy Department of the University of Woolloomooloo.
All: Goodday.
Fourth Bruce: Michael Baldwin—this is Bruce. Michael Baldwin—this is Bruce. Michael Baldwin—this is Bruce.
First Bruce: Is your name not Bruce, then?
Michael: No, it's Michael.
Second Bruce: That's going to cause a little confusion.
Third Bruce: Mind if we call you 'Bruce' to keep it clear?
[…]
Fourth Bruce: Crack the tubes, right! (Third Bruce starts opening beer cans.) Er, Bruce, I now call upon you to welcome Mr. Baldwin to the Philosophy Department.
Second Bruce: I'd like to welcome the Pommie bastard to God's own earth, and I'd like to remind him that we don't like stuck-up sticky-beaks here.
All: Hear, hear! Well spoken, Bruce!

Fourth Bruce: Now, Bruce teaches classical philosophy, Bruce teaches Hegelian philosophy, and Bruce here teaches logical positivism, and is also in charge of the sheepdip.

Third Bruce: What does new Bruce teach?

Fourth Bruce: New Bruce will be teaching political science—Machiavelli, Bentham, Locke, Hobbes, Sutcliffe, Bradman, Lindwall, Miller, Hassett, and Benet.

Second Bruce: Those are cricketers, Bruce!

Fourth Bruce: Oh, spit!

Third Bruce: Howls of derisive laughter, Bruce!

[…]

Fourth Bruce: Any questions?

Second Bruce: New Bruce—are you a pooftah?

Fourth Bruce: Are you a pooftah?

Michael: No!

[…]

Fourth Bruce: Gentlemen, at six o'clock I want every man-Bruce of you in the Sydney Harbour Bridge room to take a glass of sherry with the flying philosopher, Bruce, and I call upon you, padre, to close the meeting with a prayer. […]

An Aborigine servant bursts in with an enormous tray full of enormous steaks.

Fourth Bruce: OK.

Second Bruce: Ah, elevenses.

Third Bruce: This should tide us over 'til lunchtime.

Second Bruce: Reckon so, Bruce.

(Monty Python's Flying Circus, *2nd* season, *Episode 22,* Just the words)

All the philosophers in this department are called Bruce. This raises the question of the philosophical status of names. A common-sense view of naming practices would suggest that names allow us to pick out individual referents in the world. However, all these philosophers are called Bruce, they all work together and they call one another Bruce. For the purposes of the script, they are named *First Bruce, Second Bruce,* etc., although they themselves do not use this nomenclature. They simply refer to everyone in the Department as *Bruce.* This is akin to the Australian practice of addressing everyone as *mate* although *mate* is not intended to function as a name, rather it is an address term intended as a solidarity item.[17] The introduction of a new philosopher to the faculty is a cause for some concern, firstly because he is a *Pommie bastard,* and more importantly because his name is not Bruce, it's Michael. One of the Bruces asks Michael if they can call him Bruce, to avoid confusion. From everything we know about naming as a strategy of referring to entities in the world, or of unique definite descriptions, calling him Bruce would not be helpful. Additionally *Bruce* does not carry any sense; it does not mean anything. Now is not the time for a baptism, so that from here on in, Bruce could be a rigid designator. However, the issue in this community seems to be solidarity; identity is a matter of identification, specifically with other philosophers called Bruce. Even the *bossfella* is called Bruce, and Michael is called *New Bruce*, at least until it can be established that he has fitted in. The stereotypes of Australian speech patterns and behavior are transposed onto the blunt materialist-realist approaches of the Australian philosophers. The fact that they are all called Bruce puts the issue of naming squarely on the table. The only problem in regard to naming that they identify is when someone is not called Bruce.

This use of naming echoes the interesting observation made by Peter Alexander about Humpty Dumpty's attitude to names and the meanings of common words. Does *Bruce* have a meaning, and if so what is it? Or, on the other hand, does the name *Bruce* have a semantic or logical function, and if so, what is it? Is Bruce simply an equivalent of the address term *mate*, used as a solidarity marker, in which case, its use is entirely determined by pragmatics?

As we know, naming has an interesting status with regard to illocutionary force. The use of certain types of names indicates the relationship interlocutors have with one another. For instance, calling someone *My Lord*, or *Your Majesty* signals that the speaker is in a particular relationship to the interlocutor. Very often these relationships are asymmetrical, pointing to a hierarchical relationship between the interlocutors. Thus, in certain language communities, we find *Father/Son*, and in some cultures *Teacher/Pupil*, or *Older person/Younger person*. In many instances, it is only the status of the superior interlocutor that is indicated by some naming device, whereas the inferior status of the other is indicated by no honorific at all.

In the following joke, the convention of naming indicating relative status is flouted, in order to show that illocutionary force is really all about speaker intention and not simply about naming.

Example 36

Sergeant welcoming new troops: I will address you as Sir *and you will address me as* Sir. *In your case, you will mean it.*

In this joke, the Sergeant is essentially saying that even though all parties may name each other as equals, the soldiers should all be aware that he has a higher status than they do. So, although they will all be engaged in the practice of egalitarian and respectful name use, this is purely for form's sake, because the military is a hierarchical institution, and he is of a higher rank than they are. It is clear to all that the naming practice here is of no consequence at all, because, in the act, the illocutionary force of the Sergeant's use of *Sir* does not convey respect at all, whereas he is warning his troops that they are expected to show respect in word and deed, *i.e.*, to ensure that the illocutionary force of their *Sir* is respect. This is a difficult call, since we cannot tell people what their intention should be in speaking. One cannot order another to intend respect. All one can do is to ask for their respect. However, in this case, it is not even certain that this is what the

Sergeant is doing. In fact, what he is saying is that he has no respect for the troops, even though he may address them respectfully. Thus the force of his utterance is to leave them in no doubt as to their place in the hierarchy, relative to his.

In this chapter, I have discussed jokes that not only use language, but are also about language in some of its uses. It is necessary, in some cases, for the hearer to know consciously which particular rule or feature is being exploited for humorous purposes, and in these cases, we need to say that the joke evokes both tacit and non-tacit knowledge of language. Essentially, however, it is at least the tacit knowledge of language that is evoked whenever a joke pivots on language play.

Notes

1 This remark is generally attributed to George Bernard Shaw, a long time campaigner for spelling reform, but shown unequivocally to go back at least till 1855, a year before his birth. According to Benjamin Zimmer, on Language Log, April 23, 2008, quoting some evidence unearthed by Matthew Gordon who found it in a letter by Charles Ollier to William Hunt, this particular example was proposed by Ollier's son. In the name of historical accuracy, I should note this. Shaw has quite enough witticisms to his credit: Ollier has none of which I am aware.

2 See for instance, Crystal, 2006.

3 Aesthetic appraisals must surely be limited by some criteria. I am not aware that these do or could exist.

4 An alternative phrasing, which would work as well, is "So, the bartender gives her one".

5 See for instance, http://tvtropes.org/pmwiki/pmwiki.php/Main/ThisTropeName ReferencesItself, whence I have taken these examples.

6 As a complement to this joke, I want to note a story from my days as a student of literature. The following exchange has stayed with me.
My friend: I can't find Mimesis!
Her partner: I don't know where your mesis is.
The reference, which has stayed with me, is to Erich Auerbach's *Mimesis: The Representation of Reality in Western Literature*. Princeton: Princeton UP, 1953.

7 See *Language Log* December 12, 2004. *A misattribution no longer to be put up with*, introduced by Geoffrey Pullum, and written as a guest post by Ben Zimmer.

8 "Latin-obsessed twentieth century introverts"? *Language Log*, August 26, 2010.

9 Hempelmann, Christian. December 2000, Linguist List.

10 Using *sounds like* is a trick much exploited in cryptic crossword puzzles. See Chapter 9 for a more extensive discussion.

11 I am indebted to Daniel Janks for this joke and many others of its ilk.

12 Depending on the theory of humor one adopts, one might also focus on how the listener feels, having been taken for a fool. In general, we laugh at a joke like this, because we are impressed by how easily we have been deceived, in this world of play. Both relief and incongruity theories would have something to say about this.

13 I am indebted to Nick Riemer for this joke.

14 See Chapter 2 and 3 for discussions of 'meaning'.

15 Pooh-bear is a common noun, the NP we use to refer to any stuffed teddy bear, but that name derives from the character Winnie-the-Pooh, *i.e.*, pooh-bears were named after the character Winnie-the-Pooh in A.A. Milne's stories. *Pooh*, although the original name of the class, is now considered a shortened form of Pooh-bear.

16 Philosophers such as Michael Devitt and David Armstrong were known as typical representatives of the "hard headed Australian materialists", and it is this stereotype which is exploited here in the behavior of the Bruces. Both worked in philosophy of language and expressed strong views on the issues of naming. Devitt, for instance, is a strong supporter of the Causal theory of meaning.

17 For a detailed and insightful analysis of this term, see Wierzbicka, 1997, pp.101ff.

9

CRYPTIC CROSSWORD PUZZLES AND LINGUISTIC KNOWLEDGE

1.0 Introduction

In this chapter, I show what kinds of knowledge are required in solving cryptic crossword puzzles. In solving cryptic crosswords the aim is to find all sorts of connections—working not only with the content of the obvious sense of the clue—but with the connections between words and letters; words and their synonyms, homonyms, metonyms; words and their spelling; words and their sounds; words with other words in a string; words and their sense; and words and their reference.[1]

My interest in analyzing the clues in cryptic crossword puzzles is to highlight what they reveal about the structure and function of oral and written language; orthography; sequentiality; and how language is used to make different kinds of meaning. Essentially, cryptic crossword puzzles exploit the ambiguity of language, both spoken and written, at all levels of structure and in different contexts of use. Since crosswords are a particular kind of language game, they pose an interesting question for Wittgenstein's dictum, "meaning is use".

I argue that cryptic crossword puzzle clues require the activation of both our tacit knowledge of the rules of our language (English, in this case) and the necessarily conscious knowledge of the rules of written English and its relation to spoken English. I delineate a broad outline of the coverage of these rules.

a. These rules include our knowledge of the formal rules of ordering in written language of both letters and words; the spatial arrangement of words and letters and the rules governing how words are constructed and related to form phrases that combine into sentences.

b. They also include our understanding of the relationships between our unconscious knowledge of phonemes, morphemes, and syllables, and our conscious awareness of lexical semantics involving phenomena such as homographs, homophones, homonyms, partial homophones, synonyms, and metonyms.

c. Additionally, they include our tacit knowledge of syntax and phrasal semantics, and conscious knowledge of how these are related to the construction of written grammatical sentences.

d. Finally, they require us to understand that meaning is truly slippery and fundamentally ambiguous and that pragmatics, *i.e.*, language in use, is entirely driven by context, whatever that context may be.

In addition, I show that in reaching and recognizing the solution to a cryptic clue, we realize how we came to it: this is in certain important respects the same as recognizing how a joke that is based on our tacit knowledge of language works. In the case of a linguistic joke, a linguistic mechanism that may never have been articulated is raised to consciousness. In contrast, the cryptic puzzle requires recognition of the different levels of structure of both spoken and written language, the types of function expressions may serve, and highlighted awareness that the function of any element, meaningless or otherwise, needs to be determined in a particular context. In order to do this successfully, we need to know the rules both of spoken and written language, and be sensitive to all their possibilities. Language, as we know, is infinitely generative, and once the peculiar nature of the written system is included, the permutations and possibilities are further complicated.[2]

2.0 The Cryptic Crossword Puzzle

Cryptic crosswords are a particular sort of linguistic puzzle, an accident not present in all languages and linguistic communities. They are not anything other than play using language as a code. If we don't have a key to the code, the clues are truly impenetrable. The problem is that the rules for solving cryptic crosswords, even if available, are not easily identified as the appropriate ones for the solution, nor do they guarantee success if followed faithfully. People have to learn to do cryptic crosswords, and generally, have to want to do them, for whatever personal satisfaction they might provide. So the activity of solving crossword puzzles is an entirely unnatural, and voluntary, one.

It is not often the case that people who do crosswords can articulate a list of the rules involved in solving them and, moreover, there does not seem to be an agreed upon set of rules, although there is some convergence and consensus on the basic techniques. The rules are, in any event, descriptive of the work of past master setters, and the philosophy of some of the more famous of these (*cf.* Ximenes (D.S. Macnutt); Afrit (A.F. Ritchie)).

3.0 The Cryptic Crossword Puzzle and "Meaning"

3.1 Meaning What You Say and Saying What You Mean

In the lifetime of cryptic crossword puzzles, there has been an unarticulated agreement between compilers and solvers that the clues have to be fair. To this end, there are some guidelines that are generally followed by compilers, and as a result, puzzlers try to solve cryptic crosswords in good faith.

Afrit (the pseudonym of a revered *Listener* puzzle compiler) is known to have said, as a guideline for the basic principle of fairness for compilers, "You need not mean what you say, but you must say what you mean." This is a rather difficult statement to unravel, but for our purposes here it is crucial. In *Alice's Adventures in Wonderland*, Dodgson provides an exchange in which the problem is highlighted

> "Then you should say what you mean," the March Hare went on.
> "I do," Alice hastily replied; "at least—at least I mean what I say—that's the same thing, you know."
> "Not the same thing a bit!" said the Hatter. "You might just as well say that 'I see what I eat' is the same thing as 'I eat what I see'!"
> *(Dodgson, 1865, Chapter 7)*

"Meaning what you say" is not at all the same as "saying what you mean", for the reasons outlined by the Hatter, but also, and more importantly for our purposes, because we don't know what to make of "mean".

Thus, before we can begin to address the construction and solution of cryptic crossword clues, we need to consider briefly the notion of "meaning".[3] When solving a cryptic clue, we have to ask ourselves, "what does it mean?" and "what are we meant to do?" The compiler is bound, at some level, to say what s/he intends. Solvers are thus entitled to believe that there must be at least one way in which the clue may be read that expresses the compiler's instruction, which if followed exactly, will provide all we need for solving the clue. That doesn't mean, of course, that the compiler has to do it in an unambiguous way.

Each of the uses of the term "meaning" has its place in the solution of cryptic crossword clues. A large part of what we do in analyzing a cryptic crossword clue is to decide on which senses of "meaning" are operating in the clue.

3.1.1 Literal Meaning v. Non-Literal Meaning

Literal meaning is a property of linguistic expressions. It is calculated on the basis of a word or phrase's conventionally agreed dictionary definition, sometimes known as its "denotation". In opposition to literal meaning we may consider figurative meaning, often termed an expression's "connotation". In calculating the connotation of an expression, we need to take into account not only its literal meaning but also what we know about the world, and how language is used in that world. So, when we say, "Her heart is made of ice" when referring to a human person, we know that cannot be literally true, but we search for its truth at some other level. We consider the nature of the information we have been given, and conclude, perhaps, that we have been told something that cannot literally be true, but that nevertheless communicates some other kind of truth.[4]

In the construction and solution of cryptic clues, paying attention to literal meaning is essential. However, there are all sorts of other meanings to which we are required to pay attention. So, Afrit's guideline, "I must say what I mean" is not a guarantee of simplicity. It certainly does not entail that he has to limit himself exclusively to literal meaning, nor to any other kind. In fact, it is precisely the blurring of the many items on the list in Chapter 3 that might loosely be termed "meaning" that contributes to the cryptic nature of these clues.[5]

For the purpose of focussing on the uses of "meaning" in cryptic crosswords, I discuss the most central of these.

3.1.2 Sense v. Reference

The mathematician and philosopher, Gottlob Frege, claimed that every name (let us say, noun phrase) and to some extent, sentence, has both "sense" and "reference". He showed, using a series of examples, that an expression's sense was not the same as its reference (Frege, 1892/1980). This is best illustrated by his famous example,

The evening star is the morning star.

The evening star refers to the planet Venus. The morning star also refers to the planet Venus. However, the sense of *the morning star* is "the last star we see in the morning sky" and the sense of *the evening star* is "the first star we see in the evening sky". Although they have the same reference these two expressions each have a different sense.

Frege's argument runs as follows. "The evening star is the morning star" is no tautology: it is informative. This piece of information could be something an astronomer discovers. Therefore, the terms can't have the same sense, although, (*ex hypothesi*) they refer to the same thing. Thus, sense is different from reference.

A linguistic expression may have sense but no reference (*e.g.*, unicorns, the current king of France), but not reference without sense. Thus, sense, would seem to be the primary feature of a linguistic expression.[6]

In cryptic puzzles, we are not always sure as to whether we are to look for the sense or reference of an expression, as either might be required.

We should note also, however, that in the context of the puzzle, there are additional complications, even subsequent to establishing that we are looking for the sense of an expression, rather than its referent, since words are potentially polysemic and homonymic. Thus, determining the sense of an expression is not by any means clear-cut, and this problem is not always resolvable, even when the potential semes or lemmae may be teased apart.

3.1.3 Sense v. Intention

Many, though not all, linguists make a distinction between semantics and pragmatics (*e.g.*, Green, 1996; Blakemore, 2001; Levinson, 2000). This distinction is based on the idea that semantics is concerned with the properties of expressions, and that pragmatics is concerned with expressions in their context of use. For my purposes here, I'll assume that an expression's sense is its "linguistic meaning", *i.e.*, its definition, and that this is a semantic property of the expression.[7] An utterance, however, is always made in a context of use. Analyzing utterances in use is the business of pragmatics. Thus, "mean" in relation to linguistic expressions is quite different from "mean" in relation to speaker meaning (illocutionary force or intention) and hearer meaning (potential perlocutionary force, or the hearer's understanding of conversational communication).[8]

In cryptic crosswords, we are required to understand the compiler's stated intention, usually an instruction, often disguised, and at the same time, work out in each case, what other kinds of meaning, *e.g.*, sense, reference, definition, naming etc., s/he would have us supply.

Solving a cryptic clue requires using a certain type of literal strategy, particularly with regard to the instructions we are given. Literalness alone, however, does not get us very far. One reason for this is that, crucially, cryptic crosswords play with the distinction between "use" and "mention".

3.1.4 Use v. Mention

The use-mention distinction has a long history in Western philosophy[9] (and it is also the case that some philosophers do not agree about the clear-cut nature of its existence, *cf.*, Derrida, 1988). Without engaging in the debates about how to resolve or reconcile the problems this distinction highlights, I'll provide a few examples that make the proposed distinction clear.

1. Julia Gillard is the Prime Minister of Australia.
2. Julia Gillard has twelve letters.

In (1), at the time of speaking, Julia Gillard is the person who holds the office of Prime Minister of Australia. This is true at the time of speaking. The expression "Julia Gillard" is used to name a certain person and a true statement is being made about the political position the named person occupies at a certain time. However, in (2), a true statement about the expression "Julia Gillard" is made. The statement is that this expression is made up of twelve letters. (1) provides an example of "use", whereas (2) provides an example of "mention". We tend, conventionally, to use quotation marks around a word or a phrase when we are mentioning it.

To illustrate further, consider the riddle-like joke in (3) that exploits the distinction between (1) and (2).

3. What do Alexander the Great and Winnie the Pooh have in common? They have the same middle name.[10]

In cryptic crosswords, it is quite common to see a clue such as the following.

4. Clue: Power plant lacks a spiritual leader (6)
   Solution: RECTOR

The crucial observation to be made here is that the letter "a" should be regarded as mentioned, rather than be parsed as the word "*a*" (the indefinite article), used as a determiner preceding *spiritual leader*. In essence, the clue tells us that *power plant* (=reactor) should lack the letter "a", thus yielding a word synonymous with *spiritual leader*.

As we shall see, cryptic crosswords are a superb example of the blurring of the use/mention distinction at every level of oral and written language.

4.0 Ambiguity

As argued at length in the preceding chapters, the play with ambiguity at the different levels of structure and function that occurs in jokes taps the tacit knowledge we have of the rules of our language. In contrast, when we solve a cryptic crossword, we call upon all the knowledge, both tacit and learned, that we have about our language. Much of this knowledge is not what Chomsky would term "competence", but is rather, metalinguistic, *i.e.*, knowledge about language. In Example (5), I provide a children's joke, in riddle form, that relies on lexical ambiguity and knowledge of morphological word formation rules.[11] In Example (6) I provide a cryptic clue that is homographic, *i.e.*, it relies for its cryptic quality on the play between two different phonological realizations of the same orthographic sequence and therefore, the potential for two different senses.

5. Q: What's brown and sticky?
   A: A stick.

6. Clue: A wicked thing
   Solution: CANDLE

In both cases, that of the linguistic joke and the cryptic clue, the phenomenon that is exploited is ambiguity. In the joke, the play of verbal elements is based on incongruity, and when the lexical ambiguity is resolved through consciousness of a hitherto tacit rule, the incongruity is exposed, leading the listener to respond to the unlikely similarity between ambiguous elements with some appreciation of the humor found in the ambiguity. In the case of the cryptic clue, in order to find the correct solution, the solver has to find the ambiguity, and resolve it by careful attention to the phrasing of the clue, thus eliminating any other possible readings. When the clue is solved, this may lead to the solver feeling self-satisfied, and very often delighted at the clever detective work performed in solving the mystery.

In (5) the verbal joke exploits our knowledge *of* language, whereas in (6) the cryptic crossword clue exploits our knowledge ***about*** language, in this case, homography, which might quite possibly also include our knowledge *of* language, specifically phonology, morphology and lexis. It is likely that only a certain stripe of linguist would care about the distinction I am making about the nature of the knowledge required, but I think it is an important one to note here.

4.1 Knowledge *of* Language and Knowledge *About* Language

The crucial difference between linguistic jokes and cryptic crossword puzzles is, in essence, not at all about the formal mechanisms implicated in both, but about the nature of the knowledge each requires. Not everyone can do cryptic crosswords, although in principle, any literate person with normal intelligence might be taught to do so. Also, it is certainly not the case that everyone wants to do them or enjoys doing them. It's a matter of taste and temperament; also of leisure and choice. Linguistic jokes, on the other hand, do not require us to learn how to appreciate them. When they occur, they provide us with a flash of consciousness about some aspect of language, which, for most people, is not normally part of conscious knowledge.

Jokes based on the structure of language (such as example 5 above) tap tacit linguistic knowledge that the ordinary language user is not often conscious of. In this chapter, though, I focus on cryptic clues, because it seems to me that the cryptic crossword is one of the most extreme forms of activity in which a conscious knowledge of linguistic forms (spoken and written) is required. The cryptic crossword is a puzzle to be solved: the better our knowledge of the codes and combinations required, the greater our chances of success in solving the puzzle. It seems to me, as well, that consciousness of the rules of the particular code is not quite enough; the setter/solver of the cryptic clue must have (near) native knowledge of the language *as well*. This, I believe, is an assumption underlying the construction and solution of such puzzles. No-one is a native speaker of "Cryptic", it is merely a code, but everyone is a native speaker of some natural language.

Certainly, computational linguists have tried to program machines to generate linguistic jokes (see for instance, Ritchie, 2004) and some have tried to write programs to generate cryptic crosswords (Smith & du Boulay, 1986). In my opinion, in neither case can we expect a machine that will ever get the joke or solve the clue based on the sorts of linguistic ambiguities involved. That is because the human capacity for language cannot as yet be modeled or replicated, and the linguistic unconscious is basic to all our dealings with language, no matter what additional conscious or unconscious cognitive mechanisms are required.

4.2 What do We Need to Know to do Cryptic Crosswords?

Doing cryptic crosswords requires a conscious and active conception of how the rules of spoken and written language work. Cryptic crossword clues are largely based on eliciting what users know about language, primarily in the written form, but also about the relationships between oral and written form. In discussing the mechanisms used to compose and solve cryptic crossword puzzles, I propose to show that the formal mechanisms have a great deal in common with some of the formal mechanisms used in jokes, however, the purpose to which they are put is in some way an exercise in general intelligence: of puzzle-solving using whatever cognitive and linguistic strategies are consciously available to the user.

Solving example (7) relies on both linguistic and non-linguistic strategies.

7. Clue: Tailless creature's soul (5)
    Solution: ANIMA

This clue is based on our knowledge of synonymy and our knowledge of the order of written letters involved in word construction. It also uses a particular form of instruction, known as a disguised indicator (to be discussed at more length below).

If we parse the clue as follows, it is fairly easy to solve.

[*tailless* [*creature*]]'s [*soul*]

In solving the clue, we are expected to provide a synonym "animal" for *creature*. We are also expected to identify and follow the instruction and remove the tail, *i.e.*, the last letter of "animal", and we get ANIMA, which is a synonym for *soul*.

There are all sorts of traps that lie in wait in a clue like this. Example 7 provides a good example of some of the ways in which we can be led astray in solving cryptic clues. Firstly, from a linguistic point of view, there is lexical ambiguity in the use of *tail*. It's tempting to think of a tailless creature, as it is to consider a creature's soul. Since this is puzzle-solving exercise requiring both linguistic and non-linguistic strategies, we need to decide which strategies to use in each different twist of the clue. It turns out that we are not supposed to be dealing with tailless creatures or their souls if we propose to solve the clue, but to be following the instruction as literally as possible, once we can discern what that instruction is, *i.e.*, *tailless* (remove the tail).

In order to demonstrate how the process of solving cryptic clues yields correct solutions, I provide a brief description of some of the central mechanisms and then some examples to demonstrate how each one works. Some of these phenomena are not limited to cryptic crosswords but are incorporated within them.[12]

5.0 The Mechanisms

5.1 Similarity

In general, synonymy is the fundamental, but not sufficient, requirement that has to be met in solving a cryptic clue. In philosophical terms, synonymy is sameness of sense.

Cryptic crosswords, however, rely on sameness of both sense and reference, in a much less rigorous way. As discussed above in 3.1, these are complex calls to make, and precise equivalents are difficult, if not impossible, to find. In the cryptic crossword clue, a looser kind of synonymy is required, not as strictly defined by the term "synonymy", but perhaps by the notion of association.

Synonymy is very seldom the only requirement for solving a clue, given that the shared understanding between compiler and solver is that the clue should be cryptic (*i.e.*, mysterious, unstraightforward, enigmatic or obscure) or provide information that is hidden in some way. Additionally, sometimes what is sought is not true synonymy, but a form of metonymy, in which the solution to be found is a metonym of the "correspondent" word or phrase in the clue, known less accurately by puzzlers as the "synonym" or "definition".[13]

5.1.1 Synonymy and Metonymy

Looking for metonymy involves finding a solution that refers to a member of the class that the "correspondent" refers to.[14]

To illustrate the synonymous/metonymous relationship consider a case in which the "correspondent" is *holler*, and the solution is BELLOW.

This can be seen in example (8)

8.   Clue: Holler "Author" (6)
     Solution: BELLOW

The way the clue works is as follows. *Holler* (in the sense of "shout") can be seen as synonymous with "bellow". Saul Bellow is the name of a well-known American author, a member of the class of authors, thus a metonym of "author".

Within the fundamental principle of synonymy, a number of different clue types may be found, each using at least one (and often more) of these techniques.

5.1.2 Polysemy

5.1.2.1 Double Meanings/Double Definitions

The most common technique used in cryptic crossword puzzles is that known as double meanings, or double definitions. Essentially, the technique used in this kind of clue is to provide two words, both of which may be defined by the same answer or solution. Notice in these cases of double meanings, that when *meaning* is used, the preferred understanding is "definition". The examples that follow are simple demonstrations of the technique.

9. Clue: Savings book (7)
    Solution: RESERVE

Note that in this clue, one of the words, *book*, is multicategorial, *i.e.*, it might be construed as a noun or a verb. Using such words is a favorite trick of crossword compilers.

In this case, *savings* may be considered as one's "reserve". To *book* (a seat *e.g.*,) may be equivalent in sense to "to reserve". Thus, *savings* = reserve and *book* = reserve, and polysemously, RESERVE is the solution. The fact that *savings book* is most naturally parsed as a phrase, leading one to think automatically of a bank account is deliberate. These are the sorts of distracters that are intended to lead us astray.

The next example is a little more cryptic.

10. Clue: Oinking tendency (8)
     Solution: PENCHANT

In solving this clue, one may consider each word separately, or together as a phrase. The basic imperative in solving cryptic clues is to search for the synonymy. It seems logical to go for *tendency*, first. This is because *oinking* does not immediately suggest any words (to me) other than pig. *Tendency*, on the other hand, suggests some immediate synonyms, such as "propensity", "inclination" and, indeed, "penchant". Examining these words to see if any of them share anything with *oinking*, might prove useful. The key is "chant" in "penchant", even though of course, "chant" has nothing meaningful to share with "penchant". However, if we divide "penchant" into "pen"+"chant", we note that pigs live in pens and that their oinking noises might be construed as a kind of chant. Therefore, *oinking* = penchant and *tendency* = penchant, and PENCHANT is the solution. Note that the polysemy in this example derives from a semantically illegitimate division of *penchant* into two morphemes "pen" and "chant".

5.1.2.2 Homography

A more specific instance of double definitions relies on the fact that English has homographs, *i.e.*, words that are written the same way, but are pronounced differently. Since crosswords are a form of written English, compilers can exploit this fact (and the corollary phenomenon, homophony, discussed below).[15]

11. Clue: Metal guide (4)
     Solution: LEAD

Potential candidates for a metal that is made up of four letters are, *e.g.*, "lead" (or "gold", or "iron", *inter alia*). We need to test a number of candidates, but "lead" is an obvious one because it functions homographically. To *guide* is "to lead". Although the words are not pronounced the same way, they are spelt identically. In order to solve the clue, we need to construe *guide* as a verb in this case. "Lead" is a metonym of *metal*. For the purposes of solving the clue they are regarded as equivalent. Thus, *metal* = lead and *guide* = lead and LEAD is the solution, an example of polysemy in the written form.

The following example of double definitions is more complex. In this case, we have a clue that comprises more than two words. Essentially, the clue is made up of three phrases. However, we cannot tell what each of the three phrases is made up of.

12. Clue: Left red wine in harbor (4)

    Solution: PORT

In choosing a starting point, one normally looks at either the first or last word of the clue. Since *harbor* is the word most likely to be unicategorical in this context, it is probably good practice to start there. Thus, starting with *harbor*, we try to think of a synonym or polysemous association. "Port" is a very close synonym to *harbor* and it is made up of four letters, so could be considered a candidate. Once one has *port* in mind, it is easy to notice that *port* is also a kind of red wine, and finally that on a ship, *left* is known as "port" (and right as "starboard"). Thus, there are three terms, each of which may be defined by "port". Of course, the compiler has been very deceitful: we might well parse the clue as VP→V NP PP, where *left* is a verb, *red wine* is the NP and *in harbor* is the PP. Instead, in order to use the clue to find the solution, we need to construe *left* as an NP, *red wine* as another NP and *in harbor* as a PP, equivalent to "in port". Thus *left* = port, *red wine* = port, and *in harbor* = in port, and the solution is PORT.

The double definition clue type does not contain any instruction to the solver about how to proceed. This is unusual among clue types. An important element in most cryptic clues is the instruction to the solver. As a rule, instructions as to the operations are provided as part of the clue, but cryptically. It is necessary to analyze the structure of the clue in order to find out which of various operations the solver is required to perform in order to work out a particular answer. Such operations are called crypto-mechanisms, or disguised indicators, and are normally to be found in every clue, except double definitions and some very curly pure cryptics, discussed later. Part of the task for the solver is to discern which part of the clue is the "correspondent" and which the "disguised indicator". Clues involving homophones very often include a disguised indicator.

5.1.2.3 Homophony

Homophones, *i.e.*, words that are pronounced in the same way, but have different senses, are widely used in cryptic crosswords.[16] Functioning as the corollary of homographs, they are employed much as classic puns are in linguistic humor. As a rule, the homophone is cued by homophone indicators in the clue. These include phrases such as, "sounds like", "I hear", "we hear", "sounds", "audience", "spoken", "said", "reported".

The following example is the most simple of its kind.

13. Clue: Bend the branch, I hear (3)
    Solution: BOW

I hear is an instruction to look for homophony. One needs to parse the rest of the clue into two separate phrases. This is fairly uncomplicated here, so one gets *bend* and *the branch*. Following the instruction, we look for a spoken word that conforms to the one of the definitions of both *bend* and *branch*. *Branch* is synonymous with "bough", and to *bow* (verb) may also be defined as "to bend". We know that the solution has three letters, so we choose BOW as the answer, in the absence of any other instructions. Thus, *bend* (verb) = bow and *branch* (noun) = bough, and the answers sound alike; the solution requires a three letter word, so we choose BOW.

Note that in cryptic clues we are often not told what syntactic category we are to understand a word as belonging to. This ambiguity is crucial to the cryptic quality of the clue: it is not until we parse the clue correctly that we will crack it. In (13), *the* gives us an unequivocal indicator that *branch* is a noun. This is not actually necessary: if the clue had read "Bend branch, I hear", it would have been well formed (in fact, probably better formed than (13)).

In (14) the clue requires a similar solution process, although in this case there are absolutely no extraneous words.

14. Clue: Church service sounds correct (4)
    Solution: RITE

We are told that we are looking for homophony by the use of *sounds*. We then need to parse the clue into its component phrases, which are *church service* and *correct*. Next, we need to look for a homophonous item that matches the description of *church service* in one case, and of *correct* in the other. It's a good idea to look at *correct* first, as it is less complex than *church service*, although also multicategorial. A candidate synonym for *correct* is "right". A test of the pronunciation of *right* in conjunction with *church service* might trigger the word "rite", which is an exact homophone, and indeed, one possible description of a church service, or at least one that has a metonymic relationship to "rite".[17] The clue tells us that the word we are looking for has four letters. RITE fits, as it is a description of *church service* and sounds like *right*.

Example (15) involves somewhat more associative thinking, but essentially requires the same solution process.

15. Clue: Shakespeare, I hear, is excluded (6)
    Solution: BARRED

Shakespeare is very often used as code in cryptic crossword puzzles for "bard". In cryptic puzzles, then, as a rule, "the bard" or "bard" refers to Shakespeare, and "Shakespeare" denotes *bard* or some like-sounding form. This is a fairly well entrenched metonymic relationship in crossword lore. It is a good example of how the extension/intension distinction can be blurred.

I hear is a homophone indicator. Thus, we are cued to think of the homophones of "bard". The next part of the clue is *is excluded*. This is the "correspondent". The clue tells us that the homophone of "bard" should be equivalent in some way to *is excluded*. "Barred" might be defined as "*is excluded*". Since "bard" and "barred" are exact homophones, the solution is very neat. *Shakespeare* = bard and *is excluded* = barred, *bard* and *barred* are homophones, so some equivalent of *Shakespeare* sounds the same as some equivalent of *is excluded*, and the solution is BARRED.

In (16), the indicator that we are looking for a homophone is somewhat more disguised, and the association a little more tricky. The indicator to look for a homophone is provided by *audience*.

16. Clue: Hot dog topping gathered for the audience (7)
    Solution: MUSTARD

In this case, in our search to solve the double definition, we need to parse the relevant parts of the clue into the phrases *hot dog topping* and *gathered*. One candidate for *hot dog topping* might be "mustard". To solve the clue we need to note that "mustered" is a synonym for *gathered*, and that the solutions to each phrase are homophonous. The final solution is spelt in accord with the first phrase. We are to understand the clue as reading: "find a word for *hot dog topping* that sounds the same as a synonym for *gathered*".

Thus, *hot dog topping* = mustard and *gathered* = mustered and these words sound alike and the spelling we choose is the one that conforms to the first phrase, the "correspondent" MUSTARD.

In (17) the spelling of the solution is in accord with the answer to the final word to be defined. In this clue, we are given clear guidance that we are looking for a homophone, *viz.*, *sounds like*.

17. Clue: Sounds like an affirmative organ (3)
     Solution: EYE

We are expected to parse the clue as follows. The solution *sounds like* (the instruction to find a homophone for) *an affirmative* that also refers to an *organ*. The *affirmative* we are looking for might be "aye". It might also be "yes", but we should be conscious of looking for a homophone, and "yes" does not seem to be a candidate for that. We need not be fooled by the potential reading, *sounds like an organ*, and instead we should focus on finding an organ that sounds like "aye". There is no reason for us to assume immediately that the clue refers to an organ of the body, but in playing around looking for a homophone of "aye", it is reasonably easy to find the answer. Note in this case too, that the solution, "eye" is a metonym of *organ*, the "correspondent" word in the clue.

Thus, *an affirmative* = aye, *organ* = eye and "aye" sounds like the answer, EYE.

Of course, since homophony is a spoken language phenomenon, the cryptic crossword puzzle does not cross dialect boundaries very well. Homophones in British English are not always homophonic in American English and *vice versa*: *e.g.*, sure/shore (BE) and merry/marry (AE). Thus, for this, among other reasons to be discussed along the way, cryptic crosswords do not travel well.

5.2 Clue Types using Words as Grapheme Sequences

5.2.1 Charades in Writing

This type of clue has been so named because of its similarity to the game of the same name, in which contestants mime different words and/or syllables, which, if guessed correctly in the order in which they are presented, make up a more complex word or phrase. The straightforward way this process works in cryptic clues is that different parts of a word or phrase are put together in order, each part forming the solution to some part of the clue. The "correspondent" word or phrase for which a synonym is sought, is usually to be found either at the beginning or the end of the clue. The most important observation to be made about this sort of clue is that the parts are never etymologically related to the whole, as expressed in the solution.

In Example (18) below, the solution is found by adding together an ordered sequence of parts, which, taken together, form a synonym for the first word, MINSTREL.

18. Clue: Minstrel shows dance, gaining a buck (9)
     Solution: BALLADEER

Shows is an indicator that the solution will display what follows. One candidate synonym for *dance* (noun) is "ball". Naturally, it is not the only synonym for *dance*, but exploiting that ambiguity is in the nature of a cryptic clue. *Gaining* is another indicator, telling us to add what follows to what we already have, which is BALL. The next bit we have to add is *a*, because no word is meant to appear in a clue unless it has some purpose for the solving of the clue. So, thus far, we have BALL+A. The next part of the clue is *buck*. Needless to say, *buck* can be a noun or a verb, and even as a noun, it has at least two unrelated senses: "dollar", or "deer". If we have already put BALL+A in place, it is very easy to see that the preferred reading of *buck* is "deer", in this instance. Thus we add DEER to BALL+A and we get BALLADEER, a type of minstrel. The relationship of "balladeer" to *minstrel* is metonymic, a very common association in clues of this type. Notice that no part of the clue is etymologically related to the whole.

This sort of clue depends on the Rebus Principle. It is deeply counter-intuitive to linguists, in the sense that syllables are not morphological or semantic units *per se*. They constitute part of the phonological component of the grammar.[18] Sequential componentiality in word structure is, in fact, morphological, and can generally be accounted for in terms of hierarchical word structure.[19] Words are built by means of combining morphemes. Other than monomorphemic words (irrespective of their number of syllables) words are built along principles of morpheme combination. Syllable structure, in spoken language, and orthography, in written language, are not relevant to either morphology or semantics.

In the final product, each contributory morpheme (or multimorphemic word if it occurs) in the solution is allocated the status of a series of letters only. I note, for contrast, that the central unit of meaning in a word is the morpheme, and words are made up of one or more morphemes. However, in charade clues, solutions are built up entirely of sound or letter sequences that are unrelated in meaning to the final product. Cryptic crosswords exploit this artifact of language, one present in spoken and written language. Recognition that constructing words this way is bizarre leads to the realization that words are not constructed this way at all, in just the same way that jokes which play with sound sequences that are non-morphemic lead us to the realization that multimorphemic words are hierarchically structured, in terms of rules of morpheme combination, and not linearly constructed by linking one phoneme to another, or one syllable to another.[20]

In Example (19) the solution requires some cultural knowledge about terminology used in the USA. We need to know that the anti-abortion campaigns in the 1980s used the term "pro-life", to describe themselves, as opposed to "anti-abortion".[21]

In (19) the composite solution is going to be similar in sense to one of the senses of the "correspondent", *spread*. Note that in this case, the "correspondent" is in final, not initial position.

19. Clue: Anti-abortionist ate spread (11)
    Solution: PROLIFERATE

The solution to the clue is in the form of a charade, although we are given no indication that this is the case. Experienced solvers just know! *Anti-abortionist* may be rephrased as "pro-lifer". Again, this relationship is metonymic: a pro-lifer is one kind of anti-abortionist. *ate* is simply added to "PROLIFER" (a result that is not all that difficult to deduce if one looks at the clue, having already come up with "prolifer", and notices that there are three more letters required). Thus we get PROLIFER+ATE, which is equivalent to the verb *spread*, in one of its senses.

Yet again we see that the solution does not share any meaning component with any of its parts. This non-etymological composition seems to be a requirement of charade clues in all the cryptic puzzles I have investigated. We see also, that in clues of this sort, pronunciation has nothing to do with spelling. Thus, the change of the vowel from [ai] in 'pro-l<u>i</u>fer' to [I] in prol<u>i</u>ferate is of absolutely no consequence in the solving of this clue.

In the case of example (20) we are required to find a synonym for *consumed*. Part of the deceptive nature of cryptic puzzles is that compilers may choose from a set of clue types and each clue has its own rules for solution: for instance, in (19) *ate* is simply the sequence *ATE*, in (20) the clue may require us first to do something with *consume* to transform it to ATE, and then use the letter sequence. This is one of the tricky ways in which the use/mention distinction is exploited.

20. Clue: After operation I consumed a painkilling drug (6)
      Solution: OPIATE

The clue is solved in the following way. *After* is a disguised indicator for sequentiality, or an instruction to build a word from charade pieces. Thus, we start immediately after *after*. *Operation* is often referred to as "op", in the sense of surgery. Semantically, the rest of the clue primes us to think of surgery and other medical matters. As it turns out, the answer is not far from a medical lexical item, but, just as often in cryptic clues, the lexical clustering is there to deceive us. Our default instruction is to proceed literally: thus, after OP we add I. We then have OP+I. Thereafter we encounter *consumed*. One candidate synonym for *consumed* is "ate". Still following the instructions, we add ATE to the sum, and get OP+I+ATE. We now have a word of six letters, and we notice that this word denotes a member of the class of painkilling drugs, or indeed, "a painkilling drug". In this case, the "correspondent" appears at the end of the clue. Building up the solution is straightforward, in the sense that we follow an instruction to be sequential. However, it is a matter of judgment to decide when to use an actual clue item (I), and when to use a synonym ("ate" for *consume*) or an abbreviation ("op" for *operation*). We are guided by the number of letters, and also, as so often in cryptic puzzles, we see that using the most obvious syntactic structure of the clue does not lead us to parse its cryptic structure correctly. Parsing the cryptic structure correctly, *i.e.*, as the instruction "After '*Operation*' add '*I*' and then '*ate*' to yield the denotation", "*a painkilling drug*" tells us what to do to get a result which will produce a synonymous item for the relevant word or phrase in the clue, in this case, *a painkilling drug*.

In the cases above, examples (18)–(20), we have looked at clues involving whole words or morphemes that are used in word building as simple letter sequences. This is, of course, equivalent to the spoken language use of morphemes as simple phoneme sequences. The equivalence may be illustrated by a very simple children's riddle.

21. Q: Why could you never starve to death in the desert?
    A: Because of the sand which is there (sounds like *the sandwiches there*).

Cryptic crossword clues play with letters. Letters constitute the basic structure of written words. Like phonemes, they are meaningless elements, but in combination with other letters, they may form meaningful units. This is one of the most fundamental features of all human languages: duality of patterning. In written language, a word is simply a sequence of letters in allowable combinations and orders for that language; it forms at least one meaning unit. Sequencing of letters, and their larger units in words, is all-important. Cryptic crosswords flagrantly demonstrate what playing fast and loose with the ordering of letters can do to word meaning.

5.2.2 Letters and their Sequencing

There are a number of clue types that play with the sequencing of letters. As the instructions for reordering are usually cryptic, or only implied, I illustrate some of the less straightforward exemplars. Once the essential principle is discerned, these clues may be seen as facets of the same principle, which is to play with letters. Clue types such as these include the following procedures: transposals; reversals; deletions; additions; substitutions; acrostics; hidden clues and containers.

5.2.2.1 Transposals

In transposals, also known as anagrams, a set of letters forming a word or group of words is rearranged to form another word or group of words.

In cryptic clues, it is very rare for the compiler to tell the solver that the solution is an anagram. Instead, there is often a disguised anagram indicator as seen in example (22).

22. Clue: It rarely turns out like this in books (8)
    Solution: LITERARY

The letters to be anagrammed are those found in *it rarely*. Those who know the trick will see that *turns out like this* is the disguised anagram indicator. *In books* is, in the cryptic world, sufficiently equivalent in sense to "literary"'. Thus, the letters to be rearranged form a word, "literary", which shares one sense of *in books*.

In Example (23), we see a similar use of the technique of anagram and disguised indicator. However, in this one the letters to be transposed are positioned nearer to the end of the clue, rather than at the beginning, as in (22). Anagramming letters is a fairly straightforward procedure. The trick lies in knowing which bit of the clue has to be anagrammed.

23. Clue: Tube taken to theatre for three-act play (8)
     Solution: CATHETER

In (23) the letters to be transposed are to be found in *three-act*. The disguised indicator here is *play*. Those who know the conventional codes for anagrams will recognize *play* as an instruction to play around with the letters. A catheter is a kind of tube taken to (used in) an operating theatre. Note that "catheter" functions as a metonym of the "correspondent" *tube* here. A three-act play is something found in a theatre of a different kind. Once these techniques are noticed, or explained, the solution makes sense. If they are not noticed, the clue remains mysterious.

In Example (24), the anagram involves letters that belong to more than one word. Note that the disguised indicator is *doctor*, which tells us that we need to change the letters around (or doctor the words).

24. Clue: Doctor is venal – get a preacher (10)
     Solution: EVANGELIST

The "correspondent" is *a preacher*. We are instructed to doctor *is venal get* to find a synonym for *preacher*. An evangelist is a kind of preacher. We must rule out all the irrelevant syntactic structures here. The clue must be read as an instruction, not as a statement.

The principle illustrated in (22–24) should be clear. Essentially all the other types of clue mentioned in this section require a rearrangement of letters. The degree to which the instruction to rearrange is cryptic usually determines the level of difficulty in solving the clue. The hidden indicators are invariably multicategorial, and this is an additional reason for the difficulty in picking them out from the rest of the clue structure.

5.2.2.2 Hidden Words

A well-established technique used in cryptic puzzles is the hidden solution. In these kinds of clues, the solution is actually hidden within the clue itself, as a sequence of letters forming part of a word or group of words. Some examples make this clear.

In Example (25) the solution is found in a sequence of letters that runs across three different words.

25. Clue: Scientist finding partial evidence in Steinbeck (8)
     Solution: EINSTEIN

Thus, *Scientist finding partial evidence* **in Stein***beck* actually contains the answer, EINSTEIN. The "correspondent", *scientist*, occurs at the beginning of the clue. "Einstein" refers to a member of the class of scientists. The disguised indicator instructing us to look for a hidden clue is *finding partial*, which tells us the solution is to be found in parts of what is to follow. In these sorts of clues, spaces and capital letters have no status at all. The referent of *Steinbeck* has the function of totally distracting us from the intended solution to the clue. To be successful, we need to focus on *Steinbeck* as part of a sequence of letters. As used in the clue *Steinbeck* has absolutely no referential function at all.

Example (26) is similar to (25), demonstrating, among other things, how irrelevant referents can lead a solver astray.

26. Clue: Cheese stored in Baroque fortress (9)
     Solution: ROQUEFORT

In (26) *cheese* is the "correspondent". *Stored in* is the disguised indicator that we are to look for a hidden word. I have highlighted the relevant letters in bold: *Cheese stored in Ba***roque fort***ress*. Note that *Baroque fortress* has the additional function of leading us completely astray semantically. The denotation and connotation of *Baroque fortress* have absolutely nothing to do with the semantics of the answer. The clue is to be read completely literally. We may be **using** *store*, but *Baroque fortress* and *Roquefort* are pure **mention**. The sequence of letters ROQUEFORT is stored in the sequence of letters *baroque fortress*. And finally, the metonym: Roquefort is a kind of cheese.

5.2.2.3 Reversals

This clue type is very often combined with other types such as containers. Reversals are found in clues that require us to find a solution to part of the clue, and then to reverse the letters in order to find a match for the "correspondent".

An uncomplicated example follows. In example (27) the disguised indicator for the reversal is *back*, or more accurately here, *bring back*. The "correspondent" for which a synonym is to be found is *spies*.

27. Clue: Spies bring silverware back (6)
     Solution: SNOOPS

In order to solve the clue, we parse it as follows:

[spies] bring [silverware] back

We may consider "knives", "forks" and "spoons" to be words denoting classes of silverware. A quick look at their spellings in reverse yields only one candidate: "spoons". Then we follow the instruction to bring "spoons" back, *i.e.*, to reverse the word *spoons*. This gives us SNOOPS.

[*spies*] = *bring* [*spoons*] *back*

[*spies*] = [SNOOPS]

Example (28) demonstrates a similar process. In this case, the "correspondent" occurs at the end of the clue. The disguised indicator is *returned*. It is categorially verbal, although ambiguous as to whether it is a preterite past or a participle. Once we see *returned*, however, it should cue us to conduct a reversal of a letter sequence.[22]

28. Clue: Returned beer of kings (5)
    Solution: REGAL

The "correspondent" here is a phrase, *of kings*. We parse the clue as follows:

Returned [*beer*] [*of kings*].

Returned is the indicator of a reversal. "Lager" is one candidate metonym for *beer*. If we reverse the sequence of letters in "lager", we get REGAL, which indeed is fairly closely defined as *of kings*. As is clear, conducting the reversal is mechanical. Parsing the clue and picking up the disguised indicator, as well as the "correspondent", is where the work lies.

5.2.2.4 Deletions

This clue type indicates that some part of a word or phrase is to be deleted from a sequence of letters. Naturally, the instruction to delete is disguised. Sample indicators that parts of a word must be deleted are *endless, without end, without an end, tailless, amputated, chopped off, headless, beheaded, topless, nearly, bottomless, after the first, unfinished, heartless, heartlessly, at the centre,* inter alia. In this kind of clue, as in all others in this section, the relevant words must be seen as sequences of letters and thought of as such.

It might be noted that the particular kinds of indicators are generally metaphoric, based either on removing part of a living body or on spatial/sequential extension. Deletion clues, too, are a very clear demonstration of the way in which words can be regarded simply as the object of operations. Much though on the surface reading it may appear otherwise, in this clue type we are told what to do with a sequence of letters. The semantics of what the letters spell out are entirely irrelevant to the operation. The only semantics that are relevant in clues of this sort are those involved in the instruction, and those features of the "correspondent" element that need to be matched.

Several examples follow to illustrate these principles. At this stage, I assume the reader has grasped the principle, so I will not hammer the point home more than is necessary for a demonstration of the ambiguity that is intended to mislead the hapless solver.

In (29) the disguised indicator is *without an end*. The word before the colon, *pins*, is the "correspondent" for which we seek some synonymous item.

29. Clue: Pins: superfluous without an end (7)
    Solution: NEEDLES

Setting aside *pins* for a moment, we can parse the second part of the clue as follows:

[*superfluous*] *without an end*
This yields
[*needless*] *without an end*

Reading the instruction literally, or taking *needless* as an example of mention, not use, we lop the end off NEEDLESS and get NEEDLES. Returning to the clue as a whole, we see that NEEDLES is close enough to *pins* to be the solution.
Pins: NEEDLES
Example (30) is a fairly straightforward example of a deletion from the beginning of a word. The disguised indicator is *first off*. The "correspondent" word for which we seek a metonym is *mountain*. Since Everest is probably the most famous mountain in the world, it is likely that *Everest* would spring to mind, but it is not necessary to solve the clue that way.

30. Clue: First off most uncompromising mountain (7)
    Solution: EVEREST

The clue is syntactically in many ways ambiguous. As crossword solvers, we might parse it in the following ways, at least:

a.   [[*first off*] [*most uncompromising mountain*]]
b.   [[*first off* [*most*]][*uncompromising mountain*]
c.   [[*first off* [*most uncompromising*]] [*mountain*]

In fact, the way to parse the clue to derive the solution is to work with (c) as follows:
We need to resolve the deepest bracket first. As a synonym for *most uncompromising*, sharing many of its semantic features, "severest" suggests itself.

This gives us

[*first off* [SEVEREST]] [*mountain*]

We then follow the disguised indicator, the instruction to take the first (letter) off SEVEREST, which yields EVEREST.

[EVEREST] [MOUNTAIN]

Of course, the temptation to consider *most uncompromising* as the comparative adjectival modifying *mountain* is natural. Yet again, we need to bear in mind that we have to read against our instincts when we parse cryptic clues. The clue is generally designed to thwart our instincts, and to force alternative readings if it is to be solved. The crucial imperative is to treat language as an object, and the trick is to decide which bits constitute the objects of particular operations.

In Example (31), shown earlier as Example (4), we find another demonstration of just how literally we need to read the indicators as instructions. The disguised indicator here is *lacks*, and the metonymic "correspondent" is *spiritual leader*.

31. Clue: Power plant lacks a spiritual leader (6)
    Solution: RECTOR

We might be forgiven for thinking that we are instructed to delete a first letter somewhere, since we know that *leader* often functions as an indicator that we should do something with the first letter of a word, and we see *lacks* in the clue, which cues us to look for a deletion. However, if we go that way, we will be fooled.

The correct way to parse this clue in order to solve it is as follows:

[[*power plant*] *lacks a*][*spiritual leader*]

We are told to find a word for *power plant*, and then rewrite that word so that it lacks the letter A. This yields a metonym for *spiritual leader*. We are entitled to substitute "reactor" for *power plant*. Following the instruction, we remove the letter A from REACTOR. This gives us RECTOR. A rector is a particular instantiation of a spiritual leader.

Notice the ways in which we could be led astray: *plant* can be read as a noun or a verb; *a* can (and should, normally) be read as the determiner preceding *spiritual leader*, *leader* can cue us to look for a first letter and *lack* could lead us into deleting a first letter somewhere.

Clue types involving additions are based on the same principle. Adding letters to the beginning, end, or middle of a sequence of letters requires one to abandon all conceptions of language as following componential and compositional rules in any kind of traditional linguistic way, and simply to see letters as building blocks that fit together in different ways that can change meanings.

Similarly, clue types involving substitutions follow much the same principle as illustrated above. The solver is required to substitute 1–2 letters into a word designated to be operated on. The disguised indicators for substitutions include *instead of, in place of, is taken for* and so on. Again, the mechanism is simple: it is identifying the instruction and the "correspondent" that require us to make linguistic judgments.

5.2.2.5 Split Words/Containers

For the sake of completeness, I provide some further examples of additions that are somewhat more sophisticated, although as demonstrated above, the mechanism itself is simple. These kinds of clues require the insertion of one word or group of letters into another. The disguised indicator is usually one of a set of words like *in, inside, within, keeps, holds, contains, puts* or any others with the semantic feature that these share, more or less [+inside]. Note that here it is vital to ascertain the relevant semantic feature, and to be less concerned by the syntactic class, of the indicator.

The "correspondent" requiring the synonymic or metonymic match is to be found at the beginning or end of the clue.

In example (32) the "correspondent" is found at the beginning of the clue. The disguised indicator is *in*. This clue is a good example of how container clues work, especially in their way of incorporating the results of an exercise in synonymy, with the purely formal operation of inserting one set of letters into another set of letters to make a new word entirely unrelated to any of the semantic elements of which it is made up. Mysteriously, yet neatly, the answer is nevertheless synonymous with another key word in the clue.

32. Clue: Discovered calf in grass (8)
    Solution: REVEALED

We may solve the clue by parsing it as follows:
[*discovered*] [[*calf*] *in* [*the grass*]]

It appears from the syntax of the clue as parsed that we will find some synonymous version of *calf* literally inserted into the midst of the letters of a word that is in some way related to *the grass*. The solution to the larger bracket should yield a word similar in meaning to, or sharing some semantic features with, *discovered*.

Calf shares most of its semantic features with "veal" (although certainly not all of them). "Reed" is a kind of grass. If we insert VEAL into REED, as instructed, we get REVEALED, a word that is similar to *discovered* in one of its senses, *i.e.*, "to expose".

Thus, we get,

[*discovered*] =[[VEAL] in [REED]]

[*discovered*] =[RE+[VEAL] ED]

[*discovered*] = REVEALED

5.2.3 Combinations

It is, in fact, rare for a cryptic crossword clue to be a pure example of the type. Part of the satisfaction in compiling and solving cryptic puzzles is no doubt to be found in deciding upon the nature of the different clue types in more complex clues. This does not necessarily entail that solvers can identify a clue type by its name, but that they recognize all the procedures to be completed on the basis of a clue of only a few words.

In Example (33) we find a clue that has as a solution an anagram inside a container as part of a charade.

The "correspondent" phrase is at the beginning of the clue. We are looking for a synonymous word or phrase for *someone beyond criticism*. The solution will consist of a phrase made up of two words, one of six letters and one of three.

33. Clue: Someone beyond criticism raced wildly in boat (6,3)
    Solution: SACRED COW

We can start by parsing the clue in such a way that we might be able to solve it in stages.

[*someone beyond criticism*] [[*raced wildly*] *in* [*boat*]]

Recall that anagrams are often cued by means of a disguised indicator. One such indicator is *wildly*. We are to understand that the letters in the preceding word are to be arranged wildly, *i.e.*, in a different order. This answer is to be placed within a word that is synonymous with *boat*, more specifically, given what we know about the uses of metonymy in crossword puzzles, we are looking for a kind of boat. We might guess that *someone beyond criticism* is a "sacred cow", but it is more likely that we will come to this once we see what letters are available for solving the clue.

Thus, we solve the clue accordingly:

[*someone beyond criticism*] [(anagram) *raced*] *in* [SCOW]

[*someone beyond criticism*] [S +[ACRED] COW]

[*someone beyond criticism*] = [SACRED COW]

Note that we have used the technique of finding a synonymous phrase for the "correspondent" phrase. Additionally, we have used SCOW (*boat*) as a container, for (ACRED) an anagram of *raced*. We have put these all together in the form of a charade.

5.2.4 The Structural Elements of Written Language

For those with an intuitive or educated sense of how language works, at least in terms of morphemes and their relationship to word meaning, the kinds of procedures outlined above must seem transgressive. They are indeed deeply transgressive, if we think of language as hierarchically structured from phonemes, into morphemes, lexemes, phrases and other components that have been conventionally proposed to show compositionality. However, there are other artifacts of language, both oral and written, that have an influence on the forms of words we encounter.

Syllables, particularly, occupy an awkward place in written English as their functions have bearing on phonological and morpho-phonological processes that occur in spoken language. The status of orthography, too, is awkward. Spelling is a partial archeological record of a word's history, and perhaps of its earlier pronunciation. However, writing conventions are a large fact of our lives, and although not all of these conventions can be analyzed within the framework of linguistic theories, mastering these conventions requires knowledge of the mechanics of spoken and written English.

Written language is made up of elements in addition to those formal units, the phoneme, the morpheme, the lexeme and the phrase. Letters have the status of separate elements that can be used compositionally. Language allows us the possibility of "use" and "mention", apart from all the other ambiguities of sound, sense and sight. The cryptic puzzle plays fast and loose with all of these permutations, mixing and matching, leaving it vague as to what is being used, how it is being used and what is being mentioned.

Beyond these permutations, however, there are puzzle-type tricks that interact with the various techniques illustrated above. These are additional variables increasing the mysteriousness of cryptic crossword puzzles. They include ways of identifying and working with pieces of code. These do not rely on homophony, homography, polysemy or lexical and syntactic ambiguity. Like almost all cryptic clues they rely on the disguised indicator, and the synonym associated with the correspondent. Besides that, they appear to be based on puzzling out a code, working with the elements of written language, according to rules that the compiler encrypts and the solver decodes. When explained, these solutions seem simple and obvious, but when we come to solving a clue, we seldom know what we are looking for.

5.3 Clue Types that use Puzzle Code

5.3.1 Cryptic Techniques

In addition to the clue types discussed above, there is a store of tricks that the community of cruciverbalists shares. These are simply conventions, rather than rules, and if one doesn't know them, there is not much that can be done, other than to check the available guides for cryptic crossword solving.[23] These tricks have evolved over the years, and are mostly based on cultural knowledge and accepted abbreviations. They are not hard and fast rules, but used so often that they have a certain reliable status. I discuss such cryptic techniques for completeness, rather than in order to suggest that they tell us anything about the structure of written language.

I list just a few examples, to provide the flavor of these techniques. Strictly speaking, they are not crucial to the claims I am making about cryptic crossword puzzles, but they do form some of the input data that is available as part of Cryptic English.

These sorts of codes are often combined and used in additions, deletions and substitutions. I list them below with examples of each.

Shortened names: *e.g.*, ED, SUE, AL; **Cardinal points**: N, S, E, W; **Periodic table abbreviations**: *e.g.*, AU, AG, CU, FE; **Directions**: *e.g.*, L,R; **Abbreviations**: *e.g.*, ER (for Queen or Elizabeth), CO (for company), CE for church; RE (for soldiers—Royal Engineers); **Latin**: RE (for about) C (for about); **Letters by sound**, *e.g.*, P, Q, R, T (pea, queue, are, tea); **American States**: *e.g.*, GA, MA, LA, NY; *the* **French, Spanish, Italian** etc.: *e.g.*, LE, LA, EL; **Article**: A, AN, THE; **Love, ring, round, circle**: O; **Roman numerals**: *e.g.*, C, L, IV, V, M, D; **literal tricks** like 4th July (= Y), Beethoven's second, (= E), Swedish leader, S; **Heart of** *e.g.*, darkness: KN; **Italian river** normally cues PO; **Ancient city** normally cues UR.

5.3.2 Acronyms/Acrostics

Acrostics are very often signalled by disguised indicators such as *initially*, *primarily*, *in the beginning*, *at the start*, *leaders*, *heads*. In this type of clue, we are expected to use the first letter of each word in a given sequence to construct a new word that is in some way synonymous with the "correspondent" word or phrase. In example (34) the "correspondent" is the phrase *in Turkey*.

34. Clue:　　　Initially, I saw that Albert's nervous British uncle lived in Turkey (8)
　　　Solution:　ISTANBUL

Once we have recognized the disguised indicator *initially*, and understood that it refers to the initial letter of each word, it is a matter of straightforwardly taking the first letter of each word till we have spelt out a new word, which is ISTANBUL, the capital of Turkey.

Thus, we should read the clue as follows:

*Initially [**I** **s**aw **t**hat **A**lbert's **n**ervous **B**ritish **u**ncle **l**ived] [in Turkey]*

In Example 35, we see a particularly clever acrostic that I have borrowed from Alec McHoul.

35. Clue: Primarily something that you press to injured chin (7)
     Solution: STYPTIC

Now, this is a particularly clever clue, because not only is it an acrostic, but the solution also provides a candidate for the definition "*something that you press to injured chin*". This is called a double duty clue. Its mechanism however is the same as seen in Example 34.

The solution is reached by following the instruction in the disguised indicator *primarily*. We need to recognize the polysemy of *primarily*, choosing between the senses, at least, of "most importantly" and "firstly". We need also to distinguish whether the words in the relevant phrase are being used or mentioned. If we decide that they are being mentioned, then "firstly" or *primarily* may have the narrow sense of "the first letter" of each word. We should thus understand that this instruction refers to the first letter of each word that is to follow *primarily*. Thereafter, we proceed straightforwardly to use the initial letter of each word, which gives us the answer STYPTIC, something that is pressed to an injured chin when, *e.g.*, shaving.

So, we may understand it as follows:

[primarily [**s**omething **t**hat **y**ou **p**ress **t**o **i**njured **c**hin]]

Example 39 is syntactically very ambiguous, and can only be read as a grammatical sentence if we understand *carpet* to be a verb. Additionally, it is not immediately obvious to which part of the sentence the prepositional phrase *after transgressions* belongs. Needless to say, we discover that for the purposes of solving the clue, *carpet* is not a verb and *after transgressions* may be a PP, but that this is not only irrelevant but a deliberate distracter. It turns out that *carpet* is the "correspondent" for which we need a synonym. The disguised indicator that we have to identify is *leaders of*.

36. Clue: Carpet leaders of men after transgressions (3)
     Solution: MAT

We are intended to parse the clue as follows:
[*carpet*] [*leaders of* [**m**en **a**fter **t**ransgressions]]

Thus [carpet] = [MAT].

One of the ways in which we can be led astray in this clue is to read *leaders of men* as a complex noun phrase. Another way to be distracted is by reading *after* as some kind of instruction, which it often is in clues of the charade type, so this is a trap that even experienced crossword solvers might not avoid. However, if read literally, with the correct intuition as to what is used and what is mentioned, the instruction is clear: we are to use the leaders of the words following *leaders of*.

5.3.3 &lit (and Literally So)

This strange form of crypticness is one beloved of cruciverbalists, on either end of the puzzle. It is known as "&lit", pronounced "and literally so". In these kinds of clues, the solution contains a word or phrase that is a synonym for the "correspondent" word whilst simultaneously functioning as a description for the word play itself. In Example 37 the clue requires us to find an anagram for *evil*. This instruction is conveyed by the disguised indicator *terribly*. The anagram is fairly simple to work out. However, it should be noted, in addition, that the indicator itself is also matched semantically with the solution VILE. In general, synonyms for indicators (as opposed to "correspondents") are not found in the solutions to the regular cryptic clues as discussed above.

37. Clue: Terribly evil! (4)
    Solution: VILE

In Example 38 we see that there is a straightforward hidden solution, indicated by *in*, but ICE is not only a solution to the "correspondent" item, *a problem*, but also an example of the sort of problem, in that ice is, indeed, a problem in arctic exploration. In this clue we seem to slide from "use" to "mention" in a moebius formation.

38. Clue: A problem in arctic exploration (3)
    Solution: ICE

In Example 39 solving either part of the clue would yield the correct solution. &lit clues are often conventionally marked by means of an exclamation mark, so we are alerted to the fact that this will be a somewhat wry kind of equivalence. In this case, the solution to each part of the clue is the same, although the phrase that is yielded has an entirely different status depending on its context of use.

39. Clue: Don't touch! The clock has had amputations (5,3)
    Solution: HANDS OFF

The solution to the first part of the clue is an expression similar in illocutionary force and in semantic content to *Don't touch*, i.e., "Hands off". The solution to the second part is a literal description of what might happen if a clock underwent amputations. What could be amputated, other than hands? Thus, we might describe this amputation as "hands off" (which in no way has the same illocutionary force as the first part of the clue, but, as we know, cryptic crosswords play fast and loose with linguistic distinctions all the time; here we see pragmatic ambiguity.) The blurring is not between "use" and "mention" here, but between different kinds of illocutionary force. The very notion of illocutionary force is negated in this clue: each part of the clue yields the identical locution, and that's all we need.[24]

The solutions to all **&lit** clues share the property of being on one reading, literal descriptions, and on other readings, non-literal descriptions, or charged with different kinds of illocutionary force.

5.3.4 Cryptic Definitions

These are widely found in cryptic crosswords, particularly those in the British style. The clue forms a cryptic definition of some expression, irrespective of its syntactic category, sense or context of use. In these clues, no "correspondent" word or phrase is provided, so the helpful aspects of double definitions or synonymy, anagramming, hidden words and so on, are not available for the solution.

Homography, however, can provide additional cryptic ammunition. In Example 40 (previously Example 6) we may see a clear illustration of the way in which homography is the crux of the trick.

40. Clue: A wicked thing (6)
     Solution: CANDLE

Since crosswords are printed rather than spoken, we do not know what use of *wicked* is intended here. If we were to start thinking of *a wicked thing* (in the sense of "evil" or "bad") there would be no restriction on what we could come up with, besides the length of six letters, and whatever other letters we may have filled in already from the intersection with other clues. It is incumbent upon us to look for the cryptic aspect of the clue—that's part of the unspoken rules of cryptic crosswords: we do not expect straight clues. Our best guess is to focus on *wicked*, and explore its possibilities for ambiguity. Once we realize that *wicked* (two syllables) could be read as *wicked* (one syllable, rhyming with "ticked"), *a wicked thing* suddenly has many fewer candidate solutions. A candle is a thing that has a wick. There are probably other things too that have a wick, but I would have to search to find out what they are, so I stick with CANDLE.

Example 41 is extremely cryptic. There is absolutely no indication what we are expected to do with the clue, aside from the possibility of considering that it is a definition. Since ambiguity is the crucial aspect of cryptic crosswords, we have very little choice but to search for different kinds of ambiguity. There is little other help provided, other than the letter restriction.

41. Clue: A jammed cylinder (5,4)
     Solution: SWISS ROLL

Both *jammed* and *cylinder* are potentially lexically ambiguous, but all uses of "cylinder" that I am aware of essentially share two basic semantic features, that of "shape" and "container". This does not look very promising. So, we plump for an examination of *jammed*. *Jam* is potentially ambiguous, in both its syntactic category and its semantics. The syntactic class of *jammed* might lead us to consider that *jam* is being used as a verb, in the sense of something like "squashed". Alternatively, we can think of *jammed* as functioning adjectively, in its participial form. Even so, we have not yet resolved the ambiguity. We can think of *a jammed cylinder* as stuck, squashed or blocked. Alternatively, we can go for the more unlikely possibility that *jam* is being used in its nominal sense of "conserve", or "jelly". Because I know crossword compilers are cryptic to their core, I favor the reading of *jam* as the stuff we spread on bread. If we take that reading, we are faced with the idea of a cylinder that is filled with jam. One such cylindrical object, although it is difficult to make the immediate association, is a Swiss roll, a jammy cake shaped like a cylinder. This is a pleasing example of a cryptic clue, although it does require a certain amount of cultural knowledge, and might not travel all that well across the English-speaking world.

Example 42, a short and extremely cryptic clue, lacking any indicator, requires more than a passing acquaintanceship with the English literary canon. It is also slightly risqué in its surface reading, depending on where the search for ambiguity takes the solver.

42. Clue: Bottom-lover (7)
    Solution: TITANIA

We are challenged to think of what *bottom-lover* might be. Someone who loves bottoms? Someone who loves a bottom? Someone who loves Bottom? We have heard of bottom-feeders, but what are bottom-lovers? Unless it occurs to us that Bottom is a character in Shakespeare's *A Midsummer Night's Dream*, we will not get near to solving this clue. Once we think of Bottom in this way, we merely have to think of someone who loved Bottom. We have to know that this character was Titania. No doubt, for those with a smattering of literary knowledge, this one works beautifully. It does, however, restrict the solution of clues that should essentially be based on knowledge of the language in all its forms to those who also have a certain literary or cultural engagement with the language.

Cryptic definitions are characterized by having neither correspondents nor indicators. In this respect they are quite different from the majority of other clue types.

5.3.5 Pure Cryptics

Finally, in terms of clue types, we investigate those known as pure cryptics. There is no rule for solving pure cryptics although occasionally there is a disguised indicator, as in Example 43. In fact, this clue contains a very clear indicator, although simply identifying it is not a guarantee of solution.

43. Clue: Eight botch theft after ignoring the odds
     Solution: OCTET

First we need to parse the clue in a way that makes it look like it is possible to solve. We might start by looking for a disguised indicator. A possible candidate for the indicator is *after ignoring the odds*. As the "correspondent" is most frequently found in clue-initial or clue-final position, and we have excluded the clue-final position as it is part of the indicator, we may pursue the idea that *eight* is the "correspondent". We would then parse the clue as follows.

[*Eight*] [*botch theft*] *after ignoring the odds*.

It looks like we have an instruction to ignore the odds, which we may interpret as an instruction to ignore the odd letters in [*botch theft*]. Using only the even numbered letters if we start with the first letter as 1, this would give us OCTET. The "correspondent" is *eight*. So we are told that after ignoring the odd letters in *botch theft*, we will get a word that is synonymous with *eight*. As we do.

Example 44 is even more cryptic, containing letters but no words. We have no idea how to think about it, and certainly no indicator. We need to come up with different ways of thinking about this clue. Since there is neither guidance nor advice in the clue, perhaps we can start off by thinking of the best way to describe the clue. This might put us on the path.

44. Clue: H,I,J,K,L,M,N,O (5)
     Solution: WATER

What we see in the clue is the letters H to O in alphabetical order. If we say "H to O" aloud, we hear something homophonous with "H_2O". As we all know, "H_2O" is the chemical name for water. That's why they're called cryptic clues.

Finally, I present, without exposition, an unattributed clue. I cannot find the original source of this one, but it remains one of the finest examples of a pure cryptic I have ever encountered.

45. Clue: GEGS (9,4)
     Solution: SCRAMBLED EGGS

6.0 Pragmatics of Cryptic Crosswords

6.1 The Context

Cryptic crosswords, just like regular crosswords, have a specifically delimited context, and therefore a fairly rigid pragmatics, which varies only within a predefined visual space. Crossword puzzles are set out in a square box within which there is a grid, with the same number of squares running across and down (usually 15 by 15, although this is purely conventional). According to crossword convention, some of the squares are blacked out and some left blank. The answers to the clues are to be filled into the numbered sequences of blank squares going across in rows or down in columns. In this respect, cryptic crosswords are no different from regular crosswords, which are usually predominantly based on the user filling in synonyms for each clue in its numbered place within the grid. As with other crossword puzzles, there is only one correct answer for each of the clues. Crosswords allow for the possibility of guessing and word recognition on the basis of letters that have already been filled in during the process of solving other clues. This distinguishes crossword puzzles from quizzes of any other description; part of the fun is using the co-occurring letters from previously solved clues. In a way, then, the answers get easier the further along the user goes, because the user is providing herself with additional visual clues (letters) that help to narrow down the possible answers.

6.2 The Nature of the Interaction

Crosswords are not really mutually interactive devices. Although there is a sender and a receiver, these roles are not reversed or reversible as they would be in other co-operative interactions. The receiver does not function as a sender, nor the sender as a receiver. There is no communicative function in the interaction. It is simply a game, without winners. There is no competition. People compile crosswords for ludic satisfaction and because it would appear that the formal possibilities of spoken and written language as a code are vast, even if communication is entirely absent from the list of functions crosswords might serve. People try to solve crosswords for many satisfying reasons, but communication is not one of them. Cruciverbalism (the slightly pretentious, but self-consciously humorous name given to this activity by those who engage in it) is a use of language for personal ludic satisfaction. That cryptic crosswords have developed to a point at which some are like art forms is a tribute to the deeply non-utilitarian possibilities of language.

6.3 The Nature of the "Communication"

Like jokes, cryptic puzzles are a type of non-*bona fide* (NBF) communication.[25] This is another way of saying that our normal rules for processing language are suspended in certain kinds of communicative activities. Thus, in a riddle-style joke, we know that we are not really supposed to engage seriously with the question and try to answer it: it is simply a format or a vehicle for the humorous play. Similarly, jokes often require us to suspend our belief for the purpose of listening to the joke. We do this willingly: thus, by agreeing to participate in a certain type of activity, we accept and acknowledge that the normal rules of communication are suspended.

When we engage in the activity known as doing a cryptic crossword we agree to play by the rules of that game. The main rule is that we agree to search for cryptic information, rather than straightforward direct communication. On the other hand, we agree to seek literal, although not obvious, instructions. Paraphrasing Afrit, we are entitled to assume that the compiler says what s/he means, but it is our task to find out what s/he means and what "means" means.

7.0 So What's the Meaning of All this?

This long exposition of the different clue types, codes and coding strategies is presented here, in some detail, to show that successfully solving cryptic crosswords entails a high degree of consciousness of the different ways in which spoken and written language can be structured and used. Cryptic crossword puzzles provide, to my mind, a very striking example of pure word play that is entirely for its own sake. For me, they complement the function of the very best linguistic jokes: a deeply sensitized consciousness of the aspects of language that are generally taken for granted, either because they are unconscious, or have become automatized through our familiarity with the practices of written language.

Clearly, many of the rules or mechanisms used in cryptic crosswords are entirely foreign to the sorts of hierarchical, recursive generative rules we refer to when talking about the underlying structure of human language. Written language is a fact, however, and there are rules for written language that are not innate, nor specifically linguistic. They are, nevertheless, operations that are performed on human language in its written form. The cryptic puzzle draws not only on our implicit knowledge of the rules of our language but also on what we know about those rules and how they are used, particularly in written language.

As in any language system or subsystem, even a code as pragmatically limited as this one, in crossword compiling practice there is a natural evolution: language changes, denotations and references may change, new words and acronyms become available; compiling strategies may become hybridized; compiling strategies may develop as a result of massive changes, such as, *e.g.*, SMS text; personal style may affect choice of compiling strategies, the geographical, historical and psychological context of the compiler and the target audience will vary, and so forth. Although merely puzzles, cryptic crosswords exploit rather complex codes and coding strategies. Cracking the code means a consciousness of many of the tacit rules we follow in using both written and spoken language, and of the fact that it is only in a context that letters, sounds and words can yield meaning.

If meaning is use, as Wittgenstein held, the meanings in the language game cryptic crossword puzzles are probably nowhere near as complicated as the meanings in many of the interactions of our less orderly lives. Trying to understand this circumscribed and limited set of apparently complex codes and rules should give us cause to consider how language meanings are made in everyday use.

Notes

1 In this chapter, I analyze cryptic crossword puzzles, and not their less linguistically interesting cousins, non-cryptic general crosswords. General crosswords tend to focus on synonyms and general knowledge. Solving general crossword puzzles requires skill of a particular sort, mostly quick access to vocabulary.

2 Solving cryptic crossword puzzles also requires special knowledge, *e.g.*, of particular acronyms, agreed upon abbreviations, in-group tricks, and encyclopedic or world knowledge *e.g.*, knowledge of literature, religious texts, other languages, etc. I try to exclude these issues from my discussion of the crucial examples.

3 See Chapter 2, Section 1.3.2 and Chapter 3, section 1, for an extended discussion of meaning in relation to both pragmatics and semantics.

4 See Chapter 3, section 3 for a more extensive discussion of literalism.

5 See Chapter 3, section 1 for this list.

6 Frege's original views on sense and reference have been much disputed, particularly, in the early days of the distinction, by Russell (1905) and more recently by Kripke (1972/80). These are relevant, live debates but there is very little at stake here in the discussion of cryptic crosswords.

7 See Chapter 2 and Chapter 3 for a fuller discussion of these issues.

8 See Chapter 2, Section 1.3 for a fuller discussion.

9 See Chapter 2, Section 4 for a more detailed account of *use* v. *mention*.

10 See Chapter 8, Section 6 for an analysis of this joke.

11 See Chapter 8, Section 6 for an analysis of this joke.

12 In what follows, I have drawn on a selection of Internet guides, some cryptic crossword lore, and my own recollections for examples. Wherever possible, I have tried to acknowledge the source of the examples. Some have passed into common currency, without an accurate account of their source. Although these tricks are descriptive of what is to be found in the most highly regarded cryptic puzzles, they are by no means a guarantee of solving cleverly set puzzles.

13 I have chosen to use the term "correspondent" rather than "definition" or "synonym", since I have discussed the linguistic terms technically in Chapter 3 and am reluctant to use them loosely here. I have chosen the term "correspondent" to serve my purposes. It is not a term that I am aware has been used to date in the literature on crossword puzzles.

14 Thus, it is less common to find synecdoche, although crossword compilers are not above using this form of part-whole (as opposed to whole-part) matching.

15 In cryptic crossword lore, there are well-known ambiguities, such as *bloomer*, which is often an indicator to look for the name of a flower, and *flower*, which is often an indication to look for the name of a river. We may also find *butter*, and expect to substitute "ram"; and *master*, which is a thing with masts, *i.e.*, a ship. Further extending this, when we see *lower*, we may be expected to provide "cow"; *adder*, usually the name of a mathematician; *number*, an anesthetic or drug. *Worker* or *social worker* normally cue "ant" or "bee", as these are worker animals, or animals that work in groups. These sorts of homographs exploit the ambiguity between nominalized verb forms, and single morpheme nouns, *e.g.*, the *−er* in *stringer*, as opposed to the *−er* in *finger* (see Chapter 4, example 6).

16 See Chapter 4, Section 2.2.6 for a fuller discussion of homophony.

17 I use the more inclusive term "metonymy" in preference to making a distinction between synecdoche and metonymy.

18 See Chapter 4, especially Section 3, for a fuller discussion of syllables as opposed to morphemes.

19 Leaving aside the construction of compound words.

20 See particularly Chapter 4 on assigning structure to sound sequences.

21 This forced an interesting move by the pro-abortion lobby, who could not very well call themselves "anti-life", and thus had to call themselves "pro-choice".
22 Other examples of these sorts of indicators are "up" (in a clue running downwards), "reverse", "backwards".
23 See especially a recent, and most helpful key to the business of solving cryptic crosswords, David Astle's *Puzzled* (Astle, 2010).
24 This is an interesting parallel with Chapter 8, section 3 about the meaning is the message and the message is the message.
25 See Chapter 1 and Chapter 2 for more extensive discussion of how jokes are examples of NBF communication.

Sources of Examples

Examples 4, 8, 10, 15, 18, 24, 26, 27, 29, 31, 32, 37 have been taken from *The Online Guide to the Enigma – Solving Cryptic Crosswords* www.puzzlers.org/guide/index.php?expand=cryptics1.

Examples 7, 12, 20, 36, 40, 41, 42 have been taken from *Clue types* www.biddlecombe.demon.co.uk/yagcc/YAGCC2.html

Examples 9, 22, 23, 25, 44 have been taken from *How to solve cryptic crosswords* www.guardian.co.uk/crossword/howto/rules.

Examples 11, 16, 19, 28, 33, 43 have been taken from *The New Yorker's Guide to Solving Cryptic Crosswords* www.primate.wisc.edu/people/hamel/newyorker.html.

Examples 13, 17, 34, 39 have been taken from www.reubenspuzzles.com.au/guide.html.

Example 38 has been taken from www.crosswordunclued.com.

Example 35 has been taken from *The Times of London*, puzzle number 4322.

REFERENCES

Akmajian, A., Demers, R., Farmer, A., & Harnish, R. (1995). *Linguistics* (4th edition). Cambridge, MA: MIT Press.

Alexander, P. (1951). Logic and the humor of Lewis Carroll. *Proceedings of the Leeds Philosophical Society, 6*, pp. 51–66.

Allen, W. (1976). Remembering Needleman. In W. Allen, *Side Effects*. NY: Ballantine.

Allen, W. (1986). *Without Feathers*. NY: Ballantine Books.

Anderson, S. (2004). *Doctor Doolittle's Delusion: Animals and the Uniqueness of Human language*. New Haven, CT: Yale University Press.

Apter, M. (1982). *The Experience of Motivation: The Theory of Psychological Reversals*. London: Academic Press.

Apter, M., & Smith, K. C. (1977). Humor and the Theory of Psychological Reversals. In A. Chapman, H. Foot, (Eds.), *It's a Funny Thing, Humor* (pp. 95–100). Elmsford, NY: Pergamon.

Aquinas, T. (1981). *Summa Theologica of St. Thomas Aquinas* (Fathers of the English Dominican Province, Trans.). Christian Classics.

Astle, D. (2010). *Puzzled*. Sydney, Australia: Allen and Unwin.

Attardo, S. (1994). *Linguistic Theories of Humor*. Berlin and New York: Mouton de Gruyter.

Austen, J. (1813). *Pride and Prejudice*. Whitehall: T. Egerton.

Austin, J. (1962). *How to do things with words* (J. Urmson, Ed.). Oxford: Clarendon.

Barbiero, D. (1997). *A note on framing the innateness hypothesis*. Retrieved January 2010 from Chomsky for Philosophers:
http://csmaclab- www.uchicago.edu/philosophyProject/chomsky /innateness2.html

Bateson, G. (1976). A Theory of Play and Fantasy. In J. Bruner, A. Jolly, & K. Sylva (Eds.), *Play: Its Role in Development and Evolution* (pp. 119–29). Harmondsworth: Penguin Books.

Benveniste, E. (1966–74). *Problems in General Linguistics* (M. E. Meek, Trans.). Coral Gables, FLA: University of Miami.

Blakemore, D. (2001). Discourse and Relevance Theory. In D. Schiffrin, *Handbook of Discourse Analysis*. Oxford: Blackwell.

Blum-Kulka, S. (1987). Indirectness and politeness: same or different? *Journal of Politeness, 11*, 145–60.

Boeckx, C. (2010). *Language in Cognition*. Oxford: Wiley-Blackwell.

Borges, J. L. (1999). John Wilkins' Analytical Language. In J. L. Borges & E. Weinberger (Ed.), *Selected nonfictions: Jorge Luis Borges* (E. Weinberger, Trans.). Penguin Books.

Bowerman, M. (1982). Evaluating Competing Linguistic Models with Language Acquisition Data: Implications of Developmental Errors with Causal Verbs. *Quaderni di Semantica, 3*, 5–66.

Bregman, A. (1990). *Auditory Scene Analysis: The Perceptual Organization of Sound*. Cambridge: MIT Press.

Brown, P., & Levinson, S. (1987). *Politeness: Some Universals in Language Use*. Cambridge: Cambridge University Press.

Brownell, H., Michel, D., Powelson, J., & Gardner, H. (1983). Surprise but not Coherence: Sensitivity to Verbal Humor in Right-Hemisphere Patients. *Brain and Language, 18*, 20–27.

Burgess, C. & Simpson, G. (1988). Cerebral Hemispheric Mechanisms in the Retrieval of Ambiguous Word Meaning. *Brain and Language, 42*, 203–17.

Carlson, G. A. (1980). *Reference to Kinds in English*. NY, USA: Garland Publishing.

Chapman, G., Cleese, J., Gilliam, T., Idle, E., Jones, T., & Palin, M. (1989/90). *Monty Python's Flying Circus – Just the Words* (Vol. 1&2). London: Mandarin.

Chiaro, D. (2005). Humor and Translation. *Humor: International Journal of Humor Research, Special Issue, 18* (2), 198–210.

Chiaro, D. (1992). *The Language of Jokes: Analyzing Verbal Play*. London: Routledge.

Chiaro, D. (2008). Verbally Expressed Humor and Translation. In V. Raskin (Ed.), *The Primer of Humor Research* (pp. 569–608). Berlin and New York: Mouton de Gruyter.

Chomsky, N. (1965). *Aspects of the Theory of Syntax*. Cambridge, MA: MIT Press.

Chomsky, N. (1962). Explanatory models in linguistics. In S. Nagel (Ed.), *Logic, methodology and the philosophy of science* (pp. 528–50). Stanford: Stanford University Press.

Chomsky, N. (1986). *Knowledge of Language*. NY: Praeger.

Chomsky, N. (1978). Language and Unconscious Knowledge. In J. Smith (Ed.), *Psychoanalysis and Language, Psychiatry and the Humanities* (Vol. 3). New Haven: Yale University Press.

Chomsky, N. (1975). *Reflections on Language*. New York: Pantheon.

Chomsky, N. (1980). *Rules and Representations*. Oxford: Basil Blackwell.

Chomsky, N. (1957). *Syntactic Structures*. The Hague: Mouton.

Chomsky, N. (1995). *The Minimalist Program*. Cambridge, MA: MIT Press.

Cicero, M. (2001). *De Oratore (on the Ideal Orator)*. (J. May & J. Wisse, Trans.) Oxford: Oxford University Press.

Cleese, J. (2000). Word Association Football. In J. Cleese, *A Pocketful of Python* (Vol. 2). London: Methuen.

Cohen, T. (1999). *Philosophical Thoughts on Joking Matters*. Chicago: Chicago University Press.

Coulson, S.W. (2005). Hemispheric Asymmetries and Joke Comprehension. *Neuropsychologia, 43* (1), 128–41.

Coulson, S., & Lovett, C. (2004). Handedness, Hemispheric Asymmetries, and Joke Comprehension. *Cognitive Brain Research, 19*, 275–88.

Coulson, S., & Severens, E. (2007). Hemispheric Asymmetry and Pun Comprehension: When Cowboys Have Sore Calves. *Brain and Language, 100* (2), 172–87.

Coulson, S., & Van Petten, C. (2007). A Special Role for the Right Hemisphere in Metaphor Comprehension? ERP Evidence from Hemifield Presentation. *Brain Research, 1146*, 128–45.

Cruse, A. (2004). *Meaning in Language*. Oxford: Oxford University Press.

Crystal, D. (2006). *Language and the Internet* (2nd edition). Cambridge: Cambridge University Press.

Crystal, D. (2001). *Language Play*. Chicago: Chicago University Press.

Davies, C. (1990). *Ethnic Humor Around the World: A Comparative Analysis*. Bloomington: Indiana University Press.

Davies, C. (1990). *Jokes Around the World*. Bloomington: Indiana University Press.

Davies, C. (1998). *Jokes and Their Relations to Society*. Berlin and New York: Mouton de Gruyter.

Davies, C. (2002). *The Mirth of Nations*. New Brunswick: Transaction.

Davies, C. (2008). Undertaking the Comparative Study of Humor. In V. Raskin (Ed.), *The Primer of Humor Research*. Berlin and New York: Mouton de Gruyter.

den Dikken, M. (1995). *On the Syntax of Verb-Particle, Triadic, and Causative Constructions*. NY: Oxford University Press.

Derrida, J. (1988). *Limited Inc*. Evanston, Illinois: Northwestern University Press.

Dixon, R. (1972). *The Dyirbal Language of North Queensland*. Cambridge: Cambridge University Press.

Dodgson, C. (1865). *Alice's Adventures in Wonderland*. UK: Macmillan

Dodgson, C. (1871). *Through the Looking Glass*. UK: Macmillan.

Dodgson, C. L. (1995). *The Complete Fully Illustrated Works*. NY: Gramercy Books.

Evans, N., & Wilkins, D. (2000). In the mind's ear: the semantic extensions of perception verbs in Australian languages. *Language, 76* (3), 546–92.

Fitch, W., Hauser, M., & Chomsky, N. (2005). The evolution of the language faculty: Clarifications and implications. *Cognition, 97* (2), 179–210.

Frege, G. (1892/1980). *On Sense and Reference* (3rd edition). P. Geach, B. Max (Eds.), P. Geach, & M. Black (Trans.). Blackwell.

Freud, S. (1901/1914). *The Psychopathology of Everyday Life* (A. A. Brill, Trans.) London: Fisher Unwin.

Freud, S. (1905/2002). *The Joke and its Relation to the Unconscious* (J. Crick, Ed., & J. Crick, Trans.) London: Penguin.

Fromkin, V. (1980). *Errors in Linguistic Peformance: slips of the tongue, ear, pen and hand* (V. Fromkin, Ed.) San Francisco: Academic Press.

Fromkin, V. (1997). Some Thoughts about the Brain/Mind/Language Interface. *Lingua, 100*, 3–27.

Fromkin, V. (2000). *Linguistics: An Introduction to Linguistic Theory* (V. Fromkin, Ed.) Malden, MA: Blackwell.

Fromkin, V., Rodman, R., & Hyams, N. (2003). *Introduction to Language* (7th Edition). Thomson and Heinle.

Fromkin, V., Rodman, R., & Hyams, N. (2010). *Introduction to Language* (9th Edition). Boston, MA: Wadsworth.

Gardner, H., Brownell, H., Wapner, W., & Michelow, D. (1983). Missing the Point: The Role of the Right Hemisphere in the Processing of Complex Linguistic Materials. In E. Perecman (Ed.), *Cognitive Processing in the Right Hemisphere* (pp. 169–91). Orlando, FL: Academic Press.

Gardner, M. (1960). *The Annotated Alice*. NY: Bramhall House Clarkson Potter.

Geach, P., & Black, M. (1980). *Translations from the Philosophical Writings of Gotlob Frege*. (P. Geach, & M. Black, Eds.) Oxford: Blackwell.

Giblin, I. (2008). *Music and the Generative Enterprise*. Sydney, NSW: Unpublished doctoral thesis, University of New South Wales.

Giora, R. (2003). *On Our Mind: Salience, Context and Figurative Language.* NY: Oxford University Press.

Goel, V., & Dolan, R. (2001). The Functional Anatomy of Humor: Segregating Cognitive and Affective Components. *Nature Neuroscience 4,* 237–8.

Green, G. (1996). *Pragmatics and Natural Language Understanding.* Mahwah, NJ: Lawrence Erlbaum Associates.

Grice, H. (1975). Logic and Conversation. In P. Cole, & J. Morgan (Eds.), *Syntax and Semantics* (Vol. 3). New York: Academic Press.

Grice, H. (1957). Meaning. *The Philosophical Review, 66,* 377–88.

Groos, K. (1901). *The Play of Man* (E. L. Baldwin, Trans.) NY: Appleton.

Guiraud, P. (1976). *Le Jeux de Mots.* Paris: Presses Universitaires de France.

Guiraud, P. (1981). Typologie de Jeux de Mots. *Le Francais dans le Monde, 151,* 26–44.

Hardcastle, G., & Reisch, G. (Eds.). (2006). *Monty Python and Philosophy.* Chicago: Open Court Publishing.

Harley, H. (2006). *English Words: A Linguistic Introduction.* Wiley Blackwell.

Hatzidaki, A. (2007). The Process of Comprehension from a Psycholinguistic Approach: Implications for Translation. *Meta: Translators' Journal, 52,* 13–21.

Hauser, M., Chomsky, N., & Fitch, T. (2002). The Language Faculty: What is it, who has it, and how did it evolve? *Science, 298,* 1569–79.

Heller, J. (1961). *Catch-22.* Simon and Schuster.

Hockett, C. (1960). The Origin of Speech. *Scientific American, 203,* 89–97.

Hoffman, D. (1998). *Visual Intelligence: How We Create What We See.* NY: W.W. Norton.

Holt, J. (2008). *Stop Me If You've Heard This – A History and Philosophy of Jokes.* New York: Norton.

Huddleston, R., & Pullum, G. (2002). *The Cambridge Grammar of the English Language.* Cambridge: Cambridge University Press.

Huizinga, J. (1995/1971/1938). *Homo Ludens: A Study of the Play-Element in Culture.* Boston: Beacon Press.

Isac, D., & Reiss, C. (2008). *I-Language: An Introduction to Linguistics as Cognitive Science.* NY: Oxford University Press.

Iverson, J., Patel, A., & Ohgushi, K. (2004). Perception of Non-Linguistic Stimuli by American and Japanese Listeners. *Proceedings of the National Congress of Acoustics, Kyoto.*

Jackendoff, R. (1992). The Problem of Reality. In *Languages of the Mind: Essays in Mental Representation* (pp. 157–76). Cambridge: MIT Press.

Jackendoff, R. (1995). *Languages of the Mind: Essays on Mental Representation.* Cambridge: MIT Press.

Jakobson, R. (1937). *Lectures on Sound and Meaning.* Cambridge, MA: MIT Press.

Jakobson, R. (1959). On Linguistic Aspects of Translation. In R. A Brower (Ed.), *On Translation* (pp. 232–9). Cambridge: Harvard University Press.

Kandhadai, P., & Federmaier, K. (2008). Summing it up: Semantic Activation Processes in the Two Hemispheres as Revealed by Event Related Potentials. *Brain Research, 3* (1233), 146–59.

Kasher, A. (1977). What is a theory of use? *Journal of Pragmatics, 1,* 105–20.

Kasher, A. (1981). Minimal Speakers and Necessary Speech Acts. In F. Coulmas (Ed.), *Festschrift for Native Speaker* (pp. 93–101). The Hague: Mouton.

Kasher, A. (1991). Pragmatics and Chomsky. In A. Kasher (Ed.), *The Chomskyan Turn* (pp. 122–49). Cambridge, MA: Blackwell.

Kearns, K. (2000). *Semantics.* New York: St. Martin's Press.

Kratzer, A. (1988). Stage Level and Individual Level Predicates. In M. Krifka (Ed.), *Genericity in Natural Language, Proceedings of the 1988 Tubingen Conference. 88–42*, pp. 247–84. SNS Bericht.

Kratzer, A. (1995). Stage Level and Individual Level Predicates. In G. Carlson (Ed.), *The Generic Book.* Chicago: Chicago University Press.

Kripke, S. (1972/80). *Naming and Necessity.* Oxford: Basil Blackwell.

Kuipers, G. (2006). *Good Humor, Bad Taste: A Sociology of the Joke.* Berlin and New York: Mouton de Gruyter.

Kuipers, G. (2008). The Sociology of Humor. In V. Raskin (Ed.), *The Primer of Humor Research.* Berlin and New York: Mouton de Gruyter.

Lakoff, G. (1982). Categories and cognitive models. *Cognitive Science 2.*

Lakoff, G. (1987). *Women, Fire and Dangerous Things.* Chicago, IL: University of Chicago Press.

Lakoff, G., & Johnson, M. (1980). *Metaphors We Live By.* Chicago: University of Chicago Press.

Laurian, A., & Nilsen, D. (1989). Special Issue on Humor and Translation. A. Laurian & D. Nilsen (Eds.) *META: Journal des Traducteurs, 34* (1).

Lederer, R. (1989). *Anguished English.* Dell Publishing.

Leech, G. (1983). *Principles of Pragmatics.* London: Longman.

Levin, B., & Rappoport Hovav, M. (2005). *Argument Realization.* Cambridge, MA: MIT Press.

Levinson, S. (2000). *Presumptive Meanings: The Theory of Generalized Conversational Implicature.* Cambridge, MA: MIT Press.

Lew, R. (1997). Toward a Taxonomy of Linguistic Jokes. *Studia Anglica Posnaniensa, 31*, 125–52.

Lippman, L., & Dunn, M. (2000). Contextual Connections within Puns: Effects on Perceived Humor and Memory. *Journal of General Psychology, 127*, 185–97.

Long, D., & Graesser, A. (1989). Wit and Humor in Discourse Processing. *Discourse Processes, 20* (2), 151–66.

Lowth, R. (1762). *A Short Introduction to English Grammar.* London: A. Miller and J. & R. Dodsby.

Lyons, J. (1968). *Introduction to Theoretical Linguistics.* Cambridge: Cambridge University Press.

Lyons, J. (1977). *Semantics.* Cambridge: Cambridge University Press.

Mahoney, D. (1999). The Mechanical Mind: Bergson meets the Information Processing Model. *HUMOR: International Journal of Humor Research, 12* (2), 161–76.

Malcolm, N. (2001). *Ludwig Wittgenstein: A Memoir* (2nd Edition). NY: Oxford University Press.

Marr, D. (1982). *Vision: A Computational Investigation into the Human Representation and Processing of Visual Information.* NY: Freeman.

Martin, R. (1996). The Situational Humor Response Questionnaire and Coping Humor Scale: A Decade of Research Findings. *HUMOR: International Journal of Humor Research, 9* (3/4), 251–72.

Martin, R. (2007). *The Psychology of Humor: An Integrative Approach.* Burlington: Elsevier Academic Press.

Martin, R. (2008). Humor and Health. In V. Raskin (Ed.), *The Primer of Humor Research.* Berlin and New York: Mouton de Gruyter.

Milne, A. A., & Shepherd, E. (1926). *Winnie-the-Pooh*. McLelland & Stewart.

Minkoff, D. (2007). *Oy!: The ultimate book of Jewish jokes*. NY: St. Martin's Griffin.

Morreall, J. (1983). *Taking Laughter Seriously*. Albany: State University of New York Press.

Morreall, J. (1987). *The Philosophy of Laughter and Humor*. J. Morreall (Ed.) Albany: State University of New York Press.

Morreall, J. (2008a). Philosophy and Religion. In V. Raskin (Ed.), *The Primer of Humor Research*. Berlin and New York: Mouton de Gruyter.

Morreall, J. (2008b). Applications of Humor: Health, the Workplace and Education. In V. Raskin (Ed.), *The Primer of Humor Research*. Berlin and New York: Mouton de Gruyter.

Nilsen, D., & Nilsen, A. (1978). *Language Play: An Introduction to Linguistics*. Rowley, MA: Newbury House.

Oring, E. (1984). *The Jokes of Sigmund Freud: A Study in Jewish Humor and Identity*. Philadelphia: University of Pennsylvania Press.

Oring, E. (1992). *Jokes and Their Relations*. Lexington: University Press of Kentucky.

Oring, E. (2003). *Engaging Humor*. Urbana: University of Illinois Press.

Oring, E. (2008). Humor in Anthropology and Folklore. In V. Raskin (Ed.), *The Primer of Humor Research*. Berlin and New York: Mouton de Gruyter.

Pepicello, W., & Weisberg, R. (1983). Linguistics and Humor. In P. McGhee, & J. Goldstein, *Handbook of Humor Research* (Vol. I, pp. 59–84). Springer-Verlag.

Pinker, S. (1994). *The Language Instinct: The New Science of Language and Mind*. London: Allen Lane (Penguin).

Pinker, S. (1997). *How the Mind Works*. NY: Norton.

Pinker, S. (1999). *Words and Rules: The Ingredients of Language*. London: Weidenfeld & Nicolson.

Pinker, S. (2002). *The Bank Slate: The Modern Denial of Human Nature*. London: Allen Lane.

Pinker, S. (2007). *The Stuff of Thought: Language as a Window into Human Nature*. NY: Viking.

Portner, P. (2005). *What is Meaning: Fundamentals of Formal Semantics*. Oxford: Blackwell.

Poulos, J. A. (2001). *I Think Therefore I Laugh: The Flip Side of Philosophy*. Penguin.

Pustejovsky, J. (1995). *The Generative Lexicon*. Cambridge, MA: MIT Press.

Putnam, H. (1975). *Mind, Language and Reality*. Cambridge: Cambridge University Press.

Pylyshyn, Z. (1984). *Computation and Cognition: Toward a Foundation for Cognitive Science*. Cambridge, MA: MIT Press.

Pylyshyn, Z. What is Cognitive Science? In E. Lepore and Z. Pylyshyn (Eds.), *What is Cognitive Science?* Cambridge: MIT Press.

Quine, W. (1960). *Word and Object*. Cambridge, MA: MIT Press.

Raskin, V. (1985). *The Semantic Mechanisms of Humor*. Dordrecht: D. Reidel.

Raskin, V. (2008). *The Primer of Humor Research*. Berlin and New York: Mouton de Gruyter.

Recanati, F. (2004). *Literal Meaning*. Cambridge: Cambridge University Press.

Riemer, N. (2010). *Introducing Semantics*. Cambridge: Cambridge University Press.

Ritchie, G. (1999). *Describing Verbally Expressed Humor*. University of Edinburgh, Department of Informatics.

Ritchie, G. (2004). *The Linguistic Analysis of Jokes*. London and NY: Routledge.

Roeper, T. (2007). *The Prism of Grammar – How Child Language Illuminates Humanism*. Cambridge: Bradford Books, MIT Press.

Rosten, L. (1985). *Leo Rosten's Giant Book of Humor*. New York: Crown Publishers Inc.

Rosten, L. (1994). *Carnival of Wit.* New York: Penguin.

Ruch, W. (2008). The Psychology of Humor. In V. Raskin (Ed.), *The Primer of Humor Research.* Berlin and New York: Mouton de Gruyter.

Russell, B. (1905). On denoting. *Mind, 14,* 479–93.

Ryle, G. (1949/2000). *The Concept of Mind.* Chicago: Chicago University Press.

Sacks, O. (2008). *Musicophilia: Tales of Music and the Brain.* London: Picador.

Saeed, J. (2003). *Semantics.* Oxford: Blackwell.

Saussure, F. (1916/1993). *Saussure's Third Course of Lectures in General Linguistics 1910–11.* E. Komatsu, R. Harris, (Eds.), E. Komatsu & R. Harris (Trans.) Oxford: Oxford University Press.

Searle, J. (1969). *Speech Acts: An Essay in the Philosophy of Language.* Cambridge: Cambridge University Press.

Searle, J. (1979). *Expression and Meaning: Studies in the Theory of Speech Acts.* Cambridge: Cambridge University Press.

Shammi, P., & Stuss, D. (1999). Humor Appreciation: A Role of the Right Frontal Lobe. *Brain, 122,* 657–66.

Smith, G., & du Boulay, J. (1986). The Generation of Cryptic Crossword Clues. *The Computer Journal, 29* (3), 282–84.

Sperber, D., & Wilson, D. (1995). *Relevance: Communication and Cognition* (2nd Edition). Oxford: Blackwell.

Steiner, G. (1975). *After Babel: Aspects of Language and Translation.* Oxford: Oxford University Press.

Stemmer, B. (1999). An e-interview with Noam Chomsky: On the Nature of Pragmatics. *Brain and Language, 68* (3), 393–401.

Strawson, P. F. (1952). *Introduction to Logical Theory.* London: Methuen.

Tanenhaus, K., Lehman, J., & Seidenberg, M. (1979). Evidence for Multiple Stages in the Processing of Ambiguous Words in Syntactic Contexts. *Journal of Verbal Learning and Verbal Behavior, 18* (4), 427–40.

Thomas, J. (1983). Cross-cultural Pragmatic Failure. *Applied Linguistics, 4* (2), 91–112.

Thomas, J. (1995). *Meaning in Interaction.* Longman.

Truss, L. (2003). *Eats, Shoots and Leaves.* London: Profile Books.

Twain, M. (1889). *A Connecticut Yankee in King Arthur's Court.* Charles L. Webster and Company.

Vaid, J., Hull, R., Heredia, R., Gerkens, D., & Martinez, F. (2003). Getting a Joke: The Time Course of Meaning Activation in Verbal Humor. *Journal of Pragmatics, 35* (9), 1431–49.

van Rooten, L. (1967). *Mots d'heures: Gousses, Rames – the d'Antin Manuscripts.* USA: Viking Adult.

Wierzbicka, A. (1997). *Understanding Cultures Through their Key Words: English, Russian, Polish, German and Japanese.* Oxford: Oxford University Press.

Wilson, D., & Sperber, D. (2004) Relevance Theory. In G. Ward, & L. Horn (Eds.), *Handbook of Pragmatics* (pp. 607–32). Oxford: Blackwell.

Winter, J. (1994, July). A Pareil Tale of Bridled Passion – How I met My Wife. *The New Yorker.*

Wittgenstein, L. (1953). *Philosophical Investigations* (G. Anscombe, Trans.) New York: Macmillan.

Wright, S. (1954, November). The death of Lady Mondegreen. *Harper's Magazine.*

References to other Media

Movies

1. Adams, T. (Producer) & Edwards, Blake (Producer/Director). (1976). *The Pink Panther Strikes Again.* Amjo Productions.
2. Badalto, B., Roth, D., Arnold, S., McNeil, L. (Producers) & Chechik, Jeremiah S. (Director). (1993). *Benny and Joon.* Metro-Goldwyn-Mayer, Roth-Arnold Productions.
3. Booth, H., Deeley, M., Penington, J. (Producers) & Sterling, Joseph (Director). (1956). *The Case of the Mukkinese Battle Horn.* Marlborough Pictures.
4. Gruskoff, M. (Producer) & Brooks, Mel (Director). (1974). *Young Frankenstein.* Gruskoff/Venture Films, Crossbow Productions, Jour Limited.
5. Kaufman, G.S., Ryskind, M., Kalmar, B., Ruby, H. (Producers), & Heerman, Victor (Director). (1930). *Animal Crackers.* Paramount Pictures.
6. Mankiewicz, H.J. (Producer) & McCarey, Leo (Director). (1933). *Duck Soup.* Paramount Pictures.
7. Perelman, S.J., Johnstone, W.B., Sheekman, A. (Producers) & Mcleod, Norman (Director). (1931). *Monkey Business.* Paramount Pictures.

Radio Shows

1. Milligan, S. (Script). *The Goon Show.* Series 9, episode 4. *The Scarlet Capsule* (1959). BBC.
2. Milligan, S. (Script). *Vintage Goon Series.* Episode 8. *The Mustard and Cress Shortage* (1958). BBC.
3. Milligan, S. (Script). *The Goon Show.* Series 9, episode 3. *The £1,000,000 Penny* (1958). BBC.
4. Milligan, S. (Script) *The Goon Show.* Series 5, episode 3. *The Dreaded Batter-pudding Hurler of Bexhill-on-sea* (1954). BBC.
5. Milligan, S. (Script) *The Goon Show.* Series 9, episode 12. *Call of the West.* (1959). BBC.
6. Milligan, S. (Script) *The Goon Show.* Series 6, episode 15. *The Hastings Flyer – Robbed!* (1955). BBC.
7. Milligan, S. (Script) *The Goon Show.* Series 8, episode 1. *Spon* (1957). BBC.
8. Milligan, S. (Script) *The Goon Show.* Series 5, episode 17. *China Story* (1955). BBC.
9. Milligan, S. (Script) *The Goon Show.* Series 6, episode 18. *Tales of Montmartre* (1956). BBC.
10. Milligan, S. (Script) *The Goon Show.* Series 8, episode 2. *The Junk Affair* (1957). BBC.
11. Sheekman, A., Perrin, N (Script) *Flywheel, Shyster, and Flywheel.* (1933). NBC.
12. Speer, R., Milligan, S., Stephens, L. (Script) *The Goon Show.* Series 8, episode 14. *African Incident* (1957). BBC.

Television Shows

1. Booth, C., & Cleese, J. (Script) *Fawlty Towers.* Series 1, episode 6. *The Germans* (1975). Methuen.
2. Hodgson, J. (Creator) *Mystery Science Theater 3000,* (1988–1999) Best Brains Inc.

3. Riley, G. & J. Turner. *Kath & Kim*. ABC TV and Seven Network, Australia.
4. Swartzwelder, J. (Script) *The Simpsons*. Series 13, episode 18. *I Am Furious Yellow* (2002). FOX NETWORK.

Miscellaneous

1. Winter, J. (Writer) *A Pareil Tale of Bridled Passion – How I met My Wife* (1994). The New Yorker.
2. Borge, V. (Stage Routine) *Inflationary Language*.

INDEX

Made in the USA
Las Vegas, NV
20 January 2023

65984789R00157